THE
RELUCTANT
WARLORD

PATRICK KING entered the British film industry in 1967, as a trainee in props and wardrobe, working on films and television including 'Patton', 'Waterloo' and 'Dad's Army'. Seeking real, rather than movie, adventure he changed career in 1974 to establish his own private security consultancy working extensively in the world's many trouble spots. He returned to the media in 1987 as a freelance investigative journalist reporting for major British newspapers and as a producer/director for international broadcasters including BBC, ITV, Channel 4, A&E, PBS, and Italy's Canale 5. He has produced three documentaries associated with the Golden Triangle and the warlord Khun Sa. He is a voting member of BAFTA and the European Film Academy, and a Fellow of the Society of Antiquaries of Scotland.

Also by Patrick King:
The Piper in Peace and War (as Editor)
Kidnapping Ronnie (with Tudor Gates)
Kidnapping Ronnie (Second Edition)

patrickkingauthor.com

THE
RELUCTANT
WARLORD

PATRICK KING

*This book is dedicated to all those who like,
or would like, a bit of spice in their life.*

CONTENTS

AUTHOR'S NOTE

Myanmar or Burma?

In writing this book I decided to use the historical and recognisable name of 'Burma', rather than the official, since 1989, transliteration 'Myanmar'. The military rulers changed the name of the country after killing thousands of their citizens in the suppression of a popular uprising. They also argued that the new name was more inclusive of the country's minorities. To the Shan people and other hill tribes of Burma the word 'Myanmar', loosely translated, means union of the people, something they vehemently disagree upon. Their reasons will become clear in the book. Similarly, I stick to the old city names like 'Rangoon' instead of 'Yangon'.

Spelling. Burma is an extremely diverse nation with 135 distinct ethnic groups, from eight major national ethnic races, each with their own languages and dialects. So when names are translated from Thai, Shan, or Burmese into English they can appear in many different forms. In most cases I have retained the most common usage for the sake of simplicity, for instance, it may be necessary on occasion to use Zao instead of Sao, or I have chosen to spell the name of a place or event, such as a battle, as it was known during that period.

The Government. I have tried to avoid using too many acronyms or initialisms, as they can be confusing and even inaccurate during certain periods. For example, the Burmese (Myanmar) government was known as SLORC from 1988 to 1997, after which it was changed to SPDC. Again for simplicity, I chose to ignore those titles and refer to the government either as: The Military Government, or The Military Junta, which is what they were, or Rangoon, after the seat of government, as an informal term.

Ethnic Group. The name Tai is not a mis-spelling of Thai. It is the ethnological group name for the Shan, Thai, and Laotian peoples.

GLOSSARY

BCP Burmese Communist Party: Supported by Red China during the Mao Tse Tung era. The group was also known as the CPB (Communist Party of Burma).

CIA Central Intelligence Agency: America's foreign intelligence service.

DEA Drug Enforcement Administration: Federal law enforcement agency

KA Karenni Army: A small insurgent group.

KIA Kachin Independence Army: The armed branch of the Kachin freedom movement.

KKY Ka Kwe Ye: A Militia operating in the Shan States. It was created by the Burmese government in the 1960s to fight the tribal insurgents as well as the communists.

KMT Kuomintang: Chinese Nationalist soldiers who took refuge in Burma in 1949 and became notorious drug smugglers. Not to be confused with the Kuomintang who control Taiwan.

MI6 Britain's Secret Intelligent Service (SIS).

MTA Mong Tai Army: Name adopted after the merger of Khun Sa's SUA and Korn Zurng's TRA in 1987.

SLORC State Law and Order Restoration Council: The official name of the military junta who controlled Burma after the coup in 1988.

SUA Shan United Army: The official name of Khun Sa's private army before his merger with Korn Zurng's TRA.

SURA Shan United Revolutionary Army: Commanded by Korn Zurng, the organisation relied mainly on the smuggling of Jade and precious stones. In 1984, it merged with other smaller Shan groups to form the TRA.

TRA Tai-Land Revolutionary Army: The armed wing of the TRC commanded by Kan Jate, Korn Zurng's deputy.

TRC Tai-Land Revolutionary Council: The executive branch under Korn Zurng.

UWSA United Wa State Army: The armed wing of the Wa State Party and reinvented and renamed after the collapse of the Burmese Communist Party.

WNA Wa National Army: A large, well-armed, tribal group of drug smugglers operating in the northern Shan States near the Thai-Burma border. In the late seventies the WNA allied themselves with the Kuomintang to increase their opium trafficking.

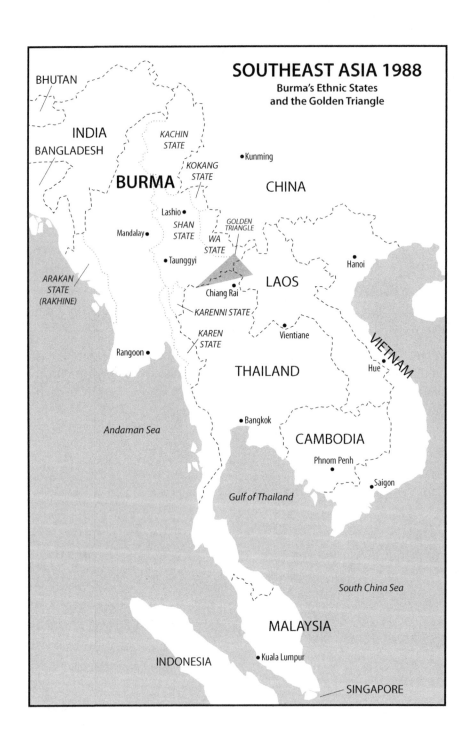

SOUTHEAST ASIA 1988
Burma's Ethnic States and the Golden Triangle

BHUTAN

INDIA

BANGLADESH

KACHIN STATE

•Kunming

BURMA

KOKANG STATE

CHINA

Lashio •

SHAN STATE

GOLDEN TRIANGLE

Mandalay •

WA STATE

• Taunggyi

Hanoi

ARAKAN STATE (RAKHINE)

LAOS

Chiang Rai

KARENNI STATE

KAREN STATE

Vientiane

VIETNAM

Rangoon •

Hue

THAILAND

Andaman Sea

• Bangkok

CAMBODIA

Phnom Penh
•

Gulf of Thailand

Saigon

South China Sea

MALAYSIA

INDONESIA

• Kuala Lumpur

SINGAPORE

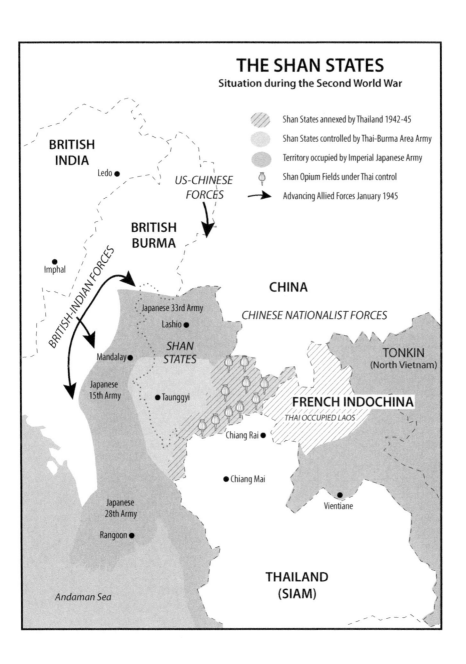

THE SHAN STATES
Situation during the Second World War

Shan States annexed by Thailand 1942-45

Shan States controlled by Thai-Burma Area Army

Territory occupied by Imperial Japanese Army

Shan Opium Fields under Thai control

Advancing Allied Forces January 1945

BRITISH
INDIA

Ledo ●

US-CHINESE
FORCES

BRITISH
BURMA

Imphal ●

BRITISH-INDIAN FORCES

CHINA

CHINESE NATIONALIST FORCES

Japanese 33rd Army

Lashio ●

SHAN
STATES

Mandalay ●

TONKIN
(North Vietnam)

Japanese
15th Army

● Taunggyi

FRENCH INDOCHINA

THAI OCCUPIED LAOS

Chiang Rai ●

● Chiang Mai

Japanese
28th Army

Vientiane
●

Rangoon ●

Andaman Sea

THAILAND
(SIAM)

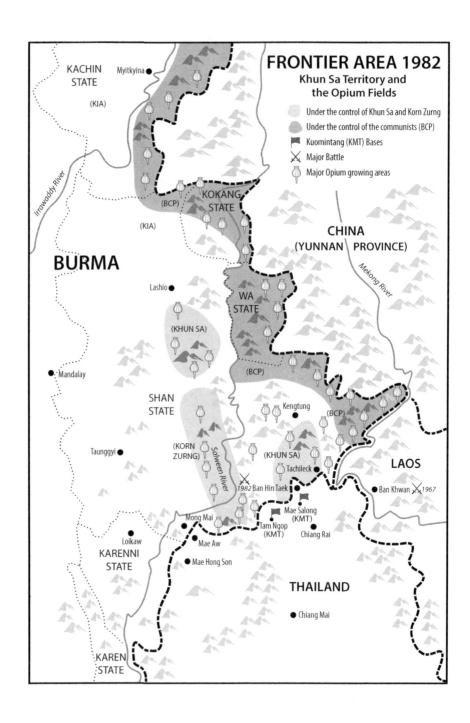

FRONTIER AREA 1982
Khun Sa Territory and
the Opium Fields

Under the control of Khun Sa and Korn Zurng
Under the control of the communists (BCP)
Kuomintang (KMT) Bases
Major Battle
Major Opium growing areas

KACHIN
STATE
(KIA)

Myitkyina

(BCP)
KOKANG
STATE
(KIA)

CHINA
(YUNNAN PROVINCE)

Irrawaddy River

BURMA

Lashio

Mekong River

WA
STATE

(KHUN SA)

Mandalay

(BCP)

SHAN
STATE

Kengtung
(BCP)

Taunggyi

(KORN
ZURNG)

Salween River

(KHUN SA)

Tachileck

LAOS

1982 Ban Hin Taek

Ban Khwan ✕ 1967

Mong Mai

Mae Salong
(KMT)

Tam Ngop
(KMT)

Chiang Rai

Loikaw

Mae Aw

KARENNI
STATE

Mae Hong Son

THAILAND

Chiang Mai

KAREN
STATE

14

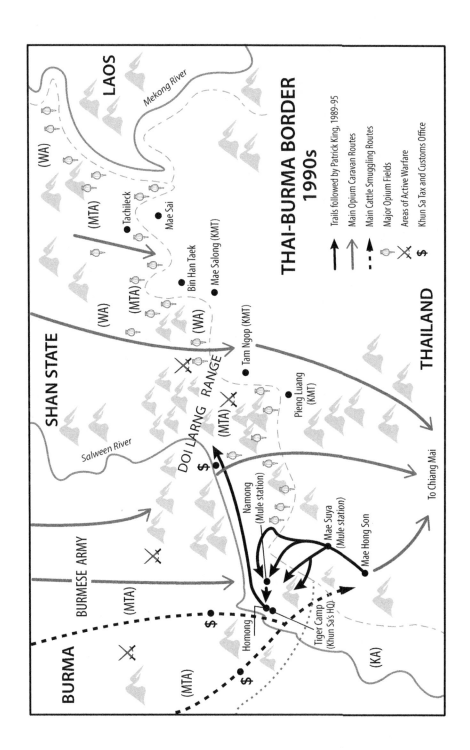

THAI-BURMA BORDER 1990s

Trails followed by Patrick King, 1989–95
Main Opium Caravan Routes
Main Cattle Smuggling Routes
Major Opium Fields
Areas of Active Warfare
Khun Sa Tax and Customs Office

LAOS

Mekong River

SHAN STATE

(WA)

(MTA)

● Tachileck

● Mae Sai

Bin Han Taek ●

● Mae Salong (KMT)

(MTA)

(WA)

(WA)

● Tam Ngop (KMT)

DOI LARNG RANGE

Salween River

(MTA)

● Pieng Luang (KMT)

THAILAND

To Chiang Mai

$

Namong (Mule station)

Mae Suya (Mule station)

● Mae Hong Son

BURMA

BURMESE ARMY

(MTA)

(MTA)

Homong

Tiger Camp (Khun Sa's HQ)

(KA)

$

INTRODUCTION

I knew nothing of Khun Sa or the Shan states of Burma (now Myanmar), where he lived, until Colonel Bo Gritz unravelled his tale. The revelations were extraordinary: assassinations, political corruption, and the nefarious activities of the CIA, all fuelled by opium money. It was fascinating.

The trail that led me to Khun Sa, one of America's most wanted men, was long and perilous. I had been informed of his fearsome reputation; dubbed the 'Prince of Death' by the media, he had reportedly had his barber's throat cut because he didn't like the haircut he'd been given. At one time this opium warlord, who controlled the infamous 'Golden Triangle', backed by his 30,000 strong private army, was considered to be the most influential figure in the world's heroin trade. I desperately wanted to make a film about him and knew that Bo Gritz, one of the most decorated Green Berets of the Vietnam War and model for the *Rambo* films, would be a key figure in my plans.

To travel across the border from Thailand into Burma using smugglers trails, was both dangerous and illegal but eventually, in 1989, I found Khun Sa in his jungle headquarters and so began a curious relationship which lasted until his death, in 2007.

When I first met Khun Sa, he was a General conducting a war. His life and the lives of his people were constantly under threat. He spoke only Shan and Mandarin, no English at all. I could only communicate through interpreters. Above all, even if these obstacles could be surmounted, I still had to win his trust and that took time. Eventually, I did persuade the warlord to tell his story and he even gave me his written permission to publish when I wrote it. But at that stage I wasn't interested in writing a book, only in making a film.

Many years have passed since I undertook the last of my nine treks to Khun Sa's jungle fortress. The one thing that has remained constant during that time are the world headlines condemning the Burmese army's atrocities against their own nationals. I have also noticed how Khun Sa's name keeps cropping up regularly in various newspapers and journals, long after his death. Many stories contained numerous errors, which have unfortunately been perpetuated over the years. Tired of reading speculative and inaccurate histories about Khun Sa, I decided to finally give my account of this extraordinary character and the bizarre world he lived in.

For this book, I decided to rely heavily on personal accounts from the many people involved in his life. Many recollections I obtained through filmed interviews. The numerous treks allowed me time to build a rapport with his closest aides and with his permission I had access to private photos and documents.

My story is set against the backdrop of the bloody insurgency war that was being waged between the nationalist government of Burma and the country's rebellious hill tribes, including Khun Sa's army. It was a turbulent and violent period that had continued for fifty years since independence in 1948. It focuses mainly on an area commonly referred to as the 'Golden Triangle'.

The 'Golden Triangle' has no official existence, no set boundaries. It is the name given to a vast ungovernable area, the size of Switzerland, and includes northeast Burma, northern Thailand, and the high plateau of Laos. It is a land of great natural wealth. A mountainous wilderness of deep valleys, covered in dense jungle and virtually impenetrable.

It is also an area whose main commodity has been the source of major wars, a product that still threatens the very fabric of Western society. This lawless region is where armed groups of men call themselves armies and where violence is a way of life.

The majority of people are Shan, but there are also many different semi-nomadic hill tribes who are poor, even by Burmese standards, and prefer to live high on mountain ridges, only accessible by narrow winding footpaths. Most cultivate and sell raw opium as their sole source of income. A portion of the crop is consumed by the tribespeople themselves, who are addicted to it. The rest is bought by drug traffickers, to be refined into heroin and transported around the globe.

Many years of war has left the land devastated. Although the world's press has always associated the Golden Triangle with warlords and drugs, the people, the politics, and the wars were, and still are, little known outside of Southeast Asia. I was to learn that the astonishing events that had taken place in this region for more than half a century, have had an everlasting effect on the rest of the world.

Politicians across the world tell us they are fighting the so-called 'war on drugs'; some even claim they are winning. But the truth is the war was lost long ago. Ineptitude and corruption both in politics and in law enforcement are largely to blame for the plague of drugs, which today, is worse than it has ever been. In this book, the reader will come to understand how this blight could have been prevented.

As for Khun Sa himself, well he never made apologies for his activities. He always claimed that he had been a reluctant warlord, forced into a business neither he, nor his people, wanted. He ruled like a king and taxed everything that moved in or out of his borders, including the opium crop. Formally indicted by the US government and officially proclaimed Public Enemy Number One, Khun Sa was contemptuous of his enemies, the CIA, and the DEA, both agencies of American policy. He claimed that these bodies were not only corrupt in their dealings but were themselves involved in the drugs trade worldwide.

The book reveals the truth about Khun Sa's youth, his family, first gang, first opium caravan and even his time as a monk, as well as uncovering startling facts on the drugs trade. His adventures include a daring escape from prison which involved kidnapping Russian doctors as hostages. His skill as a military tactician is illustrated through the many battles fought against his numerous enemies. Moreover, it explains how Khun Sa's legacy lives on. It features revealing stories and facts from people as diverse as a US presidential drug Czar, a Prime Minister, several narcotic agents, and many corrupt officials.

This man's life was quite different from that of other 'drug kingpins' such as Pablo Escobar or El Chapo. It would be far too easy to dismiss him merely as a drugs dealer. From childhood, Khun Sa's life had been influenced by violent events. There was the second world war when the Japanese army occupied his home, then a continuous insurgency war that has engulfed his nation ever since. His upbringing was also in a country where the opium culture was more than two centuries old.

On a lighter note, there were many bizarre incidents in Khun Sa's life including: ordering a pair of specially made court shoes, encrusted with semi-precious stones, for Princess Diana; there was also an American heiress who helped to sell the world's largest ruby; and how Britain's MI6 and Scotland Yard arranged for two of Khun Sa's men to visit Britain to help trap one of the notorious Brink's Mat robbery gang. He was even a friend of Prince Puren, half-brother of Puyi, the last Manchu Emperor of China.

Through taped transcripts and many conversations with the warlord, and those close to him, the work uncovers what I believe to be as total a picture of such an enigmatic personality as is possible. There is no question that Khun Sa has a place in history. He was the last warlord of his kind, a present-day Genghis Khan. Few figures have been so influential in the annals of crime and modern culture during the last half-century.

Khun Sa's rise to power is complex with different, often seemingly irrelevant pieces somehow interlocking to form the bigger picture. I have attempted to simplify these where possible, especially the political climate that existed during the various events. It is also my hope that the reader will better understand why the military junta continues to use violence and Burma remains the repressive country it is.

This is a factual story, but not a history. Forgive me if I misspelt the name of some military unit, or a date is out by a day. My purpose in writing this book is to create an objective view of the warlord and the world he lived in. I was once told, "Time doesn't change the truth, people do, by altering it". Rather a lot of fiction seems to have crept into the accounts of Khun Sa and his extraordinary life, mainly, I suspect due to lack of information. This book seeks a new perspective on him, trying to understand how he had become a freedom fighter to some, an opium warlord to others, and to the Americans, one of their most wanted men, with a two-million-dollar bounty on his head.

Patrick King
Buckinghamshire,
England, 2022.

Khun Sa, dubbed the
'Prince of Death'
by the Western media

1

Trailhead

The armed guards, who had surrounded the reception area, turned outwards, eyes alert, as Khun Sa entered. There could be no doubt he was a warlord. I studied the appearance of the man who controlled the infamous Golden Triangle in Burma, backed by a 30,000 strong private army. During the past twenty years, he had instigated the biggest drug producing operation yet seen, or so we had been led to believe by western governments.

I could not but admire Khun Sa's friendly disposition, his spirited personality, and his handsome features. His eyes were penetrating and observant, but his gaze was serious. I had pictured the warlord as a surly and arrogant despot, who had reportedly had his barber's throat cut because he didn't like the haircut he'd been given. But now I stood face to face with him I was surprised to find the infamous opium kingpin was a courteous and soft-spoken person. His bearing was far more dignified than I had expected.

Khun Sa had the air of authority that usually accompanies men of great power. He stood five feet, ten inches tall, was well-groomed and dressed in an immaculate dark green shirt and trousers, the uniform of the Shan army. There were no badges of rank, only a small patch depicting the Shan flag on one arm and the Mong Tai army insignia on the other. This was no movie-style general, dripping in gold badges and epaulettes, but rather a leader who preferred to look like his troops.

Khun Sa greeted Bo Gritz in Mandarin, and then it was my turn to be introduced. The warlord gripped my hand and looked me straight in the eye. After what felt like an eternity, he smiled and releasing my hand said, "Welcome" in faltering English. Patting me on the shoulder, he beckoned me to sit. His friendly greeting made me feel totally at ease. He bore little resemblance to the nickname he had gained in the world's press, 'The Prince of Death'.

Little did I realise then, that this first meeting with Khun Sa in his jungle headquarters, was the beginning of a curious relationship that would last for nearly a decade and would change me, and how I understood the world.

But I'm getting ahead of myself.

An American James Bond

My story begins with a genuine all-American hero or someone who was regarded as such the first time I came across him. His name was Colonel James 'Bo' Gritz, one of the most decorated Green Berets of the Vietnam War, with 62 citations for bravery and service. It is said that his exploits were the basis for Hollywood films such as *Rambo* and *Uncommon Valour*. He is an extraordinary man, by anyone's account of him. He had degrees in law enforcement, military science, and communications. He spoke Mandarin and Swahili fluently, was a trained pilot, parachutist, underwater diver, and sixth-degree black belt in Karate. All the qualifications for an American James Bond.

Licensed to kill? Well, not in the 007 sense, but he had been in command of US Army Special Forces in the sensitive Panama Canal Zone in 1976. There, he obtained information through intelligence channels that General Manuel Noriega, the notorious and former dictator of Panama, was also a drugs smuggler. Gritz personally recommended that Noriega be terminated 'with extreme prejudice', but to his great surprise was told to lay off the Panamanian general as he was 'of immense value to the highest levels of our government'.

It was Gritz who first put me on the trail of Khun Sa. He unravelled a bizarre tale of international intrigue, a suppressed scandal, and a vast conspiracy. I was hooked. As a British filmmaker, I wanted to tell the story about this oriental warlord, considered at that time to be the most influential figure in the world's heroin trade.

The warlord's name was mentioned, bizarrely, at Jennifer Fletcher's funeral, in London in 1987. I didn't know the 18-year-old, she was the daughter of my friend's work colleague, and I had been invited to hear about the events that had led to her tragic death, with a view to a story.

The naive and attractive Jennifer had gone to northern Thailand on her gap year and fell in with sweet-talking Johann, a Dutchman, who tricked her into taking heroin. The inquest revealed the dose had been too much and Jennifer died from internal bleeding. Unfortunately, the tale was a familiar one about foreign youngsters in Thailand. Interestingly, the inquest revealed the origin of the narcotics as coming from the Golden

Triangle, the area controlled by warlord Khun Sa.

The next time his name came up was in Oklahoma. I had been researching a television documentary about the legacy of the Vietnam War and in particular about the men declared 'missing in action', or MIAs, as they became known. Helping me was Jim Reser, an old friend, who had served with the elite US Army Rangers during the conflict. His brother, also a Ranger, had gone missing during a skirmish inside the Cambodian border and had been reported as taken prisoner. Nothing had been heard of him since.

By the time the peace was signed in 1973, many unlucky Special Forces and Ranger prisoners had been moved to the Laos jungles, where they were out of sight and had no official existence. This area, next to Burma, was controlled by opium 'kingpins' and it was in this context that Jim had first heard of a warlord who may have knowledge of any MIAs. His name was Khun Sa.

Researching the POW/MIA story, I encountered only opposition from the American authorities, but huge cooperation from the National League of Families, a group set up to look after the interests of those who had relatives and friends still missing from the war.

I was truly shocked at the revelations from Katherine Fanning, whose fighter pilot husband had been shot down over Vietnam. After the peace accord, his bones were solemnly returned to America. Inexplicably, she was suspicious and against all advice had the bones officially analysed, only to find that they were not her husband's. The government had lied.

In New York, I spoke to Al Boyles, another friend and retired CIA agent. He had been actively engaged in the Shan States of Burma in 1964, helping to arm Sao Ngar Khan, a nationalist leader. He had also heard of Khun Sa who, during this period, was just beginning to make his name.

Al Boyles confirmed everything I had been told in what seemed to be a government cover-up. His nephew, a Navy pilot, had been shot down over North Vietnam and the family had yet to hear confirmation that he was either dead or alive.

For the third time in as many months, the name Khun Sa had come up. The story for me was becoming more curious. I needed to find out more about the MIAs and the link with this mysterious jungle warlord. Jim Reser thought he had an answer.

Jim had heard a rumour that the government was out to 'get' Bo Gritz. I was intrigued. I knew this much-decorated soldier was something of a folk hero for his exploits in Vietnam; I also knew he had his detractors, but what possible motive could the US government have in prosecuting such a popular figure?

Gritz was not only a war hero, but also had a huge personal following because of his concern for GIs listed as missing. Gritz's theory was that many of these men still survived in slave labour camps. From the point of view of the government, such a statement was a considerable public relations embarrassment and that seemed a possible reason for their vendetta. Gritz had been outspoken on this issue since 1975 when the Americans had retreated from Southeast Asia.

American prisoners of war had also gone missing during the Korean War between 1950 to 1953, when many of the troops who were thought to have been killed in action were later discovered to have been held in secret locations, even after the armistice and the exchange of prisoners. Since the collapse of the Soviet Union in the 1990s, documents made available by the Russians have disclosed that many undeclared American prisoners were separated from their comrades and kept in solitary confinement, often in Siberian slave labour camps.

There was, however, a significant difference between Korea and the situation in Vietnam. Those who were kept by the Koreans and the Russians were mostly detained for their technical skill or strategic knowledge — pilots who could instruct them on the workings of the superior American aircraft, or officers with knowledge of troop movements. But the MIAs in Southeast Asia were ordinary GIs with no specialised knowledge, and they were deliberately ignored by their own government.

During the fighting in Vietnam, the communists made incursions from inside Laos and Cambodia. The Americans retaliated with air attacks and sent men across the borders. These attacks were officially denied by the Pentagon. When it came to the ceasefire and discussions about the exchange of prisoners, what could the United States negotiators say? "We didn't attack Cambodia or Laos, but could we have back our boys who you captured in the attacks which didn't happen?" Had it not been for its tragic implications, the situation would have seemed almost comedic.

Secretary of State Henry Kissinger had the unenviable task of negotiating with the Vietnamese. Had the United States acknowledged the existence of the missing men, he would have faced massive claims for compensation from the communists, flush after their recent victory over mighty Uncle Sam. So it was considered expedient to ignore the missing prisoners, in order that America could escape from Southeast Asia 'with honour'.

The GI who spoke fluent Vietnamese

In late 1985, the American CBS television network had broadcast an episode of its prestigious *60 Minutes* current affairs show that shocked the public. The story dealt with the possibility that the United States government had not been truthful when it stated that there was no credible proof of any American prisoners from the Indo-China theatre of war remaining overseas.

The producer of the segment was a young, Canadian born journalist and former magazine editor named Monika Jensen-Stevenson. She was amazed by the reaction to the programme. Letters and telephone calls began to pour in from veterans and families of the missing. The response encouraged her to investigate further.

The Vietnamese knew that the Americans would pay handsomely for the return of the GIs. What they did not know was that President Richard Nixon would not keep his word. It is said that he promised a sum of four and a half-billion dollars in aid to Prime Minister Pham Van Dong in 1973. That money was never paid and the Vietnamese doubtless realised they had been prudent in holding back some of the prisoners.

Was it really possible that there were American prisoners in Vietnam, Laos, or Cambodia, all those years after the war? It did seem unbelievable but there was a weight of credible evidence to suggest it may have been so.

As I had no direct involvement in the Vietnam war, it was difficult analysing such an emotive story. To establish a credible truth, I needed other independent and knowledgeable views, preferably from people who understood Americans and their armed forces. These 'insiders' were to be found, not in the United States but in London, my hometown, and among them were former members of the British special forces.

The British SAS (Special Air Service) and SBS (Special Boat Section) have a long history of cooperating with the American Army Delta Force and the US Navy SEALS. Specialists from both countries often serve on joint assignments fighting a common enemy. There is a bond between all special forces, and it was this knowledge that I wanted to tap into.

Before returning to the film industry, I ran my own security consultancy and on occasion had dealings with KAS, a British security company started by Colonel Sir David Stirling and Simon Mann, specialising in counter-terrorism. Stirling was a military celebrity, famous throughout the world not only for his exploits during the second world war but for being the father of the SAS and by definition all modern special forces.

I wanted to discuss the American MIA stories for my documentary with two men, in particular, Iain Crooke, the managing director and a former Lieutenant Colonel in the SAS, and Pete Flynn, a SAS aviation expert. I began the meeting by reminding them of our visit to Oklahoma, two years previously. The trip had been to scout a location for a private training school staffed with former SAS and Delta Force personnel. At that time Delta Force was the elite special forces unit in America and the senior officers were mostly Vietnam veterans. During their long careers, Iain and Pete had worked with American special forces on many occasions, building personal relationships with several of the commanders including the legendary US Colonel Charlie Beckwith. It was my hope they would recall discussions with these veterans that were pertinent to the MIAs. We discussed at length the possibility of American prisoners still being held by the communists long after the peace had been signed. To my surprise, both believed it was possible and, furthermore, so did most of the Vietnam veterans.

Monika Jensen-Stevenson should not have been so surprised by the reaction to her report on *60 Minutes*. Clearly, she had touched a nerve. First she was approached by the National Security Council, who were not eager for her to proceed – the sort of pressure that's guaranteed to make a good reporter more determined to seek the truth. After the programme was broadcast, the Pentagon promptly accused all the participants of lying, yet among them had been a former Director of Defense Intelligence, who was convinced that American soldiers were being held. A concerned citizen might ask whether any so-called 'missing-in-action' prisoner had ever been found. The answer was yes, and his name was Bobby Garwood.

Bobby Garwood was fairly young when he was captured by the Viet Cong. Merely staying alive in those circumstances could be difficult. A fellow prisoner advised him to learn Vietnamese which he mastered with incredible aptitude. He was a good mechanic and was put to work repairing captured and abandoned vehicles. He was useful to the Vietnamese and so they kept him alive long after the ceasefire. There seemed to be little hope of release, and there was no chance he could escape.

After fourteen years of captivity Garwood, now a fluent native speaker, risked his life by smuggling a note to a diplomat from a neutral country, which was passed on to a correspondent from the BBC (British Broadcasting Corporation). Fortunately for Garwood, the BBC made a programme about him, after which the American authorities had no option but to demand his release.

For whatever reason, the Vietnamese decided to release Garwood, who was then immediately charged by the US Army with desertion and with aiding and abetting the enemy. Although these were capital offences, his defence seemed determined to obscure the truth and advised him against testifying. When questioned by the military, he had claimed that he had been sent to collect an officer at a place called China Beach, where he was taken prisoner, but the prosecution claimed that there was no record of any such assignment. This was hardly surprising, considering the hasty destruction of documents during the American withdrawal.

Fortunately for Garwood, a witness confirmed his story. He was found guilty of the lesser charges though, and instead of being feted, he was disgraced and denied the medical benefits for his injuries. The authorities wanted him out of sight and out of mind.

But Garwood's fellow veterans refused to forget him. One of the names which kept coming up in the course of Monika Jensen-Stevenson's research was Colonel Bo Gritz. Indeed, General William C. Westmoreland, former commander-in-chief of the American forces in Vietnam, had devoted a whole chapter of his memoirs to Gritz and his daring, behind-the-lines activities. However, the reports were not all good. The magazine *Soldier of Fortune* had ridiculed Gritz with a provocative front-page headline: 'Bo Gritz, Hero or Huckster?'

I was interested in what Gritz had done to offend Washington, and my first thought was that it was something to do with the issue of MIAs. In 1983, Gritz had mounted an unauthorised mission, codenamed 'Lazarus', to rescue American prisoners of war held in Laos. He put together a team of 3 other American Vietnam veterans and 15 Laotian mercenaries with private funding, including contributions from movie stars like Clint Eastwood and William Shatner. The target was three secret POW detention centres located deep in the jungle, but within three days of entering Laos, the mission ended in failure.

In fact, Lazarus turned into a fiasco, with Gritz being arrested by the Thai authorities after his escape back across the border. But Gritz did not go down quietly, he immediately and publicly laid the blame on high-ranking US security officials, whom he claimed gave his team's jungle location away because they didn't want any POWs found. So was this private venture Gritz's clash with the powers that be, the reason they were after him?

The suggestion that prisoners of war might still be out there was unwelcome.

For the American public, for whom Vietnam was still an unhealed wound, the mere thought was hurtful. It was difficult for me, as a European, to understand the emotions Americans had regarding Vietnam and the missing prisoners of war. I was determined to keep an open mind and just as determined to find out the connection with Khun Sa. To do that I had to meet Colonel Bo Gritz.

2

The Mormon Preacher

As I flew to Las Vegas, in March 1987, I realised the elements of this story were like the unassembled pieces of a huge jigsaw puzzle. The name of Khun Sa kept popping up everywhere. I tried to get the story in perspective, for it had so far been a turbulent decade.

The eighties had begun with the United States finally resolving the humiliating hostage crisis of its embassy in Iran. President Jimmy Carter had been unable to deal with the crisis and was crushingly defeated by the former Hollywood actor Ronald Reagan. The other result of the crisis was the invasion of Iran by Iraq's Saddam Hussain, at that time considered a heroic figure by the CIA and the West.

Southeast Asia was a painful memory for most Americans, but there was a growing concern about the increasing exports of heroin from that part of the world, and the havoc it was causing on the streets of American cities. There was also a kind of collective guilt that those missing in Vietnam might yet be alive in that distant land. The idea persisted, despite repeated government denials. How much did Colonel Bo Gritz know?

Fifty miles west of the Las Vegas Strip, out in the desert, feels like another country. Sandy Valley is a sleepy hamlet that is home to around a hundred people, including Bo Gritz.

I asked him why he lived in such a remote spot. "I'm an old-style American," he replied. "I believe in freedom, and I mean freedom. Everywhere today, there are so many regulations, you can't do this, you can't do that. Out here, in the West, you can still be free. I have two small planes to fly wherever I want. I land on this dirt airstrip next to the main road and then taxi into my garage, it's big enough if you go careful. Before I got the airstrip laid, I used to land on the road itself, and then just pull off. Where else can you do that Pat, except in America?"

The man looked just like the hero he was portrayed as. Tall and burly, an athlete past his best now, he was carrying a few extra pounds, without being obese. His fair hair was beginning to grey. His eyes were blue and piercing. He was a good-looking man with a definite 'star' quality about him who could probably have made a career in the movie business.

Gritz answered my questions clearly and precisely. He gave the impression of having a prepared set of answers, as though he pressed a button and the right one came out. He was fluent but not eloquent, using plenty of Army words and phrases. He also had a sense of humour. The best example was when I asked for the correct pronunciation of his family name. "Well, Englishman, it rhymes with lights and not shits!"

Superficially, Bo appeared a good host, seeking to put his guest at ease. Yet there was a feeling that he was judging what it is he thought I wanted to hear, and how he might benefit. That was the main criticism I had heard about him. While he was revered by a large group of followers, mostly involved in the National League of Families, there were a number who claimed that he had sought to make a profit from his MIA activities. He dismissed the accusation with a shrug.

To my surprise, Bo calmly told me he was a Mormon preacher. I soon begin to build a picture of a man who was at peace with himself but at war with the government. He certainly had tales to tell, though I had no way of knowing whether they were true. He told me the story of his last trip to Southeast Asia, in search of MIAs, then his trip to Burma to meet the opium warlord, which he thought might be of interest to European audiences. It was certainly of interest to me, and it helped explain why Washington was out to 'get' Bo Gritz.

I wanted to know how the notorious Khun Sa was involved.

The Golden Crescent

In 1986, Vice-President Bush received a report which stated that Khun Sa, the opium warlord of the Golden Triangle, in Burma, had information on the whereabouts of a group of American MIAs. Bush had no option but to act on the report, which was accorded top priority because of the sensitivity of the subject. A National Security Council staff officer named Tom Harvey was ordered to check whether there was any substance to the claim. He picked up the telephone and called the only man he knew he could send on such a mission: Bo Gritz.

When the call came from the National Security office, Gritz was engaged on a project to train Afghan freedom fighters in the Nevada Desert, America's response to the 1979 Soviet Union invasion of Afghanistan.

In President Reagan's new regime at the White House, Dr David Musto

Highly decorated Green Beret, Lt. Colonel Bo Gritz

had succeeded Peter Bourne as 'Drugs Czar'. Musto had seen what had happened in Southeast Asia and he could see the same thing happening in Afghanistan where the opium growers were rebelling against the government. Musto knew that sending them arms would only encourage the kind of conflict that had raged ever since the end of the Second World War in Burma and Laos.

From the sixties, the spread of narcotics had started to become a serious problem throughout the Western world. Until then, it had affected only the disillusioned and college students. By the eighties, new sources and new types of drugs were flooding the markets. In Pakistan and Afghanistan, farmers found a ready market for a crop that was easy to grow. In Southeast Asia, the so-called 'Golden Triangle' recovered its productivity. In South America, peasants found a harvest that brought them a stable living and the same crop brought fortunes to the evil Medellin cartel. A variety of drugs flooded into the United States, mainly heroin, cocaine and its devastating new derivative, 'crack' cocaine. Addicts began to experiment and deaths from drug abuse began to soar.

Many experts argue, having researched the post Second World War period, that it was CIA support for the anti-communist Chinese Kuomintang army that created the Golden Triangle as the world's centre for illicit drug production. The agency's aid for the mujahideen guerrillas in Afghanistan throughout the 1980s raised that country to the number one position as a drug producing nation. For anyone who has ever lost someone as a result of illicit drugs, western government agencies, and especially the bad elements in the CIA, have a lot to answer for.

One of the agency's more disastrous enterprises was the part it played in the overthrow of the Shah of Iran in early 1979. For some reason, they felt that Ayatollah Khomeini was a better bet. The mullahs who ruled the country after the Shah could not allow drugs in an Islamic state, so the Afghan and Pakistani producers had to find new markets for their goods. Strangely, addiction in Iran increased and they were obliged to step up their own production.

At that time, the Pakistanis were major exporters of narcotics not only to their immediate region but also to other parts of the world. They became prominent drug smugglers into Britain, having a greater involvement in the trade there than any other group. The United States Government leaned upon General Zia ul-Haq, head of the Pakistan government, a brutal man who was not averse to augmenting his earnings with the proceeds from drugs.

The result was predictable: once the army had a taste of the profits, it decided to trade on a regular basis, and from then on, the military manoeuvres were just theatrical, to satisfy the Americans. At the same time, their real business was being internationally structured, with produce from the Afghan poppy fields being refined in Pakistan's laboratories and shipped to the USA or Europe. Within a few short years, the region had gained the number two ranking, after the Golden Triangle – the Golden Crescent was established.

Despite the disaster of Vietnam, and the miscalculations they had made installing Idi Amin in Uganda and overthrowing the Shah of Iran, the American administration had gained a taste for involvement in the affairs of other countries. Indeed, after the election of Ronald Reagan in 1981, America spent vast sums on overseas programmes. One that gave particular satisfaction was the overthrow of the communist regime in Afghanistan. Three billion dollars of military aid was given to Pakistan to facilitate this, under the control of Zia ul-Haq who, with his cohorts, had overthrown a democratically elected Pakistan government and hanged the prime minister, Zulfikar Ali Bhutto.

While much of the aid found its way to the mujahideen fighting the communists, the rest went to Zia, who used it to finance his drug operations and those of his associate, Gulbuddin Hekmatyar, another 'choice' ally.

Hekmatyar was the mujahideen commander in Afghanistan but was far more efficient as a drugs trafficker than as a warrior. As usual, the CIA was indifferent to the drug operations, provided their agenda was being served. When the Soviet Russians realised they were fighting an impossible war and withdrew their troops from Afghanistan, the complete overthrow of the puppet communist regime seemed imminent. Hekmatyar, so adept at shelling defenceless villages and murdering helpless prisoners, was unable to strike the final blow.

It was a journalist called Burns who broke the story in a front-page article for the *Washington Post* on 13 May 1990. The newspaper accused Hekmatyar of trafficking heroin and the United States Administration of turning a blind eye because it did not want to offend Pakistan. This was the simple truth.

This account of the CIA's backing of the mujahideen in Afghanistan is not a diversion from my story. In this Asian jigsaw puzzle, Khun Sa, the man that Colonel Gritz had been asked to visit was at its centre. I was sure Gritz would be a key figure in my plans, though I didn't realise he would have a different agenda.

Bo Gritz's surprise!

Bo Gritz had heard that no American agents who had entered the Golden Triangle in recent years had been known to come out alive. Even so, he accepted the commission from the National Security Office to visit the warlord with alacrity. Although he had been on a number of missions behind communist lines in search of missing prisoners of war, he had never considered Burma as a possible location.

The report George Bush had received, however, stated that Khun Sa had information about, and control over, American prisoners of war, and was prepared to surrender both the people and secrets to the United States as a gesture of goodwill. According to National Security Advisor Tom Harvey, the report was receiving consideration 'at the highest level'. Gritz was relieved to learn that the administration seemed, at last, to be taking the problem seriously.

The quid pro quo for Khun Sa's gesture was apparently that the Reagan administration should give serious thought to the granting of diplomatic recognition to the Shan land, in the north of Burma, as an independent nation. According to the report, Khun Sa had also requested American assistance in developing a legitimate agricultural economy. Gritz figured that the government of Burma would have something to say about such a move, since Khun Sa, a rebel and a self-proclaimed freedom fighter, was a painful thorn in their side. As an essential first step towards whatever move they might decide to make, the White House needed to know whether the report was a hoax.

The meeting between Gritz and Khun Sa was bitterly disappointing. The warlord had no knowledge of any missing American prisoners. The message received by the United States government had either been a crude extortion attempt, a hoax or maybe even a CIA or DEA plot to discredit the warlord.

Khun Sa, however, astonished Gritz by asking him to convey a message to the President of the United States. The gist was that he was prepared to ban the production of opium in the Golden Triangle if the United States backed Shan independence.

Khun Sa went on to detail the extent of CIA involvement in illicit narcotics. Even Gritz had never imagined how extensive this was, but it explained why American policy in the area had failed so miserably. Gritz had not travelled to Khun Sa to talk about drugs trading, but knowing what he did, he could not turn his back on it. It seemed that, far from discouraging the development of the drugs trade, the United States had been unwittingly financing it. Gritz was told that corrupt officials were lining their pockets with US dollars that were being supplied to wipe out the poppy fields.

Gritz's surprise at the information he had gleaned about the CIA and at Khun Sa's offer was nothing compared to the surprise in store for him when he got back home.

3

Erase and Forget

George Bush may have been appointed by President Ronald Reagan as his drugs czar, but the embarrassed word from his officials to Colonel Gritz, when he sought to deliver the message from Khun Sa, was to 'erase and forget' all that he had learned in the Golden Triangle.

It is possible that President Reagan was conveniently forgetting certain facts. After all, his number one drugs buster must have known if elements of the CIA were engaged in drug trafficking, particularly if it was in order to finance their worldwide covert operations.

Bush was now Vice-President and, in theory, no longer directly connected with the CIA. What did Tom Harvey mean when he told Gritz, concerning the offer from Khun Sa, that "there's no interest here in doing that" – that there was no interest in curtailing the traffic in narcotics?

However, Gritz felt determined to find out just who it was in the White House who was neither interested in stopping this trade nor in exposing the government officials who had been Khun Sa's best customers for so many years. Any doubts he may have had about what Khun Sa had told him vanished in the light of the State Department's reaction. It was clear that in some way he had stepped out of line, and he steeled himself for retribution. His reward for undertaking a dangerous mission and coming back with the wrong answers was to be threatened with criminal charges. When a clumsy attempt was made to arrest him by agents of the ATF (Bureau of Alcohol, Tobacco and Firearms), Gritz smelled a set-up and failed to turn up for the meeting. He was keen to know why everyone was suddenly being so sensitive about his trip to see Khun Sa. The blatant injustice only made him more determined to find out, as he freely confided in me and once he was sure I was not an undercover agent. I felt that he was becoming somewhat paranoid but perhaps it was understandable. He was convinced it was his duty to flush out the guilty parties in the CIA and DEA.

My meeting with Bo Gritz had come to an end. I had spent a couple of days with him, watching videos, looking at photos and taping his stories. He was a great storyteller and easy to listen to, but I was trying to make sense of all that I had learned, which required some serious analysis.

One of my parting questions to Gritz was about the fact that Khun Sa was listed as an international terrorist, which meant that the US State Department would not even recognise him, let alone do any business with him. Surely Khun Sa must have been aware of this? Gritz stated that many men who had been branded as 'terrorists' were now public heroes and national leaders, recognised at international conference tables. Yasser Arafat, the Palestinian leader, being one such example.

Gritz claimed that Khun Sa had promised to release names of American officials who had been involved in narcotics trading, believing that if the United States government made any attempt to investigate, it would prove his information correct.

But some of the people involved were still in office, and Gritz was under pressure to forget about the whole thing, as he had been advised. However, the dangers of allowing the drugs trade to flourish even more were, in his view, unthinkable. The whole moral fabric of the United States was under attack. Not only was heroin a cancer within the national body but even one of his own children had been affected by drugs. So for Gritz, this had become personal.

Gritz was also under threat of an indictment for the 'misuse of a passport', a crime which he cheerfully admitted to having committed on many occasions; using false identification was standard procedure for Special Forces operatives. He also told me that he had been warned by many friends to lie low and stay 'under the radar'. He added that he had no such intention and wanted this matter out in the open.

Gritz gave evidence before the International Narcotics Control committee. He testified that after his meeting with Khun Sa, he was convinced that an organisation within the US government was profiting from illicit drugs trading. He told the committee that it was their job to uncover and expose the members of this clique. The colonel's strong words met with the expected response. The chairman rejected the entire report as 'nonsense' and called Khun Sa 'a crazy character' and 'a criminal' and totally denied the allegations of corruption among American officials.

Interestingly, while the White House was denying that Gritz had ever gone to Burma on behalf of the Reagan administration, the State Department was at the same time blocking enquiries about Gritz's visit on the grounds that his missions were 'classified'.

Then the government did make good its threat; upon arriving home in Nevada, Gritz found that he had been indicted by a grand jury in Las Vegas for the 'misuse of a passport' and also that he was under investigation for 'conspiracy to transport explosives'. Furthermore, articles in the press portrayed the war hero as an 'unstable crackpot'. The pressure was really on. Everything I had heard on the Washington grapevine had proved true. The government, or some element of it, really had its hooks in the former Green Beret Colonel.

The plan

I was intrigued by Khun Sa, the mysterious opium warlord of Burma, from the first moment I heard his name and was determined to seek a meeting with him. However, this was easier said than done as Burma was not on the tourist map in 1989. The pro-democracy movement had been viciously put down by the Burmese military, with thousands of innocent victims murdered. The military dictatorship was condemned by the free world.

Even had it been possible to get permission to visit as a journalist, I would never have been allowed to stray far from Rangoon, and certainly not as far as the 'Frontier Area' where the insurgency war was raging. Yet this was exactly where I wanted to go. It was to the Shan States, into the real Golden Triangle, or, if you like, the lair of the dragon.

The world's press had always associated the region with warlords and opium, yet among the Hill tribes the opium culture was more than two centuries old. The people, the politics and the wars were little known outside of Southeast Asia, but the astonishing events that had taken place in this region for more than half a century, have had an everlasting effect on the rest of the world. This was especially true in the West where, since 1945, attention had been focused on the 'Iron Curtain' and the communist threat from the east, completely forgetting those who lived behind the 'Opium Curtain' and its legacy: the drug crisis facing us today.

The only direct point of contact I had with the notorious Khun Sa was Bo Gritz, who claimed to have a strong rapport with the warlord. I felt that the story of the much-decorated Green Beret hero at loggerheads with his own government was also a good tale, one that I could weave into a documentary. I had only recently returned to the industry after a twelve-year absence and needed a good story to make my name.

Ever since I was a small boy, I'd wrestled with two ambitions: to be a soldier or to be a filmmaker. I tried both. Following the family tradition of a career in the army looked less attractive to an ambitious teenager living in 'Swinging London' in the 1960s, so I tried my luck getting into the film industry. It was not easy in those days, as a large part of the industry was controlled by a powerful trade union, The Association of Cinematograph, Television and Allied Technicians (ACTT), who ran a 'closed-shop'. It was Catch 22: you needed a union card to get a job, and a job to get a union card! However, there was non-union work available in related trades such as music or the theatre. My first job, aged fifteen, was as a messenger for a recording studio in *Tin Pan Alley,* then the centre of London's music scene, for 5 pounds a week, about 14 US dollars.

A chance invitation from an old school friend to the Elstree Film Studios, north of London, where he was working as an assistant lighting technician, led to a lucky break. Passing the wardrobe department, I noticed an enormous pair of American army boots that had been placed on top of a clothes hamper. Intrigued, I read the label – Name: *Clint Walker.* Size: 14. Film: *The Dirty Dozen.* The boots were being used for publicity stills and came from Monty Berman Limited, the world-renowned film and theatrical costumiers based in London. I quickly made a note of their telephone number.

The following day I telephoned the military uniforms department at Monty Berman to apply for a job, without knowing whether there was a vacancy or not. The manager told me, not surprisingly, he didn't know what job I was talking about, but as it happened he was thinking of taking on a trainee to work in the department. The starting salary was 7 pounds a week, not too bad in 1967. With a bit of nerve and a lot of luck, I entered the industry through the wardrobe and props department, eventually receiving my all important union card working on a film called *Patton.*

During the mid-1970s, I was lured by the adventure and money offered in the fledgling international security business. Over the next few years, I found myself in some hair-raising situations as I travelled to some of the world's worst trouble spots. Despite making good money I wanted a change of career and, in 1986, formed a small independent production company providing stories, either in print or film, to the international media.

To help cover the considerable expense of undertaking an expedition to the Golden Triangle meant the need for a partner. The major British broadcasters were nervous about the idea and imposed too many restrictions, so I searched elsewhere and eventually found a willing partner in Canale 5, the Italian television company owned by Silvio Berlusconi, later Italy's Prime Minister.

At first they were reluctant, due to the potential danger of sending a crew into Burma illegally, but eventually they agreed. As a co-production we would each edit our own language version of the film, with reporter Gabriella Simone fronting the Italian film. It was now time for me to convince Bo Gritz to make yet another trek to Khun Sa's jungle headquarters. On the flight to Las Vegas, I formulated a plan. Guessing that Gritz would look good on screen, especially meeting the infamous warlord, I played on his ego. So there was no misunderstanding about money, I impressed on him that this was a European documentary rather than a Hollywood production, which meant tight budgets and low fees.

He immediately accepted my offer. I attributed this enthusiasm to his adventurous nature, but I would soon find that Gritz had his own agenda, which was quite different from mine. I knew about the troubles he was having with the United States government and had been told he was due to attend court for a minor offence that if found guilty would only be punishable with a small fine.

Then a telephone call from Jim Reser, in the United States, unravelled the truth about the severity of Bo's impending court case. To my horror, I learnt it was to be a jury trial, the result of which might prevent him leading my crew into the Golden Triangle. I could lose not only my money but my credibility with Canale 5.

In February 1989, they finally got Bo Gritz into court. He was looking forward to his appearance, seeing it as a grandstand to reveal the truth about CIA complicity in narcotics dealing, and about the obstructions put up by government to prevent missing prisoners of war from returning home. He told me afterwards that he was convinced his performance and his righteousness would be well received - "it would be like winning the Oscars"!

However, right from the beginning he was told that no such evidence would be admissible and that on no account would he be allowed to discuss in public the actions of the CIA and other government agencies. His prosecutors begged him to admit guilt on a 'technicality' upon which he would be 'guaranteed' a dismissal, but Gritz was not falling for that.

In the end, the United States government's own incompetence caused its downfall, as a jury found that the government had brought an incorrect charge against Gritz. Both judge and government had no choice but to accept the jury's acquittal, though they did so begrudgingly. The judge said: "While you are acquitted, it doesn't mean you are exonerated."

So, no academy award for Bo Gritz, instead the Oscar went to US Attorney William Maddox. Bewildered reporters asked him why the government had wasted taxpayers' money in bringing the case. Maddox stated quite bluntly that "George Bush called me up and told me to get Bo Gritz!"

With Bo's problem behind us, I was determined to proceed to the Golden Triangle as soon as possible. It was now time to tell the Khun Sa story.

The Shan are predominantly Buddhists

4

A Prince is Born

In the Shan states of Burma, the village of Hpa-Perng, by Nawngzarng (Lake of the Elephants) lies just west of the Salween River, in Lashio Province. It is the birthplace, on the 17 February 1934, of Khun Sa, although he was known then as Chang Si-Fu. Being of Chinese descent, he was given both Tai and Chinese names at birth, a common custom for those born outside mainland China. Khun is a prefix used by those born or promoted into Shan royalty. In translation Khun Sa broadly means 'pleasant prince'. Not a soul in the Shan states, then part of the British Empire, suspected the birth of Chang Si-Fu to be an ominous event, nor could they have known that the boy would grow to become a formidable soldier, a warlord who would control half of the world's supply of opium.

The ancestors of his father, Khun Ai, immigrated in the eighteenth century from Nawng Sae, an ancient Shan principality in China. One of them won a chieftainship in Lashio Province as a result of exemplary service to the local prince. Khun Sa's mother was Nang Saeng Zoom, of the Palaung Shan people and her marriage to Khun Ai was a happy one. Unfortunately, he died prematurely in 1937. A kung-fu enthusiast, he was at exercise when he started to vomit blood and died in hospital in Lashio.

His widow eventually remarried, this time to Khun Ji, the Chief of Mong Torm, a neighbouring territory. This was to prove an historic union for Chang Si-Fu as his new stepfather was an important man. Unfortunately, within two years, Nang Saeng Zoom also died and the five-year-old orphan was adopted and raised by his stepfather. A year later he was reclaimed by his grandfather, Khun Yi Sai, the Chief of Loimaw.

Khun Sa's two most prized possessions, which he was proud to show his guests, were distinguished service medals awarded to his family by the British. The first was presented to his grandfather to commemorate the coronation of King George VI. The second was awarded to Khun Ji, to commemorate the coronation of Queen Elizabeth II.

Khun Yi Sai was to prove a huge influence on his grandson. Although the young Khun Sa attended the local school, it was in the home of his eminent grandfather that he was to enjoy an instructive education. His grandfather taught him to read and write Chinese. Then he was drilled in the basics of tea cultivation, as well as horse and mule breeding. This boyhood training developed in Khun Sa a fervent love for horses, one that would prevail throughout his turbulent career as a warlord.

The splendour of nature was also the young boy's classroom. At the age of seven he received his first lessons in looking after livestock such as pigs and cattle. In the lush forests, he also learned to distinguish between edible and poisonous plants, bulbs, and berries, and between dangerous and harmless reptiles, insects and animals. Experience taught him the colours, calls and habits of a great variety of birds, and also acquainted him with the names of the indigenous trees, shrubs and grasses that covered the countryside.

Khun Sa's early childhood was a happy one. When he was eight years old, he travelled with his grandfather to Taunggyi, the capital of the Shan states. Due to its high elevation, the only access to the capital was by a winding mountainous road. Travelling on horseback was the perfect way to appreciate the beauty of his native land.

Never before had the young boy journeyed so far. They passed through wide fertile valleys between high mountains that were covered in dense forests. They carefully waded swift-running streams and crossed numerous ridges. At night they camped on open ground huddled around a campfire. Khun Sa's grandfather was impressed with the youngster, who rode like a grown-up, showed little fatigue, and paid attention to everything that was going on around him.

Khun Sa's formal education was terminated when the Second World War began. The Japanese army lost no time in attacking the country, seizing the south of Burma three days after their attack on Pearl Harbor, and bombing Rangoon in late 1941.

Thailand at war

In 1942, the Japanese army launched a surprise and devastating attack on Burma itself that rapidly swept aside the defending British and Indian forces and the Chinese Nationalist Kuomintang army, commanded by Chiang Kai-shek. Within weeks, Japanese troops had sped across the country, cutting the Burma Road, which Chiang Kai-shek's troops relied on as a supply route. By mid-1943, they had all but conquered Burma and had penetrated thirty miles into India, before they were halted at the frontier towns of Imphal and Kohima and slowly forced back.

The Thais too signed a secret treaty with the Japanese invaders that gave Thailand access to the lands of the Shan and control of the poppy fields.

The Thai's are very clever in dealing with many sides. It is the only country in the region that has never been colonised and has always been prepared to change alliances in order to be on the same side as the winners. During the First World War, once they knew the Allies were going to win, Thailand declared war on Germany. They even sent a contingent to France but by the time their troops arrived, the war had already been won. In the Second World War their policy was just a variation of the one they used in the previous world war. The Japanese were always going to enter Thailand and the Thais had no way of resisting, so they declared war on America, or at least that was what they told the Japanese. In fact, the Thai ambassador in Washington never delivered the declaration, keeping it locked up in his files. When it became clear that the Allies were going to win, the country's rulers resigned and were replaced by a pro-American government – so Thailand still managed to emerge as a winner.

Khun Sa, a bewildered seven-year-old, was witness to an event which, although no more than a minor footnote in the war history, was to have unimaginable post-war consequences. The invasion, and subsequent annexation in 1942, of part of the Shan states by Thailand can, looking back, be seen as critical to the development of the drugs trade in Southeast Asia. It was a trade that would fuel the post-war rise in organised crime in the United States, force a demoralised army in Vietnam to its knees, and bring havoc to the streets of urban America.

It would also give notoriety to the name of Khun Sa.

5

World at War

It was not simply the Japanese entry into the war and their expansion into Southeast Asia that prompted some Burmese leaders to co-operate with them. Many nationalists saw the Japanese as their liberators from European colonialism, a role the Japanese were quick to adopt. Aung San, meaning 'Victorious Diamond', was a student leader at the time and father of Aung San Suu Kyi, immediately offered the hand of friendship to the Japanese.

At the height of their military success, the Japanese conquerors offered a measure of independence to those who had demonstrated opposition to the British, including Aung San and his Thirty Comrades, the original volunteers who formed the Burma Independence Army (BIA) to fight the British. They were permitted to set up a puppet government under the control of the Japanese. Many of these collaborators were later to figure prominently in the Burmese government once the country had gained independence.

However, not all chose the path of collaboration, and Khun Sa's family remained loyal to the British. The Japanese attempted to enlist local support politically but usually managed to alienate themselves as a result of their harsh and arrogant conduct.

Broadly speaking, the Japanese found the lowland Burmese, or Burman tribe, who were seeking independence from the British, more sympathetic to their occupation. By contrast, the Karens, like many of the hill tribes, were anti-Burmese and pro-British. The Kachins, a fierce tribe who lived in the wild country along the Chinese border and regularly enlisted in the Burma Rifles, a famous regiment in the British Empire, were fiercely anti-Japanese. The Shans, the largest of the minority groups, were in the main neutral but tended to side with the British, who they believed would eventually grant them independence.

The British 14th Army, commanded by General William Slim, was a multi-national force which formerly controlled operations against the

Japanese Army in Burma. The British began to realise that conventional warfare was of little use in the jungle, so under the command of General Orde Wingate, they placed some special forces, known as the Chindits, behind enemy lines and supplied them by air. They also started to get reports of local opposition to the invaders, particularly among the northern tribes, and supplied them with the means to hit back. The Japanese army responded with such brutality that it is still remembered today, which explains why the Shan and their neighbours are less vocal than the West in their praise for Aung San Suu Kyi, who, as the daughter of Aung San the Burmese collaborator, they view with suspicion. They believe that Aung San encouraged the Japanese to brutalise the hill tribes.

Some Shans, however, were violently anti-British and spies were everywhere. Loyal Shan and Kachin fighters, supporting the Chindit columns, were constantly on guard against informers. Suspicious individuals were interrogated and if found guilty they were summarily executed. Dealing with informers was not a question of vengeance but was crucial for survival.

Retribution by all sides was an everyday part of life in the violence of jungle warfare. After an action, the hill tribe fighters would whenever possible, hide Japanese corpses which greatly disturbed the enemy. It was a subtle and local form of psychological warfare. It was of great importance to the Japanese soldiers to recover and dispose of their dead, and they would risk as much to retrieve a dead comrade as Western troops might to rescue a wounded one. If they could not remove the corpse they burned it on the spot, cutting off a finger so that at least a portion of the deceased could be buried in Japan.

The Shans proved to be tough guerrilla soldiers and were soon recruited by the British into Force 136, the cover name for British Special Forces in the Far East. Captain J.E. Smallwood, a veteran of the British 14th Army's Chindit force in Burma, asserted in 'Guerrilla Warfare behind the Japanese Lines', a speech given in London during November 1946, that the Shan had been excellent jungle fighters. He said:

"They (Force 136) proved a real thorn in the side of the Japanese lines of communication in north-east Burma. The rank and file were made up mainly of Shans, for whom the British officer in charge had the highest praise. As an organised force they were no match against Japanese regular troops but, operating as guerrillas in their native jungle, there was nothing to touch them. Although we armed them with rifles and sub-machine guns,

they were much happier with a dah or long-bladed knife, usually used for clearing the jungle and it was with these weapons that they did most of the damage."

Khun Sa's uncle, Khun Ja, fought alongside the Allies and would later be politically active after the war, but it was the tales of Shan bravery that left the strongest impression on the boy. He loved military history and took a keen interest in learning about tactics, infantry fighting and the use of heavy weapons, especially in the jungle conditions of Burma and Southeast Asia.

Khun Sa learned at an early age that every prince, every chieftain, every tribe had possessions which had to be defended against the predatory instincts of others. War was a basic ingredient of life, and military prowess was important because it was how honours and wealth were gained. Fighting men rallied around a hero, and a small gang could grow to become an army and transform a man into a general! Khun Ja's exploits were an inspiration to his nephew, and his influence remained in adulthood.

Korn Zurng

After his uncles, perhaps the strongest influence on Khun Sa was the resistance leader Korn Zurng, also known as Moh Heng. Khun Sa's political aspirations as a nationalist leader and fighter would be better understood if we also follow the career of this fascinating character in modern Shan history.

Korn Zurng was born into a well-to-do peasant family, on 20 June 1926, in the village of Htanaw, Taunggyi Province. The young boy attended school at the village monastery, which was where the children of rural families in the Shan states usually gained their education. Accepted into the monastery Korn Zurng's heart was indelibly printed with faith in the Lord Buddha's teachings.

These were fine ideals for a man who was to become an exemplary nationalist leader. He was also going to become a partner of the Kuomintang Chinese Army and would be recognised as a Shan warlord in his own right, as well as a drugs trafficker.

At the time when Khun Sa was being taken out of school, due to the Japanese invasion, Korn Zurng was sixteen years old and ready to join the resistance movement against the invaders. While training with the British, his potential was spotted by a recruiter for Detachment 101, a special OSS unit. The American OSS (Office of Strategic Services), a predecessor of the CIA, had created Detachment 101, which mainly used indigenous personal, for a variety of clandestine guerrilla and intelligence-gathering operations against Japanese forces in Burma.

By the end of the war, Korn Zurng had matured, as a result of the hardships he had suffered during his three years as a guerrilla fighter and had earned a reputation as a competent military commander. In Korn Zurng's political mind there was no doubt about the status of the Shan land, it was a separate and different country from Burma. The Burmese, of course, took a different view.

An execution

When the Second World War ended, a ceremony was held to celebrate the return of the princes, the Zaofahs or Sawbwas, the "Lords of the Sky" in English. They were the traditional rulers in the Shan States whom the British, during the empire, had allowed to continue in office just as they had the rajahs in India. In total there were 34 principalities governed by hereditary chiefs. In theory the Zaofah was the ruler, but there was also a British Resident, a political officer appointed by the British Governor, who, diplomatically, maintained the interests of the colonial power. In allowing the Zaofahs autonomy, the British had ignored their own attempts at opium suppression. At that time opium growth was limited but, when the British left, the system was in place for expansion. The Zaofahs were greedy and demanded tribute, which could only come from the seed of the opium poppy.

The patriotic Khun Ja, uncle of the young Khun Sa, was determined to attend the ceremony, a big occasion. Joining him to pay their respects, and join in the festivities, was his brother, Khun Sam. When they arrived, however, they were arrested by the police, on a trumped-up charge of collaborating with the Japanese, and told they would be sent to Lashio, the capitol, for trial. Instead, they were taken to a village across the Salween River and imprisoned in a small brick-built dwelling that doubled as the area jail. They were informed by their escort that the regional police officer would come to interrogate them before continuing to Lashio. The two brothers waited in their cell patiently, they had no reason to be suspicious and nor could they have foreseen the true purpose of their detour.

The Zaofah had secretly ordered their execution, which was to be carried out as swiftly as possible. But there was a delay as the official executioner could not be found and the captain of the guard had to frantically search for a replacement. He ordered some of his men to carry out the deed, but even with offers of money they refused. Eventually the captain found a candidate, who only agreed if his face was covered, fearing retribution.

The first the brothers knew about their imminent death was the cell door opening. The captain entered and nervously read the judgement and sentence before they were taken to the courtyard and hanged from a metal pole.

No reason was given for the executions. None was considered necessary, for the word of the ruling families was law. The Zaofah had been promised he would retain his exalted status if he became a loyal subject of the new Burma, a country that had no intention of entertaining Shan, or any other, nationalist aspirations.

The incident made an indelible mark on the teenage Chang Si-Fu, who now began to use his Shan name and traditional title, Khun Sa. It was a name that would be remembered by those who had slain his uncles, and it was a name that would be known far beyond the borders of the Shan states. Khun Sa would never forget his bitterness. And no one would ever forget Khun Sa.

6

Aung San and Independence

During the Japanese invasion, the Burmese communist party had split into two factions. One group, which based itself on the Soviet model, saw the Japanese invasion as saving them from colonialism. The other faction, led by Thakin Soe, was Trotskyite in belief and opposed to the Japanese, whom they considered also to be imperialists. In 1944, Thakin Soe founded an anti-fascist front to unite the resistance forces. It was clear by then that the Japanese were facing defeat. Even Aung San could see this and so switched rapidly to become a part of that alliance.

Aung San was welcomed into the alliance and given a military appointment. He saw a great future for this force in the coming struggle for independence from the British. This was easily won, and not because of Aung San's pressures, but because of the enthusiasm of the British Labour Party. Following their election victory in 1945, Great Britain began to divest itself of its massive empire.

For people like Korn Zurng in the Shan states, it was clear, given the goodwill of Britain's new government, that Burma was heading rapidly for independence. The British wanted a gradual transition with time to rebuild the shattered economy, and indeed the highly fragmented political system, before the handover.

It soon became clear to the Burmese communists that Aung San's pretence to national unity was little more than a sham. After their initial co-operation in the 'democratic' process, they decided to withdraw and go underground. One half, calling itself 'The White Flag', allied to China while the other, 'The Red Flag', was backed by the Soviet Union and led by Thakin Soe. These two groups began a bloody campaign of terror. There was also considerable disaffection among the Shans and other northern hill tribes. They were beginning to wonder what had happened to the promises made to them, by the British, of self-determination.

Aung San was unwilling to wait and was afraid that, if he delayed too long, other groups might supersede him and gain the spoils themselves.

The British yielded to his demands and granted independence, but in July 1947, Aung San was assassinated. He was only thirty-two years old. The assassination was blamed on a former associate, U Saw, a man who had shared Aung San's belief that the Japanese were the rightful leaders of the Orient and who had been imprisoned by the British for his contacts with the enemy. Aung San never did get to enjoy the fruits of his struggle, though he did leave behind his daughter, Aung San Suu Kyi. One day she would become the First Lady of Burma and the country's leader in her own right.

The Promise at Panlong

When Sir Reginald Dorman-Smith, the British Governor, returned to Burma after the war, he brought with him new administrative plans for the country. The British knew that the ethnic divide in Burma was a time-bomb waiting to explode if agreement between the tribal groups could not be found. So a separate plan was presented for the Shan States and the other hill regions, collectively known as the Frontier Area.

Geographically Burma is made up of a vast central depression, inhabited by the ethnic Burmese, approximately 65 per cent of the total population, and the 'Frontier Area', a broad designation for the mountainous regions bordering India, China, Laos, and Thailand, and inhabited by non-Burmese.

The Frontier Area alone includes 67 tribal groups forming 7 main ethnic groups. The Shans, the largest group, are ethnically more closely related to the Thais than to the Burmese. The word Shan is actually a British corruption of their Burmese-given name, Siam or Syam. The Shans call themselves Tai and are fiercely nationalistic. The Tai peoples refer to the descendants of speakers of a common Tai language which includes Thai, Shan, and Lao.

Under the old British Colonial government, the Frontier Areas were detached from Burma and allowed local rule, though the Governor had overall control. With the change brought about by the war and the Japanese occupation, it was decided to introduce a more democratic system to the region rather than continue with the autocratic rule of the tribal chiefs, or Zaofahs. However, most of the tribal leaders were more interested in gaining independence and the right of self-determination than the transformation plan of the British.

Prior to his assassination, in February 1947, Aung San had held a conference at Panlong, in the Shan States to define the principles of a broad federalism which protected the rights of the ethnic minorities including the Shan, Karen, Pa-O, Karenni, Mon, Chin, and the Kachin. The agreement also included the inhabitants of the Arakan (later renamed Rakhine State), home of the much persecuted Muslim Rohingya people. The British Government Observer at the conference was Arthur Bottomley, Member of Parliament (later Lord Bottomley).

Aung San also stated that the Right and Secession for the Frontier Area must be recognised, but it was Burma's responsibility to prove its sincerity so that the States would not wish to leave. With that important concession in mind, the Shans' interpretation of the Panlong Agreement was for a federation of independent states. The new constitution was ratified on 24 September 1947 and accepted by the British government.

In short, the Panlong agreement was seen by all the ethnic minorities as a solemn promise of self-determination, given by both Britain and Burma, to be achieved within 10 years of independence. It is because it was never honoured that Burma has witnessed over seventy years of continuing conflict.

Strange alliances

In those days, the problem of narcotics crime was still minor, at least as far as the West was concerned. China still remained the largest consumer, followed by Iran, though before long, Iran would become a major producer. Meanwhile, the newborn country of Burma was being lyrically painted by its leaders as a 'Garden of Eden' and where 'The Lotus Eaters' lived.

The dream was fast to change into a nightmare, beginning soon after 4 January 1948, when the British flag was lowered in Rangoon at 4.20 a.m. It was an hour specified by the astrologers as being auspicious for the cause of independence, but they could hardly have been more wrong.

From the outset, the new independent Burmese government of U-Nu, the country's first Prime Minister, was faced with problems. There were armed insurrections by the nation states, which were all determined to exercise the rights of self-determination promised to them under the Panlong Agreement. These hill tribes, having recently fought with such courage against the Japanese invaders, were experienced in battle and well-armed. Furthermore, the recently united Burmese Communist Party (BCP), the pro-Chinese organisation, having taken part in the elections but presumably dissatisfied with the results, now withdrew their deputies from the government and began to mount attacks themselves.

Where no dissent had previously existed, the Burmese had created it by their heavy-handed and arrogant tactics. U-Nu tried to impose Buddhism as the state religion, causing fury amongst the Christian tribes, the Chin, Kachin, and Karen, and the Muslim Arakans. He also upset the more traditionalist ethnic groups by instituting socialist economic and welfare policies without consultation. Conflict spread throughout the land and even to the streets of the capital, Rangoon.

One of the ironies of Burmese politics at this time was that the Shan states were still feudal. The Shan princes, the Zaofahs and the Sawbwas were the absolute rulers and behaved as such. The history books tend to record them romantically, as ancient leaders of the local people, but the reality was different.

Humble tribesmen were encouraged to rebel against their traditional rulers by successive Burmese governments. Mistrust was sown among the different tribes by a campaign of disinformation, encouraging each to believe that another had designs on its territory.

By the time the various tribes realised that they had been duped, there was another enemy to face, for the Burmese had created further mischief by feeding arms to the northern communists, the BCP. This kind of strategy has stood all Burmese governments in good stead ever since. Even today, they are still masters at fragmenting the opposition by making pacts and truces, with various groups. In effect, the government wanted to 'Burmanise' the whole union, in other words rid themselves of the insurgent troublemakers. They had played off the hill tribes against the BCP and now they were playing off the BCP against the hill tribes.

The relationship between the Burmese government and the tribes and the various political factions of the north are not unconnected to drugs trafficking. This is still the case today. The Burmese government, desperately anxious for foreign investment, wanted to present the best possible image to the outside world, not easy given their human rights record. Nevertheless, they had made efforts to come to agreements with the dissenting tribes including the Shans, and Khun Sa and other warlords who were useful as scapegoats for all the narcotics trading, in which units of their own army were certainly involved.

Khun Sa used to say of himself that if he had not existed, they, meaning various official organisations, would have had to invent him. His presence was, perversely, in everybody's interest. Journalists were able to churn out stories about him, and the DEA was able to ask for more money so

Khun Sa in the 1950s

they could go after the drug barons. It suited the Burmese army to blame him for the increase in opium production, and social workers in the West could blame him for drug problems in their countries.

It was true that Khun Sa's international stature as a bogeyman had increased. There were many other warlords in the area who were big players in the drugs industry such as the Wei brothers with the Wa, and the Yangs with the Kokang but none of them received the same level of attention. But unlike Khun Sa, the other warlords were not committed to the Shan nationalist cause and the Burmese government knew that.

It would seem that the politics in Burma could feel more like a big business deal in the end. As a mystified Western journalist once asked Khun Sa, "What is it you do 'business' business, or 'liberation' business?" Meaning are you a drugs dealer or a freedom fighter!

The Burmese government's fear was an alliance between the dissenting tribes, which is why Khun Sa was such a thorn in their side, simply because of his proven record of uniting the Shans. In Burmese politics, it is never safe to predict anything. All the insurgent armies have over the years made ceasefires with their enemies, and they all have had Chinese businessmen attached to them who wheel and deal in the drugs trade. Strange alliances form and dissolve all the time.

7

Power of the Poppy

The trafficking of opium products remains on a global scale, despite the efforts of national law enforcement agencies. The vast profits generated from illegal narcotics makes the risk worthwhile for those people who seek power. To best understand how opium and power go hand in hand, one has to understand the history of the commodity.

Khun Sa himself had never denied that the Shan people made a living from harvesting opium, "how else can they live?" he would ask. He was always quick, however, to remind people who it was who introduced opium growing to the area.

The British

When Lord Shelburne faced the cost of paying for Britain's long war with the American colonists he had a novel idea. He expanded the East India Company's opium trade, which first began in 1775. The British were only following in the paths of the Portuguese and Dutch colonists. By 1750, the Dutch were shipping more than a hundred tons of opium a year to Indonesia. Adam Smith noted in his 'Wealth of Nations' that the Dutch found opium 'a useful means for breaking the moral resistance of the natives'. This proved to be a chilling analysis for the future.

In the early nineteenth century, Britain's trade with China was controlled by the East India Company. They imported silk, spices and of course tea into Great Britain. However, the exports that Britain offered to the world failed to match those imports in value and there was a serious trade deficit. To make up the deficit, the tea clippers began to smuggle opium into China, having obtained the drug from Ottoman Turkey and India, and this caused serious social and economic problems. All protests from the Chinese were ignored and this finally led to what became known in history as the First Opium War, in 1839. It ended three years later with China humiliated.

The Chinese Imperial Army, decimated by ten years of opium addiction, was no match for the British forces. The Emperor was quickly forced to sue for peace and Britain demanded in settlement 'admission of opium as an article of lawful commerce', as well as territorial concessions, including Hong Kong.

Relations with China remained tense and this soon led to the Second Opium War, in 1856. This time Britain was joined by France. After storming Beijing, in 1860, the victorious Anglo-French army compelled China into granting more trading concessions. Within four years, Britain was in control of 80 per cent of a vastly expanded trade.

Many trading companies had also turned their attention to the West Coast of America and the new trade in Chinese 'servants'. In 1846, one hundred and seventeen thousand coolies had been brought into America and, although this trade was outlawed by Lincoln in 1862, the import of impoverished, often shanghaied or kidnapped, Chinese continued at an escalating rate until the end of the century. Many brought with them an addiction to opium and so a new lucrative trade was encouraged in the United States and the seeds were sown for America's biggest social problem of the twentieth century.

Before any modern Americans shake their heads in condemnation of this outrage, it must be pointed out that the Americans too realised what a profitable business opium was and soon wanted a piece of the action. In 1850, the head of one such company was a certain Warren Delano II, grandfather of President Franklin Delano Roosevelt.

The Chiu Chao

Towards the turn of the twentieth century, the prime movers in the opium trade became the triads, China's secret criminal network. Their name derives from a Chinese concept that identifies the three sides of a triangle as man, heaven and earth. The most sinister and most effective triads were the Chiu Chao, from Southern China. Khun Sa told me that major banks in the region are under the control of the Chiu Chao, and they finance the narcotics trade, especially in Hong Kong.

In 1997, the lease of Hong Kong and the New Territories was handed back to China by the United Kingdom. It was until that point the heroin producing capital of the world. The drug trade was a highly organised, highly efficient business. Opium from the Golden Triangle was transferred to Bangkok by the Chiu Chao traders who then sold it on for smuggling into Hong Kong. There it was refined by some of the best chemists in the world, also Chiu Chao members.

The triads are extremely nepotistic, for the reason that written contracts or agreements are not needed when dealing with family. It would certainly take a brave man, if not a reckless one, to cross them because their professional hitmen, called 'Red Poles', are quick to exact retribution. After the raw opium has been refined, the heroin is smuggled into Bangkok for transfer to the great cities of the world, anywhere that has a Chinese quarter, like London, or Amsterdam, Vancouver or New York.

Detecting the transfer of funds is virtually impossible as a result of the unique 'chit' system of banking they sometimes operate. A man walks into a Chinese gold shop in San Francisco with a million dollars. The same day, someone else collects an equivalent sum from a gold shop in Bangkok's Chinatown, and the normal banking system has been completely avoided. Even today and at a time when even the most secretive banks are beginning to co-operate with police on international drug money, the Chinese connection remains virtually untraceable.

Their livelihood, however, depends on a steady supply of the raw opium needed to process the white powder. They are the distributors. In the eighties, the man who could cut off their trade, the man who controlled the supply of opium from the Golden Triangle, probably responsible for more than a third of the heroin used by well over half a million addicts in the United States of America, was Khun Sa.

The Sicilians

Once the Second World War was over, a golden opportunity to eradicate the problem of drugs was missed. In Italy, one of Mussolini's achievements, apart from making the trains run on time, had been the virtual elimination of the mafia as a significant organisation and in France, the German occupation had driven the Corsican crooks out of business. In China, when Mao Tse-Tung's forces completed their conquest of the mainland by capturing Shanghai, they brought drug trafficking to an end.

At that time it was estimated that there were only 20,000 addicts in the United States. If the American government had acted swiftly and with the other countries, the drugs problem might have been eliminated. If that had happened, Khun Sa might have grown up to be a dealer in mules and horses or a tea planter whose only involvement with drugs would have been to supply the English with caffeine, but the problem was thought to be minor, and the opportunity was squandered.

On the other hand, the Americans felt the menace of communism had to be confronted whatever the cost and by any means available, and the successful conclusion of the war against Germany and Japan was followed by the Cold War against communism.

Foremost in the fight against the 'red menace' was the Central Intelligence Agency, established on the orders of President Harry Truman under the provision of the National Security Act of 1947. The rosy picture perpetuated by the Agency's propaganda machine was that the citizens of the United States of America could sleep more soundly at night, knowing this vast network of agents was working tirelessly to defend their way of life, but the reality was very different. The implacable desire for power by some of its more ambitious senior agents was to lead the CIA to compromise with the devil when necessary.

The hideous problem of drug addiction, which causes so much crime and misery in the United States, can be laid squarely at the door of the CIA. The poppy fields of the Golden Triangle owe their origins to the agents who encouraged the harvesting of opium, in order to finance operations against the communists.

In furthering its duplicity, elements of the CIA have supported tyrants such as Manuel Noriega in Panama, have helped to topple governments and install imagined friends of the West like Idi Amin of Uganda, and have protected criminals around the world such as Marseille's Corsican gangs. All this has been done apparently to counter the threat of communism, without the authorisation of Congress and in direct contravention of Federal law.

At the end of the Second World War, the Office of Strategic Services (OSS), enabled many Nazi war criminals to escape. Many of them ended their days in luxury in Argentina or Paraguay. This was in return for services in opposing the communists.

It is difficult today, at a time when world communism is in tatters, to understand the fear and loathing of it that existed in America immediately after the Second World War. Soviet Russia had played as large a part as the Allies in winning the conflict, but the CIA was tasked to seek all traces of communism in America, and if this meant employing criminal elements, so be it. But it also led to the CIA helping the crooks, in order to maintain them. In time, certain CIA agents found that they could also benefit from the proceeds of these illicit trades.

The Mafia in America was imported from Sicily by Italian immigrants in the late nineteenth and early twentieth centuries, having begun as a patriotic movement seeking to drive out the French imperialists. Once their noble objective had been achieved, they turned to crime. At first they preyed on hard-working Italian immigrants, principally in Boston, Chicago, and New York, forcing them to pay for 'protection' if they wanted to stay in business. Prohibition enabled the Mafia to grow. Fortunes were made by smuggling liquor across the Canadian border and by distilling their own 'hooch'. In addition, gambling and prostitution formed lucrative sources of income. Drugs trafficking did not form a part of their activities until the late 1930s when the organisation was headed by Salvatore 'Lucky' Luciano.

Before that, the control of cocaine in America had been in the hands of the powerful Jewish gangsters, principally, Bugsy Siegel, Dutch Schulz, and Meyer Lansky. Bloody feuds raged on the streets of Chicago until Luciano, a brilliant strategist, forged alliances with the other gangs and turned the Mafia into the most potent group in the country. They hired the best lawyers and had senators and judges on their payroll. 'Lucky' Luciano bears the dubious distinction of being the creator of what we today call 'organised' crime. He took the Mafia out of the back streets and turned it into big business.

Luciano's reign as 'Il capo dei capi' (The Boss of Bosses) came to an end just before the war, when he was indicted on sixty-two counts of forced prostitution. The state, knowing Luciano's deep involvement in the drugs trade, would have preferred to charge him with narcotics offences but it was difficult to make them stick. Nevertheless, Luciano was sentenced to a thirty to fifty-year term in jail. He would probably have died there except, in 1943, his country needed him.

When the US Office of Naval Intelligence was planning the first allied invasion of Europe, via Sicily, they realised that there were American citizens with contacts on the island. One such man had the connections to assist them in the invasion even though, at the time, he resided in a prison cell: 'Lucky' Luciano. Through him, they were able to make contact with members of the Mafia in Sicily, many of whom welcomed the GIs with open arms.

With the defeat of Mussolini, the Mafia were allowed to regain their hold on crime and were considered a useful ally in the struggle against communism. Free enterprise reigned again and a lucrative black market rapidly blossomed. The Mafia was back in business and the friends of 'Lucky' Luciano prospered. As a reward for his services to the Allied cause,

Luciano was released in 1946 and deported to Italy, a condition that suited him just fine. In no time at all, he was able to re-establish himself in the business of organising opium shipments from Turkey, via his French connections in the Lebanon and processing them in Sicily or France.

The finished product was smuggled into the United States through the contacts that Luciano had set up before the war. Shipments of seemingly innocent produce from Italy and France sailed to Canada, to Mafia connections in Cuba or even direct to New York, where it was received by the members of the Mafia-controlled longshoremen's union.

The contacts forged by Luciano had really paid off. In Cuba, Meyer Lansky ruled the roost. He owned most of the casinos and corrupt politicians in Havana. The whole country was a den of vice where the criminal fraternity were able to treat the island as a home from home.

The CIA's actions after the Second World War were to generate a worldwide epidemic and create the conditions that enabled the growth of a new monster, whose name would come to be synonymous with the drugs trade. However, at that time he was just a thirteen-year-old boy named Chang Si-Fu, who was living in the Shan States, in Burma.

8

The Kuomintang

To understand why Khun Sa and the Shans got involved in the drug trade, one must understand the impact of the Chinese Civil War on its neighbours. The war, which started in 1927, was fought between the Kuomintang (KMT) government of the Republic of China, commanded by Generalissimo Chiang Kai-Shek and the Communist Party of China led by Chairman Mao Tse-Tung. By 1949, the Kuomintang was defeated and retreated to the island of Formosa, now Taiwan, in the east. In the west of China, another remnant of the Kuomintang army fled into north Burma. From there, they could mount retaliatory raids into Yunnan, the neighbouring Chinese province, which had a considerable Shan population of nearly three million.

It was a retreat which was to have repercussions for the Shans in Burma, for the Kuomintang was determined to continue its war against the communists, using the Shan state as a sanctuary.

For them, the war had never ended. They were here, or so they said at the time, while they built up their forces for the great invasion of their homeland. On three occasions, twice in 1951 and once in 1952, the Kuomintang made CIA-sponsored invasions of the neighbouring Chinese province of Yunnan. The hope was that the presence of nationalist armies on Chinese soil would spark mass uprisings against the communist regime. It did not. All three invasions failed miserably. The whole notion was unrealistic, there was no way they could counter the power of the Chinese communists and they instead decided to carve their own fiefdom out of Burmese territory.

The Kuomintang spread their troops along the border with China, though had the Chinese wished to cross it, they would have done so with ease. Financed by the CIA, they occasionally made excursions into their motherland, supposedly to glean information on communist troop movements but in reality to move cargoes of opium. Certainly, in their minds at least, they were preparing for the great day when they could oust their enemies. In the meantime, enjoying the benefits accorded to them by the CIA, they engaged in illicit trade.

In the United States, the Truman Administration was fearful of communism spreading beyond the borders of China and preventing this became the number one priority. So it was that the rag-tag army of Kuomintang remnants that swarmed over the border into Burma was afforded the status of a worthwhile army, capable of upholding the democratic way of life. There followed, from 1950 onward, the systematic but covert program of supplying weapons and finances to the Kuomintang.

At first this operation was sanctioned by Congress, but the elected representatives of the people were soon bypassed. Very wisely, no doubt, because it was quite likely that some astute member might begin to ask why so much money was being used to so little effect. Congress was kept in ignorance, democracy was side-stepped. As a result, not only was the fledgling state of Burma beset with uprisings by its own disaffected tribes and the communists, it now had to cope with a marauding horde of immigrant Chinese mercenaries, clandestinely supplied with arms by the Americans within its own sovereign territory.

The Kuomintang's forays into China met with little success but they gave the CIA a justification for continuing their support. They were though a source of intense irritation to the Burmese government, who made strenuous efforts to dislodge them. As a result, they moved up

Khun Sa (right) in his twenties.

further north into the hill areas, where they found themselves located in the best areas for cultivating the poppy. Opium had been produced therefrom early in the nineteenth century, when many Chinese, driven by famine, migrated into the area. However, from the early 1880s, when the Shan States became a British protectorate, opium production was limited and strictly controlled, and in the main it continued in that way.

Under the direction of the Kuomintang, opium production skyrocketed. As the Kuomintang General Tuan Shi-Wen would later explain to a British journalist, "We have to continue to fight the evil of communism, and to fight you must have an army, and an army must have guns, and to buy guns you must have money. In these mountains, the only money is opium."

Opium was needed to buy far more than guns. These were useful for solving small local difficulties but, for the industry to expand worldwide, something much more sophisticated was needed, such as modern transportation, preferably aeroplanes.

The Kuomintang forced the hill tribes to grow opium. They set up laboratories in the jungle, with Chinese chemists refining the crop into heroin, which was exported in exchange for arms. This was the beginning of the evil trade which would grow like a cancer, overseen and it was accepted, if not prompted, by the CIA. Kuomintang soldiers filtered through the Shan states in their thousands and Loimaw, where the young Khun Sa lived, bore the brunt of this unexpected foreign invasion. Local people were conscripted for labour, taxes were levied, and all the inhabitants were subjected to harsh rule. It was indeed the Kuomintang who, by their drug-related activities, first gave this region its sobriquet of 'The Golden Triangle'.

American fears of communist expansionism meant that CIA involvement with the Kuomintang seemed to be essential. The problem was how to get supplies to the Kuomintang, hidden away as they were in the northern Burmese highlands. It was impossible to take supplies overland, so it had to be done by air.

A solution was found. A unit of American airmen known as the Flying Tigers had earned a reputation for their exploits in China during the Second World War. Their commander had been General Chennault, who now ran Civil Air Transport, a Nationalist Chinese airline that had supported Chiang Kai-Shek and his Kuomintang forces in the civil war. No questions would be asked in Congress if a 'civil' airline bought up large numbers of old air force planes, so Civil Air Transport, suffering from financial difficulties, was purchased by the CIA for one million dollars and its name was changed to Air America. What could be more appropriate for an airline upholding the national interest?

Although the CIA was given a bigger budget for its anti-communist drive, it was not enough for the Kuomintang generals, who were encouraged to increase their opium output. Transport for it would be laid on by Air America, courtesy of the American taxpayer.

This is not to say the CIA as a whole is a corrupt organisation. But there are, and always have been, ruthless elements within it who have rendered parts of it corrupt. They also tend to be overseas and shift with world politics.

It is worth remembering that the CIA consists of more than just American agents in the field. Like the DEA, wherever they operate, there is a local infrastructure supporting the agency. The influential elements within these structures have a vested interest in keeping problems active. If the agency was to completely solve a problem, the locals would all be out of a job. So the work of the CIA and the DEA is never done. The danger is that corruption takes hold and, in due course, becomes almost institutionalised.

Khun Sa's revenge

By the time Khun Sa was eighteen he was a bold fighter, a cunning hunter and a leader among the young men of his age. He had a real passion for horses and became a fine horseman. His grandfather, a horse breeder of note, gave him a stallion to keep as his own. He was devoted to the animal, riding it whenever possible. One day, while he was fishing in a local river, a squad of young Kuomintang soldiers appeared and drove away his horse and two mules. Pursuit on foot was pointless, so he ran home to collect another mount and chased after the thieves, searching all day until he finally recognised his horse in the distance. Hiding nearby until dark, he crept into the Kuomintang camp and took his animals back.

It was a few weeks before the Chinese soldiers returned, this time for his grandfather's horses and mules. The old man was thrown aside, hit with a rifle butt and his entire breeding stock was taken. Even in later life Khun Sa could still recall his grandfather and how he was forced, at the point of a bayonet, to show the soldiers the saddle for each of the mules. It was an intolerable insult, after which he resolved to regard the Kuomintang as foreign invaders who should be driven from his homeland.

Khun Sa plotted revenge. He followed the trail of a Kuomintang

unit and for three days spied on their camp and noting every move. He sustained himself on the dried meat that he bought with him, kept between his saddle and horse's back, and the few grains of cold cooked rice in his pocket. He then organised a group of his boyhood friends and staged a dawn raid on the unsuspecting Kuomintang. The daring raid was a success and he managed to acquire more than thirty assorted weapons. He had learned the lesson of cunning and surprise. He also learned that victories won against superior might are short-lived and the Kuomintang was a formidable enemy.

The Kuomintang retaliated and quickly moved to put his grandfather in custody and demanded, together with the return of the weapons, prompt discontinuance of Khun Sa's activities. The young man had no doubt that discontinuance of his life was what the Kuomintang really had in mind and having returned the arms and secured the release of his grandfather, he promptly left the area. What had happened was a lesson he was not going to forget.

It wasn't long before the news of Khun Sa's deeds spread among the Shan and his name was held in admiration by friends and in jealousy by his enemies. But, in his view, he now had a name that counted, and his band of followers was growing in numbers.

Women were always attracted to Khun Sa. He was ruggedly handsome, a look that is apparently more appealing to Shan women than ordinary handsome features. His boyhood friends saw him as a natural leader and, when he used to say things, everybody listened to him, even the older boys. It was said that he was always cut a dashing figure and had a quick sense of humour for any occasion.

By the time Khun Sa reached adolescence he was mindful of the duties he would perform one day if he became a chieftain. He realised that a chieftain, whatever the size of the clan, was the symbol of unity. Almost daily he was reminded by his elders of the importance of adhering to the customs and traditions of their ancestors. Although many of the hill tribes were Animists, the Shans were mainly Buddhists, and he was bought up as such.

Khun Sa was known for looking after his men and had many long-serving retainers. Though in later years Burmese propaganda used to allege that he travelled extensively planning drug deals, in reality, he had never been anywhere apart from Burma, Laos and Thailand and he never held a passport. He did not read Burmese and although he spoke Thai, he did not read it, and nor did he read Shan all that well. He had a better understanding of Chinese. What he knew about the United States, or the world, he gained from Chinese books, radio, and television. As a young man he had met some American soldiers in Laos and Thailand, but that was his only real experience of Americans.

9

The French Connection

By 1953, the Korean War had been fought to a bitter stalemate. Khun Sa, and others like him, puzzled as to why Americans sent their young men to die in Asia. King George VI passed away in England and Elizabeth II came to the throne. Another link in the colonial chain had gone. The King of England, as the Shans had seen it, had been the protector of their rights in the Panlong agreement. Stalin, master of Soviet Russia and its empire, also died but his spirit still lived on. There was no end to the Cold War, no lifting of the 'Iron Curtain'.

The French war in Indo-China ended in 1954 after their army was defeated at Dien Bien Phu. Khun Sa remembers the event as a milestone along the road of freedom for the oppressed people of Southeast Asia. He did not at the time realise its enormous significance, how this particular path of history would lead to the Vietnam war. He did not realise either that this same road would be his own path to power.

French involvement in Southeast Asia had begun in the mid-nineteenth century. First they annexed Cambodia and then they extended their control into Laos and parts of Vietnam. To ensure that these colonial adventures brought in revenue, they copied the British in India and China and turned to opium. At the turn of the century, they had established a highly productive trade in the drug, in the territories which now became known as French Indo-China.

Imports of opium from the Middle East and China were processed in the refineries which the French built to serve the ever-increasing number of addicts. At the outbreak of the Second World War in 1939, income from narcotics was one of the major sources of French revenue. However, the war itself seriously inconvenienced the opium trade, mainly by cutting off their sources in the Middle East. The answer was to produce more opium in their own territories until they once again had a thriving industry. In doing so, they too had sown the seeds of their own destruction.

After the defeat of the Japanese, the French began to re-establish their control over Indo-China and to reignite the drugs trade, but times had changed dramatically. First of all, the Americans, who oversaw the surrender of the Japanese in the region, were hostile to European colonialism and withheld support for the growing war.

France, which had suffered four years of German occupation, could ill afford foreign adventures, but her military commanders in Indo-China were not easily dissuaded. The clandestine opium producing operations of French intelligence began to take on markedly greater significance. Now they were needed to finance the local war in Indo-China.

The Binh Xuyen

So it was that the operations were taken over by the French military. Naturally, their activities were not open to public scrutiny, particularly in times of war, and to question them would have been considered unpatriotic. The French started to use military transport to shift the raw opium to Saigon, where it was processed in secret refineries. As production increased, they were able to export it to Hong Kong, or the Corsican smugglers used by 'Lucky' Luciano, the American mafia boss. Like the CIA, the French had no hesitation in employing local gangsters to help them such as the Binh Xuyen (pronounced Bin Su yin), a force of ruthless river pirates. Again, the similarity to the CIA was striking and they could claim honestly that the Binh Xuyen, known for dealing in prostitution and opium, were assisting them in the fight to hold back the tide of communism.

The Deuxieme Bureau, France's equivalent of the CIA, began to search desperately for local groups to take part in the fight against the communist-backed Viet Minh. They provided money and arms to the gangsters to create a local militia but, by doing so, they also succeeded in giving free rein to vicious gangs who roamed the land, spreading terror and even managing to gain control of the government. Not surprisingly, the support for the insurgents grew ever stronger.

The Viet Minh were not the strongest enemies of the French, nor the most astute. That role fell to the Americans, who were determined to end the colonial control of the European nations.

To counter the effectiveness of the fierce Binh Xuyen, the CIA gave weapons and finance to Ngho Din Diem, who would become the first president of South Vietnam. As ever, the CIA managed to raise far greater finances for their programme than the French could. The tide turned in favour of the CIA, who were far more single-minded in achieving their goal. While French Intelligence was struggling to combat communist infiltration, as well as to keep hold of the illicit trade, the CIA worked on the principle that if they gained control of the opium market, they would also be able to defeat communism.

With a seemingly powerful army of 40,000, the French felt they were a match for the communists, but the Viet Minh began to force them back. The French set up a massive encampment at Dien Bien Phu, and into this stronghold they poured men and equipment, expecting to crush the enemy in one decisive battle. It may have seemed impregnable, but it was as useless as the Maginot Line had been on the border with Germany, in 1940. The communists surrounded the garrison and dug in, and by March 1954, the fate of the French army was sealed. There was no escape, and all attempts at relief from the outside failed. In the end, there was no alternative but abject, humiliating surrender to this rabble army.

Reaction in America suggested outrage that the French had yielded to the communists and there was a determination to take up the fight against the red hordes. The CIA, though, were not shedding too many tears now that the French had bequeathed them the lion's share of the opium trade.

The French also bequeathed the Americans the yet-to-come Vietnam war.

10

Rose of the North

The first clue I had that Bo Gritz might have some kind of hidden agenda was when he insisted that Lance Trimmer should accompany us to the Golden Triangle. Trimmer had served with Gritz in Vietnam and accompanied him on his last visit to see Khun Sa but when I originally planned the trip, I had allowed only for Gritz in the budget. However, one extra body did not wildly inflate the figure and if taking him made the colonel happy, that was fine by me. Then Gritz added Gary Goldman, a combat infantry officer who had also served in Vietnam and had joined his team on their Lazarus mission, to his entourage.

Two extra people could definitely break my business plan. I protested but Gritz was adamant: either Trimmer and Goldman came with us, or the deal was off. It was the eleventh hour and Gritz was key to my plan, so I did not want to risk calling his bluff or spoil my good relations with Canale 5 and covered the extra expense myself.

The two new members of the expedition had been part of the Operation Lazarus team which, under Gritz's command, had penetrated Laos in the early eighties in search of American POWs, but I was unsure why they were coming with us. It was also strange, given that Gritz had insisted that our numbers should be kept as low as possible, which was why I had agreed a basic crew of two, sound and camera, in addition to me and Gabriella Simone from Canale 5. I also wanted to take my friend Tudor Gates, a writer and filmmaker, for us to get the best value from our short time in Thailand. Tudor would help with any extra research on the Shan, while the rest of us trekked across the border into Burma.

Gritz had told me repeatedly that trekking through the jungle in the Golden Triangle was highly dangerous and that the more of us there were, the more likely it was we would be discovered. Yet he was able to increase the size of our group by a third on a whim. Was there a purpose, unknown to me, in taking these two individuals?

As soon as his trial was over, I contacted Gritz and reported that all was in place to mount our expedition. I wanted to hear for myself what he had attempted to tell the world and to check whether the man himself was at odds with my research.

It was 21 May 1989, when I travelled to Bangkok and met the Italian crew at the Impala, an ordinary 3-star tourist hotel. Gritz and his team had insisted on making their own travel arrangements and subsequently were late arriving. Under their instruction, I had booked more rooms than I needed at two different hotels, the Impala and the Atari, that were near each other. This made it possible for Gritz and his team to stay without checking in. I was beginning to feel like a foreign spy!

Gritz's journey to Bangkok had been an elaborate one. After sending Lance Trimmer ahead, as a kind of advance guard, Gritz and Gary Goldman flew via Hong Kong to Kuala Lumpur. They met up with Trimmer in Penang, Malaysia, and from there they were able to enter Thailand without papers, before catching a train to Bangkok. After all the fuss following Bo's return to the United States from the Golden Triangle, they were all convinced they would be listed on Thai computers, hence the secrecy.

The Italian crew and I, on the other hand, were staying quite openly, as tourists. We were carrying what felt like two tons of film equipment, mainly due to the twenty heavy cans of 16mm film stock we needed to make our documentary. If challenged, we would claim we were there to shoot the scenery – we were, after all, in the Golden Triangle.

Eventually, the Gritz team turned up, two wearing sunglasses indoors. We breakfasted at adjoining tables but were not allowed to make contact until we were upstairs, in a room which had been declared 'clean' of any bugs by Gary Goldman. It all seemed like rather heavy play acting to me, but they did have some quite serious problems. On their arrival in Bangkok, they had discovered that Johnny Poon, their main contact from previous visits, was believed to have been murdered; he and his driver had disappeared without trace. They were also concerned about Barry Flynn, an American contact of theirs who lived in Thailand and was rumoured to be involved in 'funny business'. Flynn had not been a soldier, as they all were, and they shared a mutual distrust of him. A colourful character, he made claims to have been a 'gofer' for Adnan Khashoggi and had once worked for President Ferdinand Marcos, before the leader of the Philippines had fallen from grace.

The point was that they had local contacts who would be able to make the arrangements for our visit to Khun Sa. In the meantime, the 'military' contingent, as we dubbed Gritz's group, settled into their rooms. It was my first chance to get the measure of our American companions. The balding Lance Trimmer was six feet tall, heavily built and sported a large 'beer gut'. He seemed to have a good sense of humour and was obviously the foil for Gritz and Gary Goldman, constantly warding off their jokes with wisecracks. He also possessed a peculiar habit of speaking in 'pigeon English' when answering non-Americans, including me. For instance, I might ask him where Bo was and the reply was given like an Apache Brave would in the movies "He… go… to… car." Very strange!

Gary Goldman on the other hand was a former infantryman and although never in the special forces he was a keep-fit fanatic. He teamed up with Gritz on a POW rescue operation and had since become an important member of the colonel's inner circle. His hallmark was a black canvas bag on a waist belt, although he would carry it slung over his shoulder. The bag was a mini-mart of goods, ranging from tools to small plastic bottles of every medicine you could think of.

I liked the Americans, they were good fun. I also felt comfortable in the knowledge that they had a serious side if things were to get rough. I looked on in amazement at the equipment they had brought with them, including sophisticated night vision glasses. They seemed particularly excited about trying on their new French paratrooper boots that had been specially bought for this mission.

With the clock ticking the crew was eager to get moving, but we had to await our 'military orders' from Bo Gritz. There were also still lots of cloak-and-dagger comings and goings at the hotel, as exchanges took place between Gritz and his various local contacts, who were operating from a nearby 'safe house'. Everyone seemed concerned about the missing Johnny Poon and the activities of Barry Flynn, who had apparently been involved in some arms dealings with Khun Sa, but had been unable to deliver.

At last Bo received word that we could proceed on our journey. Heng, one of our guides, had finally arrived. Although a Shan, he lived in Bangkok and worked for Khun Sa's operation. He had agreed to guide our expedition into the warlord's territory.

We hired a minibus to take us to Chiang Mai, in the north of the country. On our last night in Bangkok, Gary Goldman was appointed by Bo to be in charge of our welfare and was given the very important assignment of giving the Englishmen and Italians a conducted tour of Patpong, the red-light district. Although I had been to Bangkok before, it was still an interesting experience to go with a former GI and to see the crowded streets, the pestering touts, the brightly lit bars, and the seedy shows.

The girls were impoverished villagers from the north, lured less by the bright lights of Bangkok than by the need to provide for their families. They were available for the night at the price of a drink in a top-class American hotel. Gary Goldman reminded us that the latest statistics claimed that 44 per cent of the prostitutes in Bangkok had AIDS. We took him seriously.

The chain-smoking guide

Chiang Mai used to be known as the gateway to the border area, the last stop for trek supplies, though it is over 150 miles to the frontier and supplies can be easily purchased in Mae Hong Son, which lies right on the Burmese border.

Those who can, fly from Bangkok to Chiang Mai but with Bo Gritz we had to travel by road in case he was recognised at the airport. Long-distance travel by road can be very dangerous in Thailand, where drivers care little about speed limits, though it does give the opportunity of seeing the beauty of the countryside.

It took ten hours to reach Chiang Mai from Bangkok, on a fairly straight route. On arrival we split up. The Americans opted to stay in a rundown trekkers lodge on the edge of town, while the rest of us chose the more comfortable Chiang Inn, near the centre. Tudor Gates would stay on there, to carry out the research for the film, while the rest of us continued to the Golden Triangle. Rather than rely on the Americans, I felt it would be useful for us to have a point of contact in case we were stopped crossing the border. If that happened, Tudor could act as liaison between the officials and our embassy.

Chiang Mai, 'The Rose of the North', had the atmosphere of a frontier town. Although big flashy hotels were being built for the tourist boom, which was about to happen, there were still several small shops catering for backpackers who trekked in the surrounding hills. I took the opportunity to buy some supplies for our journey. I suggested to the Italians we each invest in some hard-wearing military-style trousers, a jungle hat and two water bottles. I also advised buying Chinese army gym shoes, which were on sale everywhere. Made of black canvas with rubber soles, they were ideal for trekking and had two small air holes on each side, through which water could escape when wading through streams. Because everything was so cheap it could all be thrown away at the end of the trek.

Chinese Haw smugglers — woman gang leader

That evening we joined the Americans for dinner at a restaurant with a nice bar near their lodge. Gritz was reminded of the first time he came to Chiang Mai, in 1986 when it seemed like there had been a big explosion. There were many windows missing from buildings over a large area of the town. Gritz asked why and was told that Khun Sa's men had just blown up a Kuomintang general's mansion nearby.

It would be at least a week before we expected to see Tudor again, so we had a farewell drink with him. We also had the opportunity to meet one of Khun Sa's agents who had been appointed to be our guide. Armed with a pleasant smile Som Suk, half Shan, half Thai, was a former smuggler. He looked like a very ordinary young man, in his late twenties and not the archetypal Chinese gangster of the movies, with gold teeth and a cigarette holder. I guessed that was why he was a successful smuggler.

His command of English was reasonable, but not good enough to have a detailed conversation. I asked him if he lived in the city. "Only two types of people come to Chiang Mai — tourists and drug dealers", he replied. Then I enquired how long it would take for us to reach Tiger Camp, he just beamed, "not long, not long" between mouthfuls of noodles.

Som Suk chain-smoked throughout the meal. At one point he took a drag of his foul-smelling cigarette and, before exhaling, gulped down half a tumbler of local whisky. We all stared in amazement, as he shook his head and contorted his face before saying, "General waiting for you, yes", before polishing off the rest of the whisky. An astonished Gary Goldman joked, "Jesus if we're not careful, this guy will be arrested for being drunk in charge of a mule!"

Mule station

The drive to the northernmost Thai town of Mae Hong Son, was a winding journey over a roller coaster terrain. The scenery was breathtaking and startlingly green, except where it was veiled by clouds, which cleared to reveal heart-stopping drops at the side of the narrow roads. Approximately seven hours after leaving Chiang Mai, we arrived in Mae Hong Son.

The town, built in the mist-shrouded mountains, had a feeling of tranquillity, a Shangri-La setting, like the mystical land described in James Hilton's novel *Lost Horizon*. There were two enchanting temples next to a small lake, surrounded by a palm grove. Bo Gritz told me that on his first visit what he immediately noticed, as an aviation expert, was something quite different: he was shocked to find an airport with a 2000 metre runway, in such a remote location.

He explained why it was there. Hundreds of tons of heroin were carried by mule out of Burma, then taken by truck to the airport at Mae Hong Son and flown to the Air Force Base at Chiang Mai, before being transferred onto legitimate scheduled flights around the world.

The man behind all this drugs activity was the man we were going to find – Khun Sa. During my research I read an article in the *Far East Economic Review* which judged that his men transported and refined about 80 per cent of the Golden Triangle's opium harvest. Even the conservative US State Department had described Khun Sa's army as "the most powerful drug trafficking organisation in the Golden Triangle".

So here we were, travelling to meet someone reputed to control almost half of the world's illicit opium supply. It was a sobering thought. Little did I know then that this trek to Khun Sa's camp would, over the next seven years, be my first of nine visits. It is interesting to read the accounts written by other people of their journeys into the Golden Triangle, which suggest they faced death every step of the way. Also, any meeting with Khun Sa tends to be described like a meeting with the devil, who might be ready to order your execution at any moment.

It's true that there was a certain amount of danger, but it has to be put into perspective. The trek from the Thai border to Homong, Khun Sa's capital, is gruelling and the terrain hazardous. The greatest danger lay in crossing the border into territory which, because it did not officially exist, was a forbidden zone. On the Thai side it was also necessary to dodge the efficient Border Patrol Police, Thailand's paramilitary force who, if they catch you, would send you back to Bangkok where, at the very least, you would be severely reprimanded. Once that border was crossed, Thai jurisdiction ended and the Burmese army was very different.

Fortunately, the Burmese troops tended to stay clear of Khun Sa's Mong Tai Army, who regularly patrolled the border area we were to cross. There were also a few independent bandit gangs who roamed the frontier and there was every risk of being kidnapped by them and held in exchange for a ransom.

Having a local Shan-speaking smuggler guide was the most important asset. In order to avoid the patrols, it was best to take the high route across the mountains, although it was easy to get lost. The lowland trails along the border were not much of an alternative as both the Shan and Thai forces had booby-trapped and mined the area extensively. However, on this first trip, I found that the greater peril stemmed from my companions. Initially, Gritz and his men had seemed efficient and, in Bangkok, arrangements for our journey had moved at a reasonable pace. After arriving at Mae Hong Son, our Shan agent had taken us to the Mae Suya, a small village on the frontier inhabited by the Chinese Haw people and from where we would start our trek.

Originally from Yunnan, China, the Haw were traders and barter opium for essential commodities such as salt and sugar. It was here that the pack animals were assembled and formed into caravans, to be sent back and forth into Shanland, following the old opium trails. Narcotics and other contraband from cigarettes to coca-cola, even washing powder, were all transported on this vital supply route.

Like all villages along the border, Mae Suya had police spies, and Khun Sa's agents were anxious to keep our presence quiet. As we were after all 'farangs', or foreigners, we were an object of curiosity, and we were accordingly instructed to stay inside our minibus until we could safely be transferred into a walled compound, away from prying eyes. No one looked directly at us, but everyone was aware of our presence. There was a strange atmosphere, which was probably something to do with being on the edge of the Golden Triangle with its bandit armies and illicit trading.

The air was still, the heat and humidity oppressive and the flies were persistent. When we were in Bangkok, Gritz had told us the entire trek would be undertaken by mules but now circumstances had changed. We discovered there were not enough mules to accommodate all of us and our gear. A mule train of twenty-five animals had left that morning and there were not enough mules remaining.

In this mountainous jungle there are only two seasons, rainy and dry and we had arrived in the former. With the monsoon about to break, we had to trek at night and with only half the number of mules we needed. Watching the Americans preparing was rather like watching a Rambo movie. Apart from bringing full army equipment from America, they had sophisticated infra-red, night-vision glasses, though they found, ten minutes before we set off, that they didn't work.

They were certainly getting over-excited as the time to leave approached. They barked out orders to us, emphasising security precautions. Even 'Good morning' was classified information it seemed, or that was the impression they gave. Although I had been trained in the British Army, and could certainly take care of myself, the ways of the American military were still an eye opener for me. It began to feel like a James Bond mission, quite remote from reality.

However, I waited patiently and shared my amusement with the

Italian crew, who were invariably good-humoured. Gabriella Simone the reporter, Adriano Zecca on camera and his brother, Damiano, on sound, were professional technicians and fun to have around. Gabriella was a charming and knowledgeable companion. I was reasonably conversant in Italian and she spoke decent English, so we all managed to speak the same language.

The village Headman, who had buck teeth, kept his hair cut to a length that made it stand upright, punk-rocker style. He, unfortunately, also had a squint, which made it seem that as he was talking to you, he was actually looking at someone else. I said to Gabriella. "I think the Headman fancies you because every time he talks to Bo he looks at you and winks!" She did not understand my, somewhat juvenile, joke and for the rest of her stay kept a good distance from the poor man. Needless to say, I kept the joke going throughout the trip.

There were a few hiccups in our journey. For some reason known only to herself, Gabriella had not told her crew the nature of the shoot they were going on and when they saw the American guys acting like something out of *Apocalypse Now*, they began to get nervous. Documentary filmmakers, though, are as courageous as soldiers and are just as used to going on dangerous assignments. Once told the true nature of the assignment, they soon came round and before long we were all laughing and joking again. Of course, they hadn't seen the Colt 45 Gary Goldman was carrying!

My first reaction when I saw the gun was to pull Gritz aside and remind him of our agreement not to carry weapons. It was vital that our cover of being a film crew who had strayed too far into the jungle was believed. However, if we were stopped and searched by the border police or an army patrol and a gun was found, our cover would be blown.

Gritz just shrugged. "What about if we are ambushed by bandits?" he asked. "So firing a few rounds at them might give us time to escape". Fat chance, I thought, but there was no point arguing with him, so I let it go.

An hour before leaving we were each given a bowl of steaming noodles and some hot tea. Although we would be travelling at night and in darkness, it would at least be much cooler. The camera gear was packed into the side baskets of one mule and the cans of 16mm film stock on another.

We left at dusk, silently in single file, to the sound of gongs and the voices of Buddhist monks at their evening prayers.

11

The Dragon's Lair

The monsoon rain had made the mule trail slippery. It was like walking on ice, but most of us were used to filming documentaries in harsh conditions. We were constantly crossing streams and climbing ever higher into the mountains. Unfortunately for Bo Gritz and his companions, their French paratrooper boots didn't have holes to let the water escape, so after every water obstacle they began to squelch. Thank God for the cheap Chinese army gym shoes!

It was very difficult for those on foot to keep up. There were only three rideable mules and Lance Trimmer, who was overweight, rode on one. Gritz was having trouble with his leg and had to ride the second. The third was taken by a muleteer, who scouted ahead.

To my surprise, it was our guides, Heng and Som Suk, who were complaining the most. The crew and I were not worried because we would be more valuable alive, as hostages, if we were taken by bandits; the Shan guides were nervous because they would probably be killed if this happened. It was the Americans who tended towards paranoia, although Gary Goldman, on his own and away from his two countrymen, was comparatively relaxed.

We had to keep going until we reached Khun Sa's outer ring of security. With dawn would come patrols from any of the following: the Kuomintang, the Burmese Communist Party, Burmese army troops or various guerrilla groups, all vying for the territory, though none of them were inclined to take prisoners. We moved on.

The rain began to pour down, bringing with it another mishap when Damiano, the sound man, slipped on a boulder and hurt his arm. The muleteer, scouting ahead, had returned and seeing the Italian in trouble, offered him his mule. A nervous Damiano carefully mounted the animal. It must have been the strange smell of a 'farang' that made the mule skittish, for it suddenly bolted forward. There was a huge commotion, with us shouting, muleteers yelling and the Italians swearing. To make matters worse it was pitch black, so we all turned on our torches. The sudden explosion of light beams spooked the animal again and it began to buck and turn in a circle, like a rodeo, until the hapless Damiano was sent crashing into the thick brush.

In normal circumstances this might have seemed a comical incident, but in the dark jungle it wasn't. The Italian was covered in clay-like sticky mud, clutching his arm in pain. Gary Goldman, our medic, examined the arm which fortunately was not broken, although badly gashed and bruised. The muleteers finally caught the mule and brought him back. Damiano, his arm now in a makeshift sling, refused to remount the animal, preferring to hobble forward on foot.

As the night wore on some of our group began to struggle and the pace slowed. There was now a real risk that we might lose someone in the darkness. Adriano, Gary and myself seemed to be the fittest, so we agreed to keep an eye on the rest. The trek was endless: you descended one mountain and waded across a stream, only to begin the upward climb to the next mountain.

Mules move faster than people, and those on foot soon lost contact with the mounted party. However, there was only one obvious trail, so we plodded on. Thankfully, the rain stopped as we climbed to the crest of an extremely steep mountain, where we stumbled across the mule party taking a rest. We were all tired and glad to take a break. The mule that had bucked Damiano, a few hours previously, became agitated when the exhausted soundman passed too close. The poor Italian, who was not looking good, slumped against a tree, a good distance from the mule's flaying hooves.

I was astonished to be told it was still a two-hour ride to the Shan mule station at Na Mon. The guides confessed that because of the heightened military activity along the border, they had been ordered to take us on a much longer, but safer route. This unfortunately increased the regular journey by 4 hours, however, that was riding mules, not on foot which meant doubling that time at the very least. Heng thought it might be best if we stayed put and waited until extra mules were sent back for us, but this didn't sound like a good idea to me. Neither myself or Gary Goldman had any confidence in the guides, or in their idea of time. In reality, we could be waiting for hours in this wilderness.

Goldman suggested that Gritz and Trimmer, both still unfit to walk, go ahead on their mules while we pressed on, no matter how slowly. On reaching Na Mon they could arrange for the extra mules to come back and pick us up on route. Gritz agreed.

Heng and Som Suk, our two guides, were not happy about this decision, but we took no notice of their protestations and set off, following the mule trail, knowing they would be obliged to follow. The pair knew that Khun Sa would be less than happy if anything happened to his guests, he would lose face, but they could lose a lot more.

The monsoon opened again. In about two more hours we reached the actual border, though the only indication was a rather ominous Thai sign bearing a red skull and crossbones to warn of minefields. Just a few yards away, there was another sign announcing entry to the Free Shan State. Once across this invisible border, Shan time begins, literally. To demonstrate their independence, the Shans had created a new time zone half an hour behind Thailand and half an hour ahead of Burma.

Dawn had long gone when we finally reached the mule station of Na Mon. A wooden arch straddled the dirt track, which I presumed was the entrance as it was guarded by Khun Sa's troops. A small wooden sign read 'Welcome' in Thai. The transition between the closeness of the jungle trail, which I had just trekked through, and the almost barren, rolling terrain on this mist-shrouded mountain was striking. The views, through the gaps in the mist, were breathtaking and the air felt incredibly clean.

Smuggler's trails over cloud covered mountains

The picturesque Na Mon was only two miles inside the Shan border and looked similar to the villages I had seen on the Thai side. The settlement consisted of several bamboo shacks where the inhabitants slept and a couple of wooden huts selling food, drink and clothing to travellers passing on the smugglers trail. The place was also the gathering point for merchants, as many as 30 a day, going north to the markets to buy cattle, that originated in India and Bangladesh. The cattle were then herded back to Thailand to be sold for meat. Each animal would fetch approximately 3000 Thai Baht, about 100 US dollars. On top of this, for transiting through his territory, Khun Sa charged a tax of 500 Thai Baht, per head.

The first part of our trek had taken fourteen hours to complete. Our feet were blistered but Gary Goldman had his first aid pack, with enough medications to equip a small field hospital. When Gary tended to himself, he found his socks soaked in blood where the leeches had got to him. He then showed us the remains of one he had crushed, Gabriella almost threw up.

I was fascinated by the activity in this remote mule station. I watched the mule trains as they passed by, smiling as both smugglers and mules watched us with intense curiosity. It was a marvel to see how sure-footed the mules could be, especially with the great loads they had to carry. Watching them reminded me of stories from the Burma campaign during the Second World War, and how reliant the British and Allied Armies were on these extraordinary animals.

Tiger Camp

From Na Mon there was still over an hour's drive to Homong and Tiger Camp, the site of Khun Sa's headquarters. At long last, a small, battered pick-up truck, its gears grinding, lurched into sight. Bo Gritz and Gary Goldman squeezed into the cab with the driver, while the rest of us piled into the back. It was a bone-shaking drive on a dirt road and tempers were frayed by the time we arrived at Tiger Camp — now dubbed 'the Dragon's Lair' by the film crew!

We cleaned up and ate a good meal of rice and stew, as the sunset was obscured by cloud over the mountains. The accommodation seemed basic and although I was too tired to do much, I did go for a quick walk around the camp. I was interested to see some young recruits being instructed in a history lesson. They sat cross-legged on the parade ground and sang songs. The history lesson was in verse, I learned, and lasted two hours. As fascinating as this insight into the Mong Tai army was, all I wanted to do was to get some sleep.

The monsoon had followed us to Homong and a thick mist, that Londoners would call pea soup fog, descended on the town. The rain fell so hard on the corrugated iron roof of our sleeping quarters that it was deafening, so much so, that it was impossible to sleep soundly.

The following morning, I awoke as dawn was breaking. The walk to the outside latrine, a make-shift hut of wood and bamboo housing a simple hole, took me along a muddy path made sticky by the rain. I was advised to check inside before entering, as snakes had a habit of taking shelter there during the monsoon. About 40 metres away was a pool for personal hygiene and general washing, the water diverted from a fast-flowing stream by bamboo split in half. The jungle shower was also fed by split bamboo, and very cold. "Invigorating" remarked Gary Goldman, which at six in the morning I could have done without.

Dawn had barely broken when I heard the sound of young men singing in the distance. As it drew closer there was a definite martial air to the rhythm. "It must be the army singing a cadence," said Gary. As we were the only two awake, I suggested going to the parade ground to take a look.

"Boy, can you believe that we're in the middle of the jungle on a fucking parade ground?" said Gary, as we watched columns of young recruits being put through their basic drill. "And there he is," I pointed to a smart-looking Shan soldier barking out orders. "The quintessential sergeant major, all armies have them". We laughed as we sat on a grassy mound that gave us an excellent view. The three hundred young Shans, who kept sneaking looks at the two of us, marched back and forth across the sandy parade ground, watched by their eagle-eyed instructor.

I explained to Gary that in the British Army, the parade ground is regarded as holy and belongs to one man, the regimental sergeant major. My basic training had been at the Highland Brigade Depot, in Bridge of Don, Scotland. The parade ground was the size of a large football pitch. Its primary use was for parades, training and drill. The rule was simple: unless on parade, you always walked around the perimeter and never across the ground.

Watching the Shan sergeant scolding some poor soldier reminded me of my drill sergeant, a short, barrel-chested man from the Black Watch Regiment, whom we nicknamed 'Black Doom'. Standing to attention almost 100 feet away, he hollered commands with such ferocity that his entire body reverberated, and the soles of his boots would carry him

Meal break during the Monsoon

forward a few inches, like a cartoon.

Watching the sweating recruits in the Mong Tai Army, it seemed that nothing had changed. Feeling relieved that we weren't the ones being shouted at, we marched off, in step I may add — old habits die hard!

Meals, meetings or any socialising took place in a large wooden pavilion, which had been built with three open sides and a corrugated iron roof. Strangely it had a warm and welcoming feel, especially after the 'invigorating' open-air shower. A regular sight, perched near the entrance, was a Burmese Roller, a purplish-blue bird with pale blue wings. This exceptionally beautiful bird would wait patiently for any titbits that came his way.

Adjacent to the pavilion was an open-air kitchen, where the young Shan chef practised his culinary skills. As guests of the Mong Tai Army, we had to follow their rules, one of which stated that meals were served twice a day, at 7.30am and 4pm.

I have enjoyed eating breakfasts all over the world and have often been amazed at the eating habits of people, so early in the morning. The Shans were no exception and our morning meals at Tiger Camp proved to be elaborate spreads, wonderfully prepared. On our first morning, we were treated to a light soup made with exotic jungle vegetables, followed by chicken pieces with cabbage, spicy green beans and boiled rice. As Western guests, the ever-grinning chef had cooked us a special plate of fried potatoes, which he presented with much pomp. Whether it was the energy we had used on the long trek or just the fresh air, we all fell on the mountain of food like a pack of wolves, enjoying every morsel. The exception was Damiano, the Italian soundman, who Gary Goldman had recently nicknamed 'Mister Gloom'. After a mouthful of rice, he refused to eat anymore. I was amazed, what did he expect to find in this lost world of the Shan — Caffe Latte and Brioche?

After breakfast we met Khernsai Jaiyane, who showed us around the Liaison Office. He was the chief officer of this important department and responsible for all guests who visited the Shan territory. A well-educated man, with an excellent command of English, he had been private secretary to Khorn Zurng, the Shan patriot and mentor of Khun Sa. When the two Shan leaders merged their organisations to form the Mong Tai Army, Khernsai was appointed to be Khun Sa's primary translator and Press Officer. Among his many tasks was to write the responses, in English, to all official communiques arriving for Khun Sa, or the Tai Revolutionary Council, the political wing of the Shan freedom movement. Over the next few years Khernsai and I would become firm friends.

Working with Kernsai, were Kampang and Seng Jo, two key figures in the liaison team and again, both had a reasonable command of English. Seng Jo had been appointed our minder for the duration of the visit. An interesting man, who had been a member of the Burmese Communist Party before deciding to join Khun Sa in the early eighties. As a reward for his distinguished service on the frontline, the warlord gave him money to open the first gem shop in Homong. Seng Jo and I would also become good friends.

Kampang had the responsibility of controlling the border entry, which meant that anybody wishing to visit Homong must deal with him first. Once invited, the visitor was given a minder for the duration of their stay. Not all visitors had the opportunity to meet Khun Sa in person and if they did, it was probably only once.

Later that first morning I found out that Bo Gritz had been granted an interview with Khun Sa the previous night. The warlord had wanted to know about Barry Flynn and Johnny Poon, who Gritz had previously introduced him to, and both of whom had apparently scammed Khun Sa for money. That did not augur well. To make us all the more jittery, we suddenly found the pavilion surrounded by heavily armed soldiers. We were all silent, not knowing what to say or do. The feeling of helplessness was not a pleasant experience.

We need not have worried. Khun Sa had decided to make a surprise early visit to meet us. He seemed satisfied that Gritz had indeed been so involved with his indictment in the United States that he had no idea what the others were doing. Furthermore, they certainly had no right to do whatever it was in his name. Our formal interview with Khun Sa had been arranged for the next day. In the meantime, his appearance was to show us that, whatever Flynn and Poon might have done, he was still good friends with Gritz.

Khun Sa shook hands with each of the crew in turn, his friendly welcome putting us totally at ease. He bore little resemblance to the nickname he had gained in the world's press, 'The Prince of Death'.

Draped across the back of the pavilion was a large Shan flag, made up of three horizontal stripes of yellow, green and red, with a white circular moon in the centre. With Khernsai translating Khun Sa explained its significance: "Yellow denotes the colour and origin of the race. Green the rich natural resources of the country. Red is for bravery and the moon represents purity and the peace-loving nature of the people."

The author introduces Khun Sa to the Italian film crew

It soon became apparent to me that this flag was an important symbol of Shan resistance and their long struggle for independence from Burmese oppression. I would also learn how the uprising and other historic events of the fifties influenced the young Khun Sa.

Shan children harvesting opium poppies

12

A Real Bad Guy

There is a tendency among people today to look at the 1960s as being the great age of protest and rebellion, but the 1950s was no decade of gentle acceptance. Across the world, people strove for independence and self-determination. In Europe there was an abortive Hungarian uprising against the Russians. The Basques in Spain, and EOKA successfully in Cyprus, struggled for independence. In America's own back yard, Cubans began to fight for, and eventually won, their release from the corrupt Batista regime. All over the world, what had been deemed impossible happened and the sun began to set on the British Empire.

Wherever these struggles took place, the major powers sought to influence the outcome. The Soviet Union encouraged the North Koreans to invade South Korea. In Egypt, the CIA backed a military coup allowing Colonel Nasser to become leader. Then when Great Britain and France attempted to occupy the Suez Canal, which Nasser had nationalised, the United States humiliated its allies by forcing them to withdraw under the threat of financial ruin. The irony was that their man Nasser, in the end, sided with the Soviets.

The young Khun Sa and his comrades also longed to be part of this revolution and rid themselves of the yoke of misery imposed on their people by the Rangoon government. But the Burmese government at that time were worried less by Shan nationalists and more by the Kuomintang.

In the 1950s China was the main supplier of arms to most of the communist groups of Southeast Asia. The United States supported the Kuomintang, and when it was clear they could never reconquer China, allowed them to create havoc in Burma. The Burmese government of U-Nu appealed to the United Nations, and the United States was shamed into evacuating their faithful followers to the island of Taiwan, where the main body of the defeated Chinese Nationalists had retreated.

This Burmese success against a super-power was short-lived. With a policy, since independence, of state control, isolation and repression, the country fell into a state of chaos and the economy virtually collapsed. The local CIA agents soon found enough allies in the Burmese army to force U-Nu out of office, which taught him a lesson about the might of a super-power. This was unwarranted interference by the United States into the affairs of a sovereign state but, worse, they must surely have known who would take over.

General Ne Win was by any standards a 'real bad guy' and probably the most influential figure in Burma following independence. A military dictator who had never had any respect for the democratic process and who increasingly built up a structure of control that allowed him to take an iron grip on the country. Imprisonment without charge, torture and murder increasingly became the accepted practice. Tyrannical governments have ruled Burma ever since.

During the Second World War, Ne Win was one of the Thirty Comrades who secretly went to undergo military training in Japanese occupied China. Under the watchful eye of his Imperial Japanese Army instructors, he learned how to subjugate people with brutality. He had been particularly inspired by 'sanko seisku', which was central to the Japanese counter-insurgency strategy. Translated, it meant "the three all policy" — "burn all, kill all and destroy all".

Once he was in power, Ne Win masterminded a strategy called 'The Four Cuts', that was designed to cut the links to funds, food, intelligence and recruitment for the insurgency.

By now it was crystal clear to Shan leaders that Britain and the West were indifferent to their right to self-determination, and that Burma would never recognise the Shan states' right of secession that had been promised by the Panlong Agreement. Khun Sa had learned that freedom was something the Shans and the other minority peoples, would have to fight for.

Resistance

In the Shan states, Khun Sa will be remembered not simply as a drugs runner but as the one man who was able to unite all the meaningful Shan factions into one cohesive political body. However, it was not achieved without a great deal of difficulty.

By the mid-1950s, Red China backed BCP (Burmese Communist Party) had embarked on a policy to destroy Shan national unity by encouraging war among the different Shan groups. In 1958, Sao Noi, a Shan adventurer,

Homong

had founded another resistance group called 'Noom Serk Harn' ('young brave warriors'), recruiting high school students from Mandalay and Rangoon. He invited Korn Zurng to join them in their struggle.

The twenty-three-year-old Khun Sa, who disliked the BCP as much as the Kuomintang, saw this moment as the birth of the Shan resistance movement. It was at seven o'clock in the morning, an auspicious time, at Hueipu, on the eastern bank of the mighty Salween, when thirty-one original warriors participated in the solemn ceremony of drinking the blood of loyalty. They vowed to free the Shan states and drive out the alien force. It was the 'Norm Serk Harn' from which all other armed movements either grew or would draw their inspiration. 1958 was also the year the secession should have been the right of the Shans, 10 years after the signing of the Panlong Agreement, and therefore of particular significance.

In 1959, Korn Zurng was wounded during a raid on a Burmese garrison in Mong Ton township. Because of the poor condition of the roads, it took some days for him to be taken to a hospital, but by then it was too late for them to treat the wounds to his arm, which had to be amputated.

It was in November of the same year, that the Battle of Tangyan was fought between the Shan and the Burmese, an incident renowned in Shan history, despite the fact that they suffered a defeat. It lasted fifteen days and among the participants was Bo Deving, who had been a commander of the Security Guard for Khun Sa's stepfather before becoming a famous freedom fighter. 'Bo' is a title conferred on a leader, usually a military officer. Like Korn Zurng, Bo Deving would also become a mentor to Khun Sa.

It was the proliferation of these nationalist factions and their constant attacks on Burmese garrisons that created the climate for a political coup and General Ne Win took over the government in 1962. He promptly abolished the constitution and any faint hopes that the promises of secession would ever be honoured disappeared. The result of the general's hard stance was that Shan resistance increased.

Since the Burmese Army moved into the Shan states back in 1952, all the resources of the Shan lands had been in the hands of the Burmese military and a few greedy businessmen. Every Shan and hill tribe peasant was fair game for the Burmese soldiery: their rice taken to feed the troops, money stolen, sons press-ganged for forced labour, wives and daughters raped or sold into prostitution. Accordingly, to escape the marauding Burmese soldiers, thousands sought refuge in the mountain areas and deep forests, where the only cash crop to survive on was opium.

However, in this frontier region, the opium trading activities of the various Shan movements were causing corruption and rivalry within their

Refugees flock to Khun Sa in search of safety

ranks. This led to internal quarrels which in turn led to military inefficiency and by 1964, the smaller groups eventually broke up. Despite the chaos of disbanding armies and political parties, Korn Zurng managed to achieve a measure of success by uniting several smaller movements into the Shan State Army (SSA), perhaps at that time the most authentically politicised Shan group.

Well aware that the Shan resistance war was now beginning to take off in earnest, General Ne Win created a new self-defence militia to combat the nationalist and communist insurgents. This military group was the Ka Kwe Ye, soon to be known and feared as the KKY. These two events, the creation of the SSA, and the KKY were before long to be curiously linked, through Khun Sa himself.

General Ne Win's first major enactment was what he called "The Burmese Way to Socialism", which in reality was no more than a policy of total nationalisation. The government took control of every facet of trade, from major networks and corporations to the humblest shop. The result was economic collapse.

The other likely recipe for disaster is when the military feels it is the answer to a nation's problems and takes over the reins of government. Combine the military and extreme socialism and you get the absolute certainty of disaster, which is what happened in Burma.

With a shortage of legitimate funds, the regime inevitably turned to opium to pay for the KKY, the formation created to counter the dissident movements. Inevitably the commanders of this force built up their own little armies to oppress the minorities and line their own pockets from the proceeds of drug trafficking.

Khun Sa, ever an opportunist, was one such commander, given charge of the strategic and geographically important Loi Maw Militia. The problem that had faced him as leader of an independent military group was how to fight the Burmese and the Kuomintang simultaneously, or, if that were not possible, which enemy he should regard as the most dangerous.

A solution was provided by Colonel Maung Shwe, the Burmese commander in the Shan state. The colonel, impressed by the young Khun Sa's guerrilla band, offered him the status of a volunteer militia chief and a free hand to build its strength in return for a pledge to fight the Kuomintang and the Communist Party of Burma. These were the Shan's natural enemies and Khun Sa accepted the offer. The strength of his anti-communist forces, and the support he gained from local merchants who, by their nature, were averse to any form of socialism, grew and soon spread into Kentung, which bordered Laos.

Khun Sa had no stomach to serve his Burmese masters, any more than he had for the Kuomintang. Eager as ever for Shan independence, he brought his Loi Maw militia over to the newly formed Shan State Army, to join Korn Zurng.

Khun Sa's force was designated as one of the brigades of the Shan State Army, with its operational area on both sides of the Salween River. Khun Sa set about his tasks with relish. Although, like everyone else with such heavy responsibilities, of feeding his men and their families, his bills could only be picked up by taxing the drugs traffickers, and he was aware of the disastrous effects of such trading. He knew he could not stop it because sales from the poppy were the lifeblood of the peasants, but he would make sure only the rich would be sufferers.

It was Khun Sa's opinion that education was the best possible preventative measure so far as the drugs problem among his own people was concerned, and built more than eighty schools in the Shan Territory as a result.

Korn Zurng was delighted to recruit such a forceful personality as Khun Sa into the ranks of the Shan State Army, but sadly his presence proved a divisive factor and the unity that Korn Zurng had fought so hard for was short-lived.

Another important player in the region was General Jimmy Yang of the Kokang Force, another guerrilla group, of ethnic Chinese origin, wanting its share of the opium trade. Jimmy Yang was a member of the Kokang State royal family and his sister Olive had been a previous leader of the armed band. His chief of staff was Lo Hsin Han, who had also led a KKY group and established himself as an independent warlord. The leaders of the Kokang Force viewed Khun Sa more as a rival than an ally.

Fighting broke out between the factions, with both sides appealing to Korn Zurng to back them. He replied that he had been elected by a democratic process and they should solve their problems in a democratic way rather than by fighting among themselves. All disputes should be settled politically, he told them, with the military option being used only as a last resort. This was how he hoped Burma would eventually solve its own border problem and the Shan state would gain its freedom. For the time being though, any fighting between factions of the SSA could only play right into the hands of the Burmese occupation forces.

Korn Zurng's words were heeded and the destructive warfare came to a temporary halt, allowing Khun Sa to resume his campaigns against his favourite opponents, the other occupying force, the Kuomintang. The Kokang Force however broke away, actually to co-operate with the Kuomintang and stayed involved in the drugs trade for many years to come.

Khun Sa holding raw opium

13

Behind the Opium Curtain

Two trucks arrived to pick us up. Gritz and his men clambered into one, while the crew and myself got into the other. I was surprised to see Gritz's vehicle speed off in the opposite direction to us. I had no idea where they were going and no one would tell me. Seng Jo explained our schedule for the morning, which was basically to travel around Tiger Valley, meeting and filming the people, most of whom had been victims of Burmese oppression. The Shans were also very open about the opium growing and were prepared to answer all questions put to them.

No sooner had our vehicle left Tiger Camp when we were intercepted by a white Toyota pick-up truck. Several soldiers jumped off it and surrounded our vehicle. Driving the Toyota was Khun Sa, who with a big smile waved to us before barking orders to Seng Jo in Shan. Still smiling, Khun Sa beckoned us to follow. Seng Jo explained that the General, as he was more commonly known there, had decided to show us the sights personally. Gabriella and I quickly glanced at each other; what amazing luck!

Our first stop was Visutthi Monastery, the first of six Buddhist temples built by Khun Sa in his territory. The temple accommodated about 60 monks and novices and was an important focal point for the people of Homong, especially during cultural festivities. Most Shan males have tattoos on their bodies, especially the chest and arms. The tattoos are inscriptions from the Buddhist teachings called the Sutra, a genre of ancient and medieval Indian texts. I was told that Buddhism had made the Shans generally a calm and organised people who show little sign of the cruel and violent history they have had to endure.

We then filmed a primary school before going to the new hospital, which consisted of 20 huts in various stages of completion. The clinic and dispensary gave free treatment to all, except many of them had to undertake long journeys to take up the offer. The patients being cared for in the wards were mostly soldiers suffering from malaria, pneumonia or hepatitis.

Visutthi Monastery

Homong had a resident population of 5000 civilians, who went about their business in an orderly way. It was hard to believe that this town had been literally carved out of the jungle just a short while ago.

The tempo of events during the past few years had moulded Khun Sa into an experienced military tactician and an astute ruler. The stringent training he received during his time with the Kuomintang, the part he played in the supremacy between rival Shan resistance groups had taught him that if a leader became complacent sooner or later he would be destroyed. Khun Sa's life was dominated by a desire for greater power, which meant leading an army mightier than his rivals. He dreamed of building an impregnable jungle fortress, a bastion which even his fiercest enemies would hesitate to challenge.

When Khun Sa and his army retreated from his base in northern Thailand to Burma, in 1982, he began looking for a new stronghold. It had to be near the border and close to the strategic Doi Lang Range, where the fertile valleys were ideal for cultivating opium. To gain control of this important area he had to fight a bitter war against the Kuomintang. By 1985, he felt confident enough to order his people to select suitable sites for the erection of permanent settlements in a beautiful area known as Tiger Valley. Hundreds of soldiers and civilians were involved in the building of the new town, which he named Homong. It was well sited, circled by mountains and many streams.

As this was to be the new Shan capital, he erected his military headquarters, Tiger Camp, on the outskirts. The compound had to be large enough to accommodate 3000 soldiers. There was no time to rest, for the warlord was impatient to complete the military installation before the monsoon season.

It was while these building projects were in progress that an important development took place. From all over the Frontier Area survivors from the barbarity of the Burmese Army arrived to plead with Khun Sa that they be allowed to stay in the safety of his territory. They were warmly welcomed by the warlord because the arrival of the refugees meant new recruits for his Mong Tai Army. Not only new recruits but men and women who hated the Burmese with a vengeance. In the course of the next two years a quarter of million people would seek refuge with Khun Sa.

Agent Orange

As we toured the mountainous countryside Khun Sa described how in the dry season, the land became bone hard. With the monsoon, it became a muddy quagmire. The winter months brought biting winds from the Himalayas. It may be a very beautiful place, but it is not paradise.

He also explained how the red earth, although fertile, was difficult to farm and the techniques of terraced cultivation had to be learnt by all the Shans. Where possible peasants grew rice and root vegetables as their main sustenance. The Rural Development Scheme was the brainchild of Khun Sa, who eagerly promoted it to new refugees arriving in Homong. He was dispensing homes and financial assistance, as well as crops, buffaloes and cattle to all those who entered his protected area. I was able to speak freely, aided by an interpreter of course, with soldiers, villagers and refugees. They all had some shocking tales to tell about the Burmese army.

It hadn't taken long to realise the drug policy that the Burmese military government presented to the world was a sham and why American policy in the area had failed so miserably. It seemed that, far from discouraging the development of the drugs trade, the United States had been unwittingly financing it. Corrupt officials in Burma were lining their pockets with the US dollars that had been supplied to wipe out the poppy fields.

I spoke to Shan refugees made homeless by the employment of chemical warfare against their villages by the Burmese, entirely for political reasons, Khun Sa insisted. Then the warlord went on to explain how he could eradicate the production of opium. The Shan farmers needed to learn about alternative crops to replace the poppy fields. He wanted the

American government to sanction a mission in the Shan States for this purpose. He had calculated that it would cost a fraction of what it was costing the United States to fund the DEA's efforts in Burma. Khun Sa had no doubt that he could affect the eradication of the opium trade in the area because, he insisted, the Shans engaged in it only to pay for the cost of protecting themselves. "If I can gain independence for my country, eight million people will rejoice, but if I can stop the narcotic problem, the whole world will rejoice!" Khun Sa said.

Congressmen and similar influential observers had been taken by the Burmese on expensive helicopter flights, courtesy of the American taxpayer, to see for themselves the poppy fields set ablaze. They returned to base satisfied, and then took home the news of how efficient the DEA was being. They did not know that a burned field was perfectly acceptable to the opium grower. Once the crops had been picked, the flames were extremely useful in burning out the undergrowth and helping to enrich the soil, ensuring a healthy crop in ensuing years.

Any veteran of Vietnam will tell you about the deadly effects of the chemical 2,4-D, or 'Agent Orange', as it was commonly known. Burma had been ordered by Washington to spray the poppy fields with it, and the aircraft and equipment had been supplied. The original intent was to stop the growth of opium, but the Burmese use of the deadly chemical

cocktail was subtly different, they used it to stop the growth of unrest in these border areas. Their real targets were the villages that were known to be sympathetic to the Shan nationalist cause, Khun Sa's people.

Most of us knew that Agent Orange would kill all vegetation with which it came into contact and that it was highly toxic to both humans and animals. It is a persistent organic pollutant and can remain toxic for many years. Particles that cling to the soil in sprayed areas are carried by water into streams and lakes before being consumed by fish and waterfowl, easily entering the human food chain.

A letter subsequently published in the *New York Times* on January 13th 1989, from Edith T. Mirante, director of Project Maje, an organisation dedicated to spreading awareness about human rights and narcotics issues in Burma, confirmed what Khun Sa told us:

"Narcotics corruption is all-pervasive in the Burmese military, from the shadow dictator Ne Win on down. Military vehicles and ships are routinely used to transport opium extorted from tribal people as 'taxes' and 'quotas' by the Army.

Also, United States anti-narcotics aid (the controversial herbicide, 2,4-D) has been used in a selective and prejudiced manner by the Burmese Army to drive 'security risk' hill tribe people from their land, while major traffickers conduct business with impunity. United States donated aircraft are diverted to ferry troops and cargo in the battle zones. Senator Daniel Moynihan has commented: 'In Ne Win perhaps we have been dealing with an Asian Noriega.'

Burma's drug deluge (now reaching New York streets in the form of Chinese white heroin) can end only with a peaceful solution to the frontier war that provides equal rights for all ethnic groups and a free, healthy economy".

It soon became clear to me that the Shans regarded Khun Sa as their saviour. They called him by names of respect – 'teacher' and 'lao ban', meaning 'old boss'. Unlike other armies of 'freedom fighters', there were no cases here of young men being 'press-ganged' to fight unwillingly for the cause. All refugees, from all tribes, of Burmese oppression were welcomed and given assistance to re-establish themselves, so it was hardly surprising that their young men chose to fight.

When we returned to Tiger Camp, I spent the rest of the day exploring the place. A wooden house, to the left of the main entrance, served as Khun Sa's office and sleeping quarters when he was in the camp. The building, surrounded by a well-cultivated garden full of flowers, overlooked the other huts where recruits were being instructed in various military arts.

The soldiers were very young, some of them no older than twelve years. They looked happy enough and were well fed, well clothed and housed in spotless barracks, that would have made any sergeant in the Grenadier Guards proud. No matter their age, every soldier was paid 150 Thai Baht a month, approximately $4 US dollars. To the impoverished Shan families any extra money was an incentive to send their sons to the army.

I also spoke to other soldiers, who were older and plainly battle-hardened, as they returned from the frontline. A bitter war was being waged about thirty miles to the east in the Doi Lang Range, where the Mong Tai Army were fighting their old enemy, the Wa. The former communists, previously known as the BCP, wanted to capture Khun Sa's major strongholds in Doi Lang, which guarded the economically important opium growing regions. At that time, the Mong Tai army was one of the best trained and equipped private military forces in Southeast Asia, probably second only to the Khmer Rouge in Cambodia.

The art of smuggling

The pattern of opium trading in the Shan states had not changed over the years. First the traders negotiate with the tribal people in the hills who grow the poppy. Deals are struck usually before harvesting. Because there is stiff competition, auctions for the cash crop sometimes happen ahead of time, similar to dealing in the futures market. The traders also cultivate a relationship with the village headman to secure continuous supplies, a system which is also preferred by the growers, who are guaranteed the money.

Opium poppies take three months to grow, which means that if the weather is good, two crops a year are possible. When the poppies are ready, the harvesters, mainly women, use a special tool to scrape grooves into the seed pod. Over the next three days, a resin weeps from the deep cuts, which is then collected. This sticky substance is raw opium which once collected, is moulded into round bundles, each weighing about a kilogram. Approximately ten kilos of raw opium are needed to make one kilo of heroin, depending on the morphine content. Although there is more money in the morphine base made ready for the traders, the tribesmen know it doesn't keep as well as raw opium, which is easy to store and can be buried anywhere. Raw opium is also pliable and can be moulded into

shapes that mean it can be hidden around car wheels, for instance.

The heroin refineries were secretly scattered along the Thai-Burma border. Originally, the smugglers along the border preferred to refine the opium themselves, making it lighter and less bulky to transport, but they realised that it was better to smuggle raw opium into Thailand where it could be processed in less volatile areas. Once the opium crop is secured, the trader deals with the organisers who supply the money, which may come from Europe, Japan or the United States. Their job is to smuggle the refined product out of the country.

Unfortunately for the DEA, it was often accused by its enemies of also being involved in the drugs business, and not just enforcing the law. The American organisation had come under severe criticism over the years, often unfairly since its operatives were doing a difficult and extremely dangerous job combating the drugs trade around the world.

Naturally, when the Shans referred to the involvement of the DEA in the drugs trade, hackles in Washington began to rise. Most people's image of a DEA agent was of a clean-cut, all-American boy from Iowa, but there were not many of those to be found in Southeast Asia. The Shan accusations were usually levelled at the locally recruited Thais, Laotians and indeed, the Shan themselves, who made up a large percentage of the DEA personnel in Southeast Asia. They recruited these people for undercover work, which does not mean they were all corrupt, but some of them were. Some were even coerced into corruption by the use of threats against their families.

Opium has always been lucrative and the problem for those working on the border was how to withstand the temptation of instant wealth. I spoke to Shans, Burmese and Laotians about opium smuggling along the border, to find out how the substance was able to get through so easily. All agreed there were many Thai military figures active in smuggling, which made life easier for the organisers. Unfortunately for the many honest Thai troops, who do a tough job for little pay, many of their high-ranking comrades were making a fortune. The smuggling usually occurred when the troops left an area and the heroin was packed into their equipment. Who is going to stop an armed force to check the cargo?

A Shan intelligence agent explained to me how the corruption worked. A corrupt general will issue troop movement orders to a local commander, who is also on the take. The orders are to shift military cargo to wherever they want the real freight to go. Military movement orders, when issued by a general, are never questioned and are certainly not checked by civilian policemen.

During that period, Malaysia had also become a distribution centre for heroin from the Shan states. According to some Shan officials, Penang in northern Malaysia was a good example of where the organisers work. This may seem strange, considering Malaysia's draconian punishments for drug dealing, but I was told by Khernsai: "The smuggler's motto is the most dangerous place is the most safe place because you have to pay only the one really powerful person. If it is not a dangerous place, you have to pay many, and there are more chances of mistakes. Malaysia is dangerous, but money can soothe it for everybody."

The Shans admitted they could only collect their opium taxes with the cooperation of the villagers, who were obliged to report every deal. The deals were double-checked and, if there was any attempt at cheating, the crop and money were confiscated, and the culprits were effectively put out of business. If the traders tried to avoid the taxes, then retribution was swift and sure.

Foreigners very rarely ventured into the Golden Triangle to buy heroin and the occasional individual who tried to set up a deal was soon caught, the Bangkok jail was full of them. The big dealing foreigners stayed in Chiang Mai and used the local organisers, thus ensuring the opium warlords that payment of any taxes is guaranteed.

*Military training starts
at twelve years old*

14

Lunch with the Warlord

In the days before smartphones and tablets, I never ventured far without a deck of playing cards. Then, no matter where you were in the world, people loved to play cards. Sometimes, I would instigate a game with fellow travellers or just play solitaire. I also enjoyed performing the odd card trick, when appropriate, a useful tool if you didn't speak the local language. One day in Tiger Camp, we were all chatting and sipping tea in the pavilion when I decided to perform a card trick on Seng Jo. He chose a card, had a secret look, then returned it to the deck which he shuffled before returning it to me. After mumbling "abracadabra", and other meaningless words, to distract the victim, I spread the deck on the table and out popped his chosen card. Magic! The audience applauded and of course wanted the trick repeated. The golden rule is, never show a trick twice to the same person, well not on the same day.

We were in high spirits when Khun Sa dropped in for his customary morning visit. Seng Jo immediately told him about the magic card trick. Khun Sa smiled, and everybody turned towards me. "The General wants you to show him the trick", ordered Seng Jo.

"Aghh," I thought. This particular trick needed time to set up, so I moved to plan B and performed a variation. Fortunately, everyone enjoyed that one as well, especially the General.

With Khun Sa in a good mood, I took the opportunity to ask his permission to go to a heroin refinery. Everyone looked aghast at the audacity of asking such a question. The warlord, a chain smoker, took a long, long draw on his cigarette, staring at me whilst in deep thought. It was the longest drag on a cigarette I had ever seen. After a minute he exhaled the smoke from his lungs and stated that there were no refineries in his territory. His advisors nodded their heads in agreement, and relief I suspect.

However, he would personally take me, meaning the film crew, to a village where the opium was kept, so we could witness for ourselves how

Akha tribe opium growers with Khun Sa

the poor hill tribe people existed. I was elated. Gabriella and the crew couldn't believe how lucky we were to be given this access. I'm not sure what the lucky omen was: the card trick or, that long puff on the cigarette!

The Headman of the Akha village only had one eye, an injury from one of the numerous opium wars he had taken part in. After greeting the Headman, Khun Sa barked some orders and several Akha women, dressed in their traditional costumes, each brought out a packet of raw opium, wrapped in brown paper and secured with string, placing them on a straw mat. The ten packets, each weighing one kilo, apparently had a total street value of $250,000 US dollars - a lot of money.

Seng Jo explained to me, that generally speaking the Akha don't like to cultivate opium but it's part of their culture to smoke it. "So much so, that any Akha man who doesn't, is considered to be a woman." He said, matter-of-factly.

Khun Sa then made a great show of unwrapping one sealed packet, then with a large pair of scissors, cutting through the centre of the ball of raw opium, to expose the resin inside. Beckoning me forward he thrust the raw opium resin towards my nose, which gave off a horrible, acrid smell. He laughed. It was an amazing photoshoot that filmmakers can only dream about. I was told afterwards by Seng Jo, that he believed it was the first time Khun Sa had ever been filmed with raw opium in his hands.

No sooner had we finished filming in the Akha village, when more good fortune came our way. Out of the blue, Khun Sa invited us back to his house for lunch.

At the house we were ushered into a terraced area where a long table has been set for the meal. About 15 meters away was a small wash house where we were allowed to freshen up in. To our delight we found it contained a Western-style toilet and the only one in Homong! Even Damiano the Gloom, managed a grin in appreciation of our luck.

The meal turned out to be a splendid affair, with the 20 different dishes having been prepared by Khun Sa's personal, Sechuan trained, Chinese chef. Forever the generous host the General had decided that neat cognac should accompany the meal and two bottles of VSOP Remy Martin, his favourite tipple, appeared. We were taken aback when he poured us each a tumbler full of the amber liquid, consuming nearly half a bottle himself. About thirty minutes into the lunch, a bleary-eyed Khun Sa suddenly stood up and left the room. We were told he had retired for a nap and we would be taken back to Tiger Camp. That was it, lunch was over.

Khun Sa the Horseman

It was late afternoon when the crew gathered on the parade ground to film the recruits lowering the flag and singing the Shan anthem, which took place every evening. Adriano was positioning his camera on a grassy mound, when suddenly Khun Sa, now suitably refreshed, trotted into view, mounted on a splendid black pony with three other horsemen following.

Although the horses were trotting at some speed, it wasn't a gait I had seen before. They appeared to be floating. Seng Jo explained that Burma ponies were trotting in a style called "athegya", similar to that of equestrian teams at horse shows. He assured me that it was a comfortable way of riding, "you just sit firmly in the saddle and the pony carries you along smoothly." Apparently, the local ponies could trot like this for miles without tiring.

I told Seng Jo that I found something pleasurable in watching good riders, although I did not ride very well myself. This was a shame, as my father, Richard King, had been a champion show jumper, winning trophies for his regiment and the British Army.

When Khun Sa rode over to talk to us I asked him if he minded galloping around the parade ground while we filmed. He was more than happy to oblige. The result was some wonderful footage of the general charging towards the camera. You could easily imagine him as an ancient Mongol horseman in Genghis Khan's army.

Khun Sa looked every inch the warlord he was. Little did I know at the time, how my curious relationship with the warlord would develop over the next seven years. During this period, I would learn as much about Khun Sa as any 'farang' could. I would gain a new perspective about the man and would come to understand more about the CIA and their historic role in Southeast Asia.

Smelling raw opium!

15

Across the Mekong

By the time of my first meeting with Khun Sa, in 1989, he had become the most famous drug lord in the world, an outlaw that nobody could catch. What was extraordinary in his rise to power had been the ability to recover from so many mishaps, that would have discredited lesser men, and still bounce back. His ascendancy was due to one of the most bizarre chain of events in Asia's drug story. The key characters in this corrupt saga, operated in Thailand and across the Mekong River, in Laos and South Vietnam.

In 1962, no one took much notice of the CIA encouraged coup by a group of ambitious South Vietnamese army generals. The CIA, never able to keep their fingers off the puppet strings for long, had backed General Khanh as the new head of South Vietnam. His rule was short-lived, mainly because he had to spend most of his time trying to pre-empt counter-coups planned against him. In doing so, he neglected to control the country with the same vice-like grip his CIA masters expected.

The CIA realised it had made a major error. The President had to go. In their search for a replacement, they found the perfect candidate. Air Vice Marshall Nguyen Ky was the head of the South Vietnamese Air Force, and a man already on their payroll. He had the necessary ruthlessness and had joined forces with the equally vicious General Nguyen Noc Loan. The locals in the know regarded this pair as a couple of 'cowboys', which is what they call high-powered crooks. The CIA breathed a collective sigh of relief. They knew that they had found their men.

The American President, Lyndon B. Johnson, was determined to be tough against all communists. Under his leadership, the United States of America increased their support for South Vietnam. No one imagined at that time how far the United States could become involved, still less what the unimaginable outcome would be. Who would have guessed that by 1975, over 58,000 Americans would lose their lives?

While the American government was loudly trumpeting its support for

Chinese Haw smugglers

freedom, the agents of that freedom in the CIA were steadily building up their opium supplies and their markets. Air America tirelessly flew their missions, from farmer to refinery and from refinery to trafficker. When media awareness of the problem began to grow there would be a public burning of the latest seizure, organised by the DEA, and which justified the enormous share of the budget they received. It also put up the price of opium.

If commodity trading was good enough for the CIA, it was good enough for Khun Sa. On New Year's Day in 1960, he set up an underground movement that was dedicated to ridding the Shan states both of the Kuomintang and its Burmese betrayers. Still a young man, he took the first step of building up a small army for himself. Drawn by his charismatic personality, it soon grew to be several hundred strong. In terms of local groupings, that was a force to be reckoned with.

He settled around the towns of Tang-Yan and Ving Ngun close to the Wa states in the north and was soon escorting large caravans of opium to Thailand and Laos. Defending caravans was an important skill and one that Khun Sa excelled in. This ancient form of warfare came from the Chinese Muslim mule breeders who lived along the old trading routes of Asia. Tea and spices transported by mules were regularly attacked by bandits, so a system of protecting the convoys was developed. Khun Sa had mastered the principles behind the ancient system during his time with the Kuomintang and it was now proving very successful for his own group.

At this time, the Kuomintang were the principal traffickers in the area, followed closely by General Ouane Rattikone of Laos. Although they had funds from the CIA, ostensibly for the purpose of keeping up the pressure on Communist China at the border, it was insufficient for their needs, and they soon began to claim a share of the opium riches.

The Kuomintang suffered a serious setback when the Burmese, infuriated by the activities of these foreign mercenaries, co-operated with Communist China in a violent attack on the main Kuomintang base at Mong Pa Liao. The 10,000-strong garrison was no match for a force of 25,000 and was forced to escape across the border into Laos. This was not the place for the Kuomintang to be since General Rattikone had no desire for such competition. He appealed to the United Nations and, as a result, most of the defeated garrison was transported to Taiwan. The few who remained went off to re-group.

One unit of the Kuomintang, consisting of around two thousand men, stayed in Laos secretly, protected by the CIA, who had brokered an agreement with the Royal Laotian Army for the Kuomintang to assist them in the fight against the Pathet Lao, the communist movement fighting to overthrow the pro-western Laotian government. They would also, of course, be used to help the Laotian army in its more important task of transporting opium for the CIA. With such corruption, there was little prospect of their being able to hold back the fanatical Pathet Lao, who were determined to drive out the foreign invader, particularly the American devils.

When, a year later, the Kuomintang garrison at Nam Tha was in danger of falling to the communists, the CIA conspired with the Thai government to allow their forces to move south, crossing the Mekong River to safety. They remained in northern Thailand for many years much to the annoyance of Khun Sa.

Rivalries inside the Kuomintang caused their troops to divide into the 5th Army, which was commanded by General Tuan Shee Wan and headquartered in Chiang Rai Province, and the 3rd Army, led by General Li Wen Huan, in Fang district. General Li was to become a principal character in the Khun Sa story.

By 1963, Khun Sa's strength had grown and his influence spread to the

Laotian border and even spilled over into northern Thailand. He now had the power and declared himself leader of the Shan independence struggle. He named his group of guerrilla fighters the Shan United Army. It was no misnomer for he had trained them into a formidable and disciplined fighting force, with barracks, arms and equipment. Even today, in the Shan lands and other parts of the region, when veterans discuss the exploits of the Shan United Army they claim it was in the battles that Khun Sa proved so remarkable as a tactician. On 15 June 1964, he held a special conference in Loi Maw, where the veteran Bo Deving, was chosen as political leader of the group and a decision was taken to extend forces into bordering Thailand. The Kuomintang were becoming seriously alarmed by Khun Sa's growing strength.

Itchy palms

In Thailand, the United States found a regime that they could rely on for support against the spread of communism throughout Southeast Asia. It was right-wing and anti-communist. The fact that it was also oppressive and criminal was irrelevant to the Central Intelligence Agency. They knew

Family man in Thailand!

that the Chinese communists could overrun that part of the world with little difficulty and the Chinese were aware that such a move would bring about a full confrontation with the Americans. The Russians, who still held sway over the Chinese, were not yet prepared to allow this. At that time, the atomic bomb was a genuine deterrent. However, this did not stop the communists from attempting to spread their tentacles through guerrilla warfare.

In 1947 Thailand was led by General Phin who, with his henchmen, had honed their skills running the drug trade in the Shan States during the Second World War, under the auspices of the Japanese army of occupation. Phin's security forces endeared themselves to the CIA by their harsh methods of repression.

Whereas the Burmese found the Kuomintang a serious nuisance, the Thais positively welcomed them and allowed them to settle along the borders, protecting them from any possible communist threat. An added bonus of this move was that the Kuomintang now had access to the Thai drug network, permitting the crooks in the government to benefit further.

So aid money from the US Treasury poured into what was no more than a token of defence against the communists, but a great boost to drug trafficking.

General Phin promoted one of his former aides, Lieutenant Phao Siyanan, to be the Head of Internal Security. In 1951, he crushed a democratic uprising with such viciousness that he gained promotion to the rank of general and the approval of the CIA.

General Siyanan, like all his contemporaries, suffered from 'itchy palms'. To further his own ends, he developed the strength of his force and its field of operation, until Thailand became the major source of drugs from Southeast Asia. His network of agents had a grip on the entire region and since the CIA chose to act as advisers to his force, they were clearly aware of what he was doing.

When international pressure from the Western countries was brought to bear on Thailand to control its drug activities, General Siyanan and his colleagues found a solution. They were able to assure everyone that the Kuomintang was the problem and that they would take steps to control them. The result was a pantomime in which a heavily armed Kuomintang caravan was apprehended by Siyanan's border police. 'Taken by Surprise', the Kuomintang would then flee from the handful of policemen, leaving behind their precious cargo. The drugs were then transported to General Siyanan, who would notch up another victory for his drug enforcement policy and earn the gratitude of the United States.

However, corrupt leaders like Siyanan had to watch their backs as well as guard their frontiers. He forgot this and, in 1957, was toppled by a coup and fled to Switzerland, and of course his many numbered bank accounts. Doubtless, he has lived happily ever after, protected by the gnomes of Zurich.

The problem facing a government that takes over after a long period of corruption is that the exchequer has usually been bled dry. Siyanan's successors knew they could not get the economy under control without engaging in the illegal opium trade. The new government decided it would earn international approval and solve the financial crisis at the same time, by limiting the sources of supply and the outlets for sale, to those which they controlled themselves. They took decisive action by raiding all the opium dens, seizing the stocks, and destroying them in a well-publicised propaganda exercise.

The reward for this was an increase in the aid they received from the United States and an acceptance as a country with a good record on narcotics control. There were instances where foreigners suffered the death penalty when caught attempting to smuggle narcotics contrary to Thailand's strict laws. Naturally, these laws did not apply to the lawmakers themselves, who continued to draw handsome profits from the illicit trade, though much more discreetly than in the days of General Siyanan.

In 1965, Thailand was now a quiet place where a businessman could live in peace, and the price of raw opium had considerably increased. And that is why Khun Sa was living there.

16

The 1967 Opium War

The late 1960s saw the United States becoming increasingly entangled in Vietnam. Over half a million American service personnel were now engaged in the war, which was costing the country a fortune to wage.

The CIA's covert activities were costing millions, and the source of the money wasn't just the American taxpayer. It was clear that a substantial amount of the money that was being used to conduct operations in the region was through the trafficking in opium, even if it was by proxy and through intermediaries. Manufacturing the raw crop into heroin made it easier to transport, reducing its bulk by a factor of ten, and laboratories, in the deep jungle territory of the Golden Triangle, were set up by the various factions to carry out this work.

Khun Sa's army was growing rapidly and required daily sustenance, so the profits derived from the poppy were vital. Although his troops guarded the business, no single member was allowed to smoke opium. The Shan Army's method for dealing with addiction in its own ranks was swift and brutal. In the rare event of his soldiers becoming addicts, they were given one chance to beat their craving. If they failed, they were executed.

Contrary to popular myth, the young warlord did not get involved with the growing of opium, nor with its refinement into heroin. From the earliest days of his career Khun Sa, always a lateral thinker, realised it was not necessary for him to do that. The crop was not for internal consumption, it had to be exported, in whatever form, and he controlled the territory from which it originated. So anything that moved along those jungle trails, he taxed, setting up command posts and customs houses wherever there were lines of communication, however crude. As all governments in history have discovered, the easiest way to make money is through taxation.

In February 1967, Khun Sa delivered what was, in effect, a declaration of war to the Kuomintang. He demanded that their caravans trading in the Wa states, which were now within his sphere of influence, pay him the same amount of tax as Khun Sa's own caravans had to pay the Kuomintang when they crossed the checkpoints on the borders of Thailand or Laos. The gauntlet had been thrown down.

In June of that same year, Khun Sa supervised what was then the greatest drug caravan in history, three hundred mules carrying sixteen tons of raw opium bound for Laos. The value of the cargo was half a million dollars in Chiang Mai, at 1967 prices and represented in bulk a year's supply for every addict in the Western world.

At that time, the Kuomintang thought of themselves as Lords of the Golden Triangle, and to have Khun Sa daring to make such a display in their fiefdom was a loss of face that could not be tolerated. That the caravan was escorted by such a large force of armed men was an insult that could not go unpunished. They were already aware of the growth of Khun Sa's private army, and they had no doubt that the profit from this trip would enable him to expand even further. They decided that the upstart would be taught a lesson once and for all.

The Kuomintang marched out to destroy Khun Sa and confiscate his huge cargo. All internecine rivalries, which were a common feature of the Kuomintang, were set aside, as two armies under Generals Li Wen-Huan and Tuan Shi-Wen combined. There would be ample time in the future to resolve their minor differences.

Khun Sa's destination was Ban Kwan, a border town on the banks of the Mekong River and the location of one of General Rattikone's secret refineries, in the guise of a sawmill. A train of this size could not move without being observed and the Kuomintang informers passed on its location. The nervous, but confident Kuomintang soldiers waited in ambush by the Mekong River and as the long line of Shans came within distance, they struck, though with no great effect. The Kuomintang were perhaps unpractised as a fighting force since its business for some time had been little more than local oppression. On the other hand, Khun Sa was a natural strategist and had employed basic defensive techniques by keeping some of his troops a short distance behind. After the initial surprise of the attack, it was the Kuomintang who got the real shock when they suddenly found themselves being the target of a counter-attack, this time from the rear. Before they could recover, the Shans had withdrawn into Ban Kwan.

There, Khun Sa's men, after commandeering all boats on the adjacent river, hastily got the villagers to evacuate and dug in around the sawmill. By the time the heavily equipped, and consequently slow-moving, Kuomintang forces arrived, the Shans were ready for the siege. The two sides began to test each other. The Kuomintang formed a tight ring around

Khun Sa's army confront the Kuomintang

the village but could not break through. The Shans were well-protected but could not break out. It was a classic Mexican stand-off.

Then, the villagers who had escaped informed the nearest garrison of the Royal Laotian Army, whose commander notified General Rattikone of the battle taking place inside his property. Rattikone sent the commander to deliver a message, ordering both sides out of the area. The Kuomintang refused to move unless they were paid a large sum in compensation. Khun Sa, who for diplomatic reasons had himself remained on the Burmese side of the border, radioed his troops and ordered them not to move either, until the transaction they had been sent there for was completed.

After a few days of skirmishes, the Kuomintang launched an all-out attack and the two sides engaged in a fierce battle. When news of this was conveyed to Rattikone, he was furious. He was doing his best to fulfil a massive order for the GI's in Vietnam, his best customers. Khun Sa, the man who was supposed to supply him, had compromised him by engaging in a battle. What was even worse was that it was being fought on his territory!

But Rattikone was nothing if not resourceful. He calculated that he could turn this situation to his advantage and gave orders for some of his best troops to stand by and dispatched the Royal Laotian Air Force to attack. Both the Shans and Kuomintang suddenly found themselves under assault by a continuous air bombardment, while still taking potshots at each other. At the same time, the advancing Laotian troops effectively cut off any chance of retreat by land.

When Khun Sa heard what was going on, he guessed that the wily general was taking advantage of the situation to get his hands on the opium for free. He knew that the position was hopeless, so instructed his men to escape with as much of their cargo as they could. Thanks to their pre-planning, they were able to pile what they could into the river craft they had confiscated and make their way back into Burmese territory, though they had to leave behind their dead and much of the opium.

The Kuomintang were much more heavily armed and could not escape. Rattikone attacked with vast reinforcements, part of which was ordered to deliver the opium to him. By nature he was a vindictive man, but on this occasion he was prepared to release the humiliated Kuomintang in exchange for a modest personal backhander. When they were finally allowed to withdraw into Thailand, it had cost them some seventy dead, a considerable number of heavy weapons and ten thousand American dollars.

By contrast, Rattikone felt he had come out of the affair very well. He had enhanced his reputation by defeating two foreign invasions, he had some pocket money and he had acquired most of his supplies of opium — free of charge! On the debit side, his refinery and lumber mill had been destroyed but this could be easily and cheaply rebuilt.

This little battle on the Laotian border has become known locally as the 1967 Opium War. Perhaps it is an exaggeration to describe this clash as a war, though it did set the scene for the succeeding wars between the various warlords in the region.

Although he did not see it that way, Khun Sa had always been reported as having lost perhaps almost a million dollars' worth of arms and opium. Khun Sa's point of view was that he was playing for major stakes with major players and that the experience would prove to be worth a million dollars. He had tested his resources and not come out too badly considering that he had such a small force. Some five hundred men had only given way in the face of a massive show of strength by the Laotian army and air force.

What was more, Khun Sa believed he had beaten the Kuomintang, in that he had met and stood up to their attack, although outnumbered and with nothing like their firepower. Even better, the Kuomintang had been humiliated by Rattikone while the Shans had survived their ordeal with honour.

Khun Sa told me that after the battle he went to see General Rattikone, who was outraged at his audacity. Khun Sa replied calmly that he had only transported the opium and still had to account to the owners of it. If he lost face with them, he would be out of business and Rattikone would have lost a major and, more importantly, a reliable supplier. Rattikone blustered but could not fail to see the truth of the argument. In the end he made certain that Khun Sa was paid for his delivery and the warlord's honour was intact.

The event was still a serious blow to Khun Sa, but not a crippling one, and he had always possessed a remarkable resilience. He needed it for, now openly posted as an outlaw, Khun Sa was a target for everyone, not least the CIA and the comparatively new but increasingly powerful Drugs Enforcement Administration, the DEA.

17

More Men with Itchy Palms

The CIA remained as active in Laos as in Thailand and Vietnam, even though, back in the United States, President Nixon was denying any American presence there. It had assumed control of running the operations that the French intelligence services had been running, and those clandestine activities were financed by trading drugs. Their Hmong guerrillas in Laos grew the poppies and the opium was transported to Saigon by Hmong paratroopers. At one stage, the CIA maintained an army of 30,000 tribesmen to carry out this operation.

This period saw the meteoric rise of a young officer called Vang Pao, who until his death in 2011, was living on a ranch in Montana. Pao was typical of the kind of person that enjoyed the patronage of the CIA. He had become a soldier when only thirteen years of age and first came to prominence at the Battle of Dien Bien Phu, where he led an attack by Hmong tribesmen in a brave attempt to relieve the French garrison.

Pao gained rapid promotion in the Royal Laotian Army and by the time he was a major he'd been noticed by the CIA and placed on the payroll. He was undoubtedly a gallant and able officer but also suffered from 'itchy palms'. Dissatisfied with his army pay and the 'top up' he received from the CIA, he began to pay himself extra from the money intended for his men. When the embezzlement came to the notice of a Laotian army colonel, he asked Vang Pao to explain the discrepancies. Vang Pao's response was a botched attempt to murder the colonel, who naturally, informed his superior, Major General Ouane Rattikone.

Such a crime should have led to death by firing squad and Rattikone would have had little compunction about ordering it, but he was a shrewd man and realised that, by pardoning Vang Pao, he would place the young officer in his debt and would earn the gratitude of the CIA for saving their man. What Rattikone's political organisation needed most of all was money, and that could only be raised by the sale of opium. In this, Vang Pao was an expert.

General Rattikone used Vang Pao to make contact with the various Shan nationalist groups, who were financing their insurgency by drug trafficking. Vang Pao had already noted the successful activity of Khun Sa and brought this rising young star to the attention of Rattikone. Vang Pao knew Rattikone didn't want to trade with the Kuomintang. Indeed, if anything, he wanted to break their near monopoly and needed someone with the temerity to challenge them.

Another part of the enigmatic Khun Sa puzzle fell into place.

In Laos, Prime Minister Phoumi was doing everything such a Machiavellian character could do to ensure democracy was being stifled. His determinedly anti-communist stance earned him rich rewards from the United States, as well as his enormous income from the drugs trade which General Rattikone directed for him.

Vang Pao's star also continued to rise. After his fright, when he had to beg for mercy from General Rattikone, the cunning Laotian army officer became much more expert in choosing whom to serve. He allied himself to the Hmong cabinet minister, Touby Lyfoung, by marrying his son and daughter to the minister's children and continued to gain favour with the CIA by shifting opium from the hill tribes.

Senior officers in the Royal Laotian Army received negligible salaries, even General Rattikone was paid only two hundred dollars per month, but they had little difficulty in augmenting their pay from other sources. This meant dealing in the opium which continued to flood out of the Shan lands. With Rattikone acting as his agent, prime minister Phoumi was said to be netting a hundred thousand dollars each month. Whatever Rattikone's share was, it obviously wasn't enough and so in 1964, he organised a coup to overthrow Phoumi and the take-over of his illegal businesses. Rattikone became the grandmaster of the opium trade.

The CIA were furious at this coup against their man and set about initiating a counter-coup. However, they were distracted at the time by the dangerous developments in South Vietnam and the attempt failed.

Vietnam connection

In June 1965, Air Vice Marshal Ky was appointed Prime Minister of South Vietnam. His appointment led to the promotion of Nguyen Ngoc Loan to Major General and controller of anti-corruption, the police and central intelligence. It was a vast amount of power for one man, but Ky could not have chosen better. The opposition National Liberation Front had been growing from strength to strength, but Loan was prepared to use any dirty trick or form of oppression to stifle legitimate protest. Loan justified the faith Ky had shown in him and the CIA approved.

Any criticism against the state was dealt with promptly and effectively. To oversee the important drugs trafficking operations, Loan appointed another rough character named Mai Den, or 'Black Mai', as Head of Foreign Espionage Operations. Black Mai's brief was simple, to streamline the trade between Laos and South Vietnam.

Once again, in this incredible tapestry, a valuable thread ran back from the CIA to Ky, through Loan and Black Mai, to General Rattikone in Laos, through Vang Pao to Khun Sa in the Shan states.

A new power struggle began to form in South Vietnam, between Air Vice Marshall Ky and General Nguyen Van Thieu, the senior officer of the military junta. In1965, Thieu became the titular head of state and Ky accepted the post of Vice President, though it meant a considerable loss of power.

However, Ky still held one very strong card, or, rather, his ally Loan did. Major General Nguyen Ngoc Loan retained his position as head of the National Police but more importantly, he still controlled the funds provided by the Americans. As long as they were able to hang onto these, they were probably a match for President Thieu, until Ky suffered a series of blows that weakened his position. The public perception of the disagreement between Ky and Thieu led to a growth in support for the insurgents. Then in 1968, the Viet Cong and the North Vietnamese People's Army joined forces to launch a series of devastating, surprise attacks throughout South Vietnam. Known as the Tet offensive, after the Tet holiday, it was the largest military operation conducted by the communists up to that point in the war.

One unfortunate incident during the offensive did not help the duo. Loan suddenly gained global attention when the international press released photographs and film footage of him executing a handcuffed Viet Cong prisoner called Lem. Nguyen Lem had been arrested and handcuffed for killing the wife, six children and eighty-year-old mother of a military officer by cutting their throats. Loan was outraged on seeing Lem and summarily executed him with a shot, from his sidearm to the temple, effectively blowing his brains out for the world to see, in what became one of the most enduring images of the Vietnam war.

Then a few months later, Loan was injured by machine gun fire from a helicopter gunship and had to have his leg amputated. The attack also caused the deaths of a group of Ky's closest aides. Ky's power gradually began to decline until, by the early 1970s, it had all but disappeared. General Tran Thien Khiem became the new power in the land, with control of the police and customs authorities; Ky retained control of the air force, which enabled him to keep a stake in the movement of drugs.

There was a positive explosion of demand for heroin in two markets. The first was in exports to the United States of America, and the second was the epidemic of addiction among the GIs serving in Vietnam. Khun Sa once told a reporter, "The Americans were not defeated by the North Vietnamese but by their drug addiction."

18

A Plague of Corruption

Today, the armed forces of the United States of America is an all volunteer military force, well trained and very effective. But from 1940 until 1973, both in peace and war, men were conscripted to fill the ranks of all the services. To the Americans it was known as the 'draft' and the majority of the GI's fighting in Vietnam were drafted. Most came from poor families, with a proportion of Afro-Americans well in excess of their share of the population. Any rich kid who wanted to avoid the draft had little difficulty in doing so, though it took money. So the bulk of the troops had no interest in the war and could probably not have told you where Vietnam was before they were sent there. Once there, they were subjected to long periods of boredom interwoven with short periods of extreme violence against a tough and resourceful enemy.

In their disaffection they were ripe for introduction to drugs, in particular heroin, and there was plenty of it about. It was sold openly on the streets and brought into the camps by the civilian employees. It was estimated that by 1971, as many as 10 per cent of GIs were addicted to the drug and many have never recovered from its effects.

The growth in the number of American addicts created serious problems for the Laotian General Rattikone, because satisfying the demand was a non-stop operation. Worse was to come. Following repeated incursions from Laos into South Vietnam, through Cambodia, by the communist Pathet Lao, the South Vietnamese army retaliated by sending their men in hot pursuit. Air cover was desperately needed and Rattikone's supplies were almost brought to a standstill since so many air force planes were being inconsiderately commandeered for war purposes instead of drug trading. Fortunately, the CIA was on hand to help and arranged the removal from office of Prince Sihanouk, the titular head of Laos. Rattikone was then able to re-engage the Laotian aircraft to fly regularly between the capital Vientiane and Saigon, in Vietnam. Business was back to normal.

Although he no longer enjoyed the privileges of political status, Air

Vice Marshal Ky still controlled the drugs trade in Saigon, through his association with General Rattikone. Of course, none of these senior military figures could ever be caught with drugs personally, as they always worked through intermediaries. Ky and Rattikone used a Chinese racketeer by the name of Huu Tim-Heng. He had a Pepsi-Cola franchise which gave him the dual benefit of being able to move about freely without arousing suspicion and also to buy the chemicals needed in the drugs refinement processes.

Like Ky, South Vietnam's President Thieu took every precaution to ensure that he was not incriminated. He could use the officers who had been so helpful in his election, men of the army and the navy, who were able to transport the drugs under the guise of carrying out manoeuvres and operations. Chief among them was General Quang, another upright citizen who had mastered the art of taking 'backhanders'. His official title was Presidential Intelligence Adviser, but he was beginning to supply almost as big quantities of drugs as Ky himself. The Thieu-Quang double act managed themselves in much the same way as the preceding Ky-Loan administration. The rotten Generals were getting richer by the day.

The South Vietnamese assault on Cambodia, which had been such a nuisance initially, ended happily for the drugs trade because it opened up the mighty Mekong River as an additional supply route. The senior officers were now able to make use of their navies to assist in transportation.

In the late 1960s and early 1970s, the Chinese were the principal organisers of the drugs trade on behalf of the US military. Back in the United States, the Mafia had a sizeable share of the takings but felt that their involvement could be further developed. They began to send in their own experts who started to make contacts through NCOs, sergeants and corporals who were willing to do business. Meyer Lansky, a major organised crime figure, sent one of his lieutenants, Frank Carmen Furci, to oversee the organisation in South-East Asia. Santo Trafficante Junior, another of Lansky's henchmen, visited the region to ensure that supplies got through for dispatch to the Caribbean and the United States. Heroin by this time was big business on the North American continent.

A new and unexpected supply route to the United States was provided courtesy of the US Mail, inadvertently, of course, when the GI's hit on the idea of sending supplies back in their letters home. As a result, some of them were able to start up businesses or buy their own houses after their release from the service. By this time, the Golden Triangle had become a major source of heroin for the United States, supplying something like a third of the demand.

The plague of corruption had spread so wide in South Vietnam that few observers doubted the coming collapse. Any attempt to reverse the moral decline seemed impossible. It was clear to many intelligence services, including the CIA, that the Republic of South Vietnam would soon be overrun by the communist North.

The North Vietnamese could also see that the South was vulnerable, and their 1975 spring offensive was the beginning of the end. The Americans had gone and so had all the major perks. All those who had brought about this hideous state of affairs, including General Thieu and Air Vice-Marshal Ky, were flown to safety in the United States, along with their wives and families, and their millions of dollars, while the small fry were left to face the music.

Southeast Asia still had a big part to play in American history. But now the stage would move to Burma and the lead player would be Khun Sa.

19

Naming Names!

My first visit to Tiger Camp was now nearly over and so it was time to discuss tactics for the important filmed interview with Khun Sa. We all had different agendas. For Bo Gritz, finding any MIAs was a priority. Gabriella and the crew wanted footage and a story for their Italian broadcaster. I was filming an independent documentary about Khun Sa and his private army. Was he really fighting for independence against an oppressive Burmese government in Rangoon, or was he just a warlord with a mercenary force protecting the opium profits?

We all had a common interest in testing the offer Khun Sa had made to the West that he could halt the flow of opium from the Golden Triangle. We had argued extensively about whether Khun Sa could be serious, and whether any such scheme would be workable.

I was also interested to know how much the CIA itself had participated in any narcotics smuggling, and whether Khun Sa was prepared to give the names of those involved. On that point I was to reach a compromise. At this time, he would not identify those individuals with whom he was dealing. He would, however, or so he said, give proof of past CIA involvement. That was all we could hope for.

The location designed for the interview was the pavilion adjoining Khun Sa's residence. It looked out onto a pond full of exotic fish with lanterns hung from trees. For the centre of a rebel army encampment, the surroundings were curiously serene.

The discussions began. First, I heard Khun Sa. Kernsai, his trusted aide, interpreted. The general was articulate and convincing. The state which he visualised did not grow poppies and refine them into heroin. Instead, alternative crops could be grown. There are forests of hardwood to cultivate, mines to exploit and precious stones and metals, he said. There could even be tourism.

Khun Sa said he had detailed plans for agricultural reform which would outlaw the poppy, and for an infrastructure which would make the

Khun Sa names names!

initiative viable. This would be expensive and would, he freely admitted, have to be funded by Western capitalist sources. But which, he asked, would be better value for the billions of dollars in aid being spent at the time, to continue to fund the crooked government and army officials who cynically channelled their millions of profits into Swiss bank accounts and Western investments, or to spend a much smaller amount on a noble experiment which could be fully overseen by American or by United Nations observers?

He was very amusing on the subject of politicians. There are three types of politicians," he told me, counting them on his fingers. "There is the idealist who cares only for the right and wrong of the issue, and never for the chances of success or failure. There is the business type who cares nothing for right and wrong, but only for success or failure." Then he spelt out the third type, making it pretty clear that he fell into this classification. "A true statesman," he told me, "cares both for the right and wrong, and takes into account the chances of success or failure. He will not engage in activities which may be morally right but promise no chance of success. He also avoids those which offer every chance of success, but which are morally wrong. He only does things which are both morally right and promise practical success."

All of us sitting there knew of politicians who could learn something from that little homily. He then made me laugh with a story which incorporated this teaching. "A pet parrot," he said, "whose master was away, saw his mistress committing adultery. He confided in a fellow parrot that he was going to tell his mistress she should not do this bad thing. The other parrot counselled against it, but the first parrot told her, anyway. His mistress, fearing he would repeat this accusation when his master returned, understandably killed the parrot".

"To the Lord Buddha," Khun Sa explained to me, "a thing should be said or done when it is not only right but advantageous. Otherwise, it is best left unsaid, undone." He left us with a final, mysterious warning "Catch not the shadow and lose the substance."

Like Gritz, I knew it would take a major campaign even to dent the prejudice held against someone like Khun Sa, though both of us could see the logic of the warlord's arguments. For Gritz, it was similar to the prohibition of alcohol in the United States after the First World War. The government then claimed it could not do business with people like Al Capone, in order to get them to give up their liquor interests. But prohibition failed, which raises the even trickier question: would the legalisation of hard drugs remove the criminal element dealing in them?

The very illegality of opium allows the trade in it far greater profits than could be yielded from any other commodity. That trade produces an enormous cash flow that has created a multitude of criminal networks on a global scale. It can buy police, soldiers and ministers at the highest level. In some places, it can even buy the judiciary, which makes the rule of law a mockery. Lose the rule of law and society collapses. Therein lies the conundrum.

No group of men could be more exposed to opium than Khun Sa's soldiers, yet their addiction problem was practically zero and their discipline was strong. Although they guarded the opium crop, they were not tempted to try it; the penalty for smoking opium was severe.

Drug users were taken to the Drug Rehabilitation Unit on the outskirts of Tiger Camp. First time offenders could expect 'cold turkey' treatment: they were put in a hole and kept there for a month, giving them time to reflect on their habit. The next month or two was spent in a large wooden cage with other drug users, only being let out for a few hours a day to work and exercise. Once they were considered to be cured, they were returned to their army unit and the slate was considered wiped clean. For the second offence, the same treatment was applied, but for double the time. The third offence warranted the death penalty, which was carried out in front of the other troops by a couple of blows to the back of the head with a bamboo club, the same way that drug dealers were executed. The treatment was highly effective, but hardly one that would be accepted in the West.

The principal benefit of legalising the drug would be the eradication of crime associated with the production, transport and distribution of it. Then America and Europe would be spared if narcotics were limited and legally available?

Khun Sa's answers were in Mandarin, he named prominent individuals who had been involved in the Golden Triangle drugs trade. It is always difficult to appreciate what is said in a foreign language. Bo Gritz told us that Khun Sa specifically indicted Theodore Shackley, a former CIA Deputy Director of Covert Operations, as being in charge of US involvement in the opium trade between 1965 and 1975. He also named Thomas Clines, CIA deputy station chief at the same time, who resigned in 1977 to go into the arms business, followed two years later by Shackley. Another associate was General Richard Secord, who would later be prominent in the Irangate enquiry.

Gritz told me Khun Sa had also named a now deceased Mafioso boss, Santo Trafficante Junior, who had taken over from Meyer Lansky in the early seventies. Trafficante was already on the international list of the Federal Bureau of Narcotics as "a powerful Mafia figure in Florida, acquainted with most of the major sources of supply of narcotics in Central and South America." He had previously been involved in the heroin smuggling operations of both Lucky Luciano and Meyer Lansky.

Trafficante never had the international high profile of these other notorious gangsters and was deliberately unassuming. It is unlikely that Khun Sa would ever have heard of him had he not been involved in the Golden Triangle drug trade. I knew about Trafficante but wouldn't have guessed he had travelled this far.

I was surprised to hear the name of Richard Armitage, a former Assistant Secretary of Defense for International Security, mentioned as having handled the relevant financial transactions, including profits from narcotic deals, mainly through banks in Australia. When George Bush was elected President, he nominated Armitage as Assistant Secretary of State, but Armitage resigned rather than face Congressional scrutiny. If what Khun Sa said about him was true, he was well advised to do so. However, I was dubious about the claim that this man was so deeply involved.

Another name that Khun Sa mentioned was Jerry Daniels a former

CIA station chief in Thailand who was the case officer assigned to General Vang Pao, commander of the Central Intelligence Agency's secret Laotian army during the Vietnam War. Daniels had died under suspicious circumstances in Bangkok and was buried on Pao's ranch at Missoula in Montana, Daniels' hometown. The millions of dollars Pao paid for the ranch and two other luxurious homes could hardly have come from his Army salary.

Bo's Hidden Agenda

Bo Gritz was obviously biased in his opinions and when I subsequently discovered that Khun Sa had been tricked into giving us those names, I had to ask questions about Gritz's motivations. For example, he seemed to have a special dislike for Armitage and did not like it when I suggested the claim against this man might be a mistake. On reflection, I believe that the real reason he offered to take me to the Golden Triangle was his long-standing hatred towards certain US government officials.

Gritz was desperate to attack the one group of people he deeply resented, those he held responsible for mishandling the situation of the MIAs, many of whom were senior government agents with the CIA and had served in Asia. Gritz believed that this group had abused their power by disregarding the constitution of the United States. Because the issue of prisoners of war is such a sensitive one to the American people, in the days following the Vietnam War, many mistakes were made. Instead of being honest, some American officials chose to lie about the missing POWs, which turned into a cover-up that Gritz despised.

I believe that Gritz thought that the only way to deal with this nest of vipers was in their own way, underhandedly! After all, he was a product of the same school of covert operations and would use whatever method necessary to expose those who had engaged in corruption.

The colonel had a large following in the mid-1980s when his name still had a certain mystic quality about it. He was a much decorated war hero but unfortunately, a decade later, he became known as a fanatic, and his extremist views, anti-government rhetoric, and the building of survivalist fortifications in the Idaho hills to survive an impending Armageddon had done little for his image.

The Bo Gritz at the time of my first visit to Tiger Camp was a different man. Eventually, I was to make three films with him, and we spent many hours in the back of a minibus together, so I got to know the man quite well.

He had been disillusioned about the Vietnam war and its sorry ending. He served in the war for a total of four years and the role he had played seemed to trouble him, he had burned many villages and was responsible for the deaths of at least 400 of the enemy.

There was no doubt that Gritz was obsessed with the issue of the MIAs. It seemed natural that he should set up the Lazarus Mission and enter Laos in search of the missing POWs. Gritz believed with absolute conviction that he had been betrayed by the CIA in Laos. He put the failure of his mission firmly at the door of the CIA and from then on, he made it his business to gain revenge.

The rumours of CIA involvement in the drugs trade had been circulating for many years, but nobody had been able to prove it. Over the years, Gritz had built up a network of contacts in United States government departments and, once he realised that the very men he wanted revenge on might have been involved in drugs and illicit arms sales, he became more determined than ever.

Gritz was also extremely anti-narcotics, feeling that drugs were the biggest threat to the American way of life he loved. Like a plague, it had affected nearly every school in the Western world, and his teenage daughter's addiction served only to increase his hatred for those he believed to be ultimately responsible.

Gritz knew that Western governments were losing the war on drugs and as a former soldier in the special forces, he also knew that difficult problems needed to be tackled with unorthodox methods. That is why he advocated dealing with Khun Sa, although he didn't agree with the warlord's justification of the Shan opium trade.

I believe Gritz admired the Shan people and wanted to help them. His second marriage was to a Chinese woman, and he made every effort to understand the oriental perspective. His military successes in Vietnam were achieved mainly while leading a force of 250 Cambodian mercenaries, known as the "Cambodes", and he understood their way of thinking.

The core of his plan was to get Khun Sa to name the corrupt American officials in front of me and the Italian film crew. He reasoned that, as a European filmmaker, I would give the recording credibility and the CIA would be exposed as being at least partly responsible for the drugs epidemic on the streets of America. The problem was that Khun Sa knew the names of the local CIA and DEA chiefs in Thailand, Laos and Burma who had been involved, but not those of the bigger fish that Gritz wanted.

As a result of this, Gritz told Khun Sa the people he should name. Khun

Sa no doubt believed they were guilty, after all, Gritz acted like a friend of the Shan and had been a colonel in the Green Berets so must have known what had gone on and his argument certainly sounded convincing. Most importantly, the Shans believed that Gritz was working directly with the United States National Security Council which had very close links to the president. After all, his first mission to Khun Sa had been at the request of George Bush.

Gritz didn't name names himself, because he reasoned that if he did, his claims would be put down to sour grapes and he would end up with further trumped-up charges back home. By putting the names in the mouth of Khun Sa, they gained the backing of the world's greatest expert in the murky world of heroin trading.

What did Khun Sa get in exchange for his help? Gritz had ingeniously drawn up a six-year plan for the Shan Council which would, in effect, offer to stop opium production. Although it was based on the same formula as previous Shan plans that had pledged to reduce the opium supply in exchange for aid money, there was a difference. This time, Gritz said he would personally organise the aid money for the first year. Once the United States saw the plan working, he told the Shans, they would be more inclined to support the scheme.

Gritz must have realised that Washington would never take the plan seriously, but the Shans were convinced. Gritz told them he planned to raise the first year's aid by asking forty-eight businessmen to each contribute one million dollars to a fund, which would recompense the Shans for their reduction in opium during the first year, in return for the rich mineral wealth of the Shan states. Khun Sa and his close advisers believed Gritz, thinking that he had access to the Oval Office.

Whether Gritz believed it himself or whether it was all part of his plan for revenge on the men he held responsible for the failure to return the MIAs, is impossible to say. But I never heard of one businessman signing up for the fund and if there was any attempt to get the Shan support plan into operation, it didn't amount to anything.

Gritz had another ploy to gain Shan support, which finally answered my questions about why Gritz had been so insistent on Lance Trimmer joining our expedition. The former sergeant had come to Tiger Camp because of his military skills as an armourer and ammunition technician. The Mong Tai Army had previously mentioned to Gritz that they were having problems with some dated stocks of ammunition and that they had suffered casualties from accidents due to misfires and explosions.

Trimmer set about checking the stock. By this simple act of assistance, Gritz earned a reputation as a friend of the Shans and the co-operation he needed from Khun Sa.

I do not believe that Gritz's hidden agenda was an attempt to make money because he didn't. His intention was clear enough, he wanted to get the men he was after by whatever means possible and the one he hated above all was Richard Armitage.

An interesting, independent view of Armitage is to be found in the library of *Time* magazine, where on 4 May 1987, there appeared an article about Ross Perot, the man who recorded an all-time high vote for a third runner in the US presidential elections of 1992. Perot, a Texas billionaire, patriot and extremely powerful man, received information that Armitage was a drugs smuggler and arms dealer. Being the kind of man he was, he wasted no time in confronting Armitage himself, demanding that he resign his government post. Armitage, predictably, denied everything, so Perot went to see fellow Texan and then Vice-President, George Bush. He got no help from that source and nor did he from William Webster, then Director of the CIA. So he went to Frank Carlucci, nominally Armitage's boss. Carlucci told Perot to "stop pursuing Armitage". Carlucci, it should be noted, was Deputy Director of the CIA when George Bush was in charge!

At that time, all I knew was that Khun Sa had held up a piece of paper on which was written three names as if he had written them himself. I have that on film, and my subsequent investigations into these names, when I returned first to Europe and then to the United States, did not really substantiate the allegations made against them.

My last night in Tiger Camp was spent having a drink with the crew and our newly found Shan friends. We were sad to be leaving, though Gritz and his team decided to stay on in Homong for a few more days. Our return to Thailand was uneventful. We were taken on a route that avoided the Thai Border Police, who by now would know that foreigners were in Homong, thanks to their network of informers. Thai goodwill was essential to the Shans if their much needed supplies were to keep rolling across the border. The presence of 'farangs' in the Shan states did not please the Thais and when the informers reported any sighting of foreigners, the police would immediately tighten the whole border.

Perhaps because we had been guests of the general himself, any informers who were aware of our presence must have kept the information to themselves. The Border Police patrols that were around appeared to be routine and we were able to get back to Thailand safely.

20

Public Enemy Number One

The completion of my first trek to Khun Sa's jungle headquarters had left my head spinning. It took a while for me to absorb all the stories I had heard and the sights I had seen in the Shan states. The connection between the resistance movements and narcotics, the Burmese government and the CIA, was complicated. The general public had become tired of the drug related news continuously regurgitated in the newspapers or on television. They told the same story of corruption and despair but had no answers.

By the 1990s, the major Western countries had been hit with a drug epidemic of astonishing social and economic proportions. Responses to the problem, from the major economies of Britain, Germany, France, Italy and Japan had been completely ineffective. The proliferation of drugs in the United States had actually become a public embarrassment. It seemed that criminals and dealers were trading with impunity. Public outrage was high, and the press took up the cry against the government. The authorities were desperate to turn the 'heat' down.

In March 1990, at a press conference called by Richard Thornburgh, the United States Attorney General, it was revealed that in the previous December federal prosecutors in Brooklyn, New York, had filed a sealed indictment against Khun Sa.

He was accused specifically of being the owner of a 2,400 pound shipment of heroin bound for New York and intercepted at Bangkok in 1988, at that time the largest single heroin seizure ever made. He was further accused of importing 3,500 pounds of heroin into New York City over a period of eighteen months. Khun Sa was now officially, 'Public Enemy Number One'.

The New York Times next day quoted the head of the DEA, John Lawn, as calling Khun Sa "the self-proclaimed king of opium" and federal prosecutors styling him "the most powerful drug trafficker in the Golden Triangle." This same John Lawn, by the way, had on the 8 May 1986, sent a message to General Noriega reading: "I would like to take this opportunity to reiterate my deep appreciation for the vigorous anti-drug trafficking policy that you have adopted." So what did he know?

When I asked Khun Sa, on a subsequent visit, about the indictment, he shrugged it off. Instead he asked since I knew of the CIA's involvement, and since President Bush had been at one time head of the CIA, why did I find it surprising. He had a point.

In the same month, the indictment was filed against Khun Sa, some twenty-five thousand combat troops invaded Panama to arrest Manuel Noriega. That particular general had become too big for his boots and his friends, including one George Bush (senior), had turned against him. Noriega was brought back to Miami to face charges of conspiring to smuggle cocaine into the United States. He was found guilty and sentenced to forty years in prison. He was granted early release in 2007 and extradited to France, where he was again found guilty and sentenced to twenty years in prison. In 2011, he was returned to Panama to serve the remainder of his sentence. He was never allowed to make public what he knew about the CIA and what his relationship with them was during his long years of power, when he was actively engaging in drugs trafficking with their knowledge and assistance. He died in a Panama hospital in 2017. For all of its drama, Noriega's arrest had no impact on the Caribbean cocaine trade.

The same year as the indictment, Khun Sa wrote a letter to Margaret Thatcher, the Prime Minister of Great Britain, and asked me to deliver it. Mrs Thatcher was my Member of Parliament as well as patron of the business club I belonged to and my former wife baked cakes for her. I had met her on several occasions, and she occasionally greeted me "as the cake lady's husband". Included in this letter was information that Irishmen, possibly members of the IRA (Irish Republican Army) had sent envoys to Khun Sa. At that time, the Provisional IRA had been waging a guerrilla war against the British armed forces in Northern Ireland and due to their indiscriminate bombing of civilian targets in mainland Britain were classed as a terrorist organisation. Though there was general public disbelief that the outlawed Irish Republican Army could be involved in drugs trading, many in the intelligence community believed it generated income to purchase arms.

Apart from the IRA information, I prepared a short report on the Shan resistance movement and sent a video copy of the film we had shot the previous year to put the Shan case to the Prime Minister. Although Mrs Thatcher was otherwise occupied at the time – this was when the leadership coup was being successfully organised against her – she showed great interest in the Shan problem. By the time a reply was received, however, she was no longer Prime Minister and a letter to me from the Foreign Office only re-stated Britain's official position, which was not to take a position on the Shan cause.

Interestingly the letter, signed by Douglas Hurd the Foreign Secretary, also dismissed any IRA involvement in the narcotics business. It is now clear that the organisation certainly had been involved in this kind of activity.

A short time later, I was approached by a top official in the Drugs Investigation Unit of Her Majesty's Customs & Excise Department, to whom presumably the letter and tape had been passed on. The unit was desperately seeking ways to control and prevent the flow of drugs into the United Kingdom and the official was prepared to visit the region to see what could be done. Indeed, the law enforcement agencies in Britain and Europe, like the DEA in America had obviously failed in their efforts to win the so-called "war on drugs".

Curiously, a report from the United States General Accounting Office dated 1992, had examined the DEA's operations in Southeast Asia and rebuked it for the "poor performance" of some of its staff who, it said, lacked "the knowledge, skills and abilities recommended for their positions." It also stated that the overall quality of the DEA's intelligence analysts assigned to that area had "significantly declined since the late 1980s." The British official asked for my guidance. I was ready to accompany him on a visit to the Golden Triangle and to make the necessary arrangements for him to meet Khun Sa but, once again, the Foreign Office was to intervene and veto any constructive attempt to solve the problem for fear of 'upsetting' Burma's brutal military regime.

Since the 1970s official US policy had been to condemn the ruling military junta in Rangoon for its direct involvement with major drugs trafficking groups in the region, as well as for gross violation of human rights. At the same time, however, in a classic case of the left hand not knowing what the right hand is doing, the DEA had been praising the junta for its 'vigorous anti-drug policies'. When democracy finds itself opposed to the interests of big business, it usually loses out.

In January 1988, a House of Representatives news release announced a study mission by the Select Committee on narcotics abuse and control, leaving for Southeast Asia. The Chairman, Representative Charles B. Rangel, noted: "The large amount of opium produced in Burma and illicit narcotics trafficking through such nations as Thailand, Malaysia, and Singapore, make it important for the Select Committee to visit Southeast Asia at this time. Not only is heroin addiction debilitating, but intravenous drugs abuse is a major vehicle for the transmission of AIDS in America. We want to see what we can do to stop this twin tragedy from continuing to spiral in our land." This is the same Rangel who had previously dismissed all approaches by Khun Sa, for the United States to do something about its drug problem in Southeast Asia, completely out of hand.

In February 1989, the United States government finally removed Burma from a list of countries eligible to receive aid for combating the drugs trade, when American satellite images showed that drug production in Burma was increasing at an alarming rate and intelligence reports suggested high-level official complicity in the trade.

In July of that year, a new DEA attache, Angelo Saladino, arrived in Rangoon and immediately pleased his hosts by openly disagreeing with official US policy: he believed the United States should continue its generous indulgence of the ruling junta and thus aid what the DEA laughingly called its narcotics suppression activities.

In February 1990, a Burmese government delegation, led by the Foreign Ministry's Director, General Oh Gyaw, visited Washington to lobby for resumption of American anti-narcotics assistance. They met with Charles Rangel, then Chairman of the Committee on Narcotics in the House of Representatives, and senior DEA officials, much to the embarrassment of the State Department because the delegation included Brigadier General Tin Hia, commander of Burma's 22nd Light Infantry Division. This unit had never, so far as is known, participated in any anti-narcotics raids but which was known to have played an active and enthusiastic role in the 1988 massacre of student protesters.

To coincide with the visit, the Rangoon authorities had authorised the first public drug burning in Burma. Such occurrences were common spectacles in Thailand and other drug producing countries, where the DEA was said to be paying up to 80 per cent of the local street value of drugs confiscated by local law enforcement agencies. This was seen by them as just another way of dipping into Uncle Sam's bottomless purse.

In 1992, Saladino was replaced by Richard Horn, who lasted only a year before being recalled to Washington. Horn's crime was an attempt to seek radical resolutions, meeting with officials of the Wa wing of the Communist Party of Burma's rebel army, which had approached the DEA with drug eradication proposals similar to those of Khun Sa.

Although US government officials had steadfastly refused to meet with Khun Sa himself, or open any official lines of communication with him, Congressman Rangel had met with Lin Mingxian, a former BCP commander turned government militia commander in the hills north of Kentung, a man whose group was fast becoming one of the most powerful drug trafficking organisations in Burma.

The difference between Lin Mingxian and Khun Sa was, of course, that one was a puppet of a military dictatorship while the other was a patriot, dedicated to the cause of Shan independence.

A special pipe for the village Headman

21

A Dopey Smuggler

No sooner had I returned to London from the Shan lands, that I wanted to go back. I couldn't explain it, but the desire to immerse myself completely into the story of the Shans was overwhelming. I realised, however, that a few filmed interviews could never do justice to the extraordinary life of Khun Sa and I had to go back to find out more, as soon as possible.

Strangely, an opportunity presented itself in November 1989, while I was in Dhaka, Bangladesh, to discuss producing an information film for the government. Serious rioting had erupted on the streets of the capital, forcing an emergency to be declared. Foreigners had been advised to stay in their hotels until order was restored and my meeting with General Ershad, the President of Bangladesh, had been postponed for ten days. Northern Thailand was only two short flights away, so I decided to seize the moment and arrange a last-minute trek into Shan land.

On arriving in Chiang Mai, I telephoned Mr Mook, who worked directly under Khernsai Jaiyane, one of Khun Sa's closest aides. I asked him to seek permission for me to visit Tiger Camp. A few hours later he called me back, the answer was yes.

In Thailand, like other Asian countries, it is vital to have a local person, a 'fixer', who is sufficiently well-connected to smooth the way through any problems you may encounter. As I had to cross the border illegally into Burma, Mook thought Heng, who I remembered from my first visit, would be the best man but unfortunately he was unavailable at such short notice. Luckily an associate called Toby was available.

Toby was a short plump Shan with curly hair, which I presumed had been permed. His attire of a dusky pinkish bomber jacket and white shoes were not exactly inconspicuous making him look more like a pimp than a guide. Although a supporter of Khun Sa, he was not directly employed by him or the Mong Tai Army. Looking every inch the villain that he probably was, he boasted of being able to find anything for a price. Within minutes of our meeting he pulled a dirty white cloth from his pocket, which he carefully unwrapped, revealing four tiny pink coloured stones.

"Wubies — very good — you want, good" he said thrusting them towards me.

A smuggler by profession, Toby earned his living arranging for commodities to be smuggled across the border to the various insurgent groups. Because he obviously knew all the clandestine routes, or so he said, and with so little time at my disposal, I had no alternative but to hire him.

It was late afternoon when we finally drove into the sleepy border town of Mae Hong Son. Parking his Toyota pickup next to a public telephone, Toby, who had fortunately swapped his pink jacket for blue and his white shoes for brown, called a number he had been given to receive further instructions. As he spoke into the receiver, his chubby face broke into a wide grin. The contact had suggested we go straight to a small village nearby as there was probably a mule train going to cross the border sometime that night.

The village was just off the main tarmac road, hidden from view by dense foliage and reached by a narrow dirt track. I didn't recognise the place. I had assumed we were going to Mae Suya, the village we gathered in only a few months before.

"Are you sure this is the right place" I asked Toby. He grinned, choosing

Many tribesmen are addicted to opium

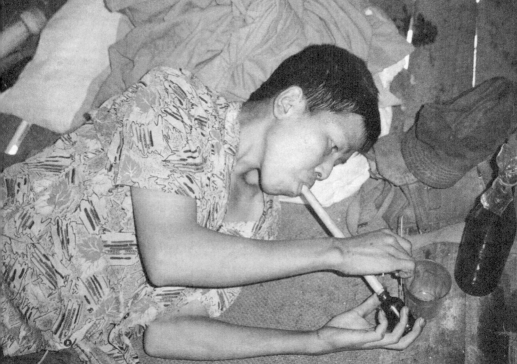

to ignore my question.

We were met by a young man, wearing a traditional sarong wrapped around his waist, who beckoned us towards a large hut. Three men emerged from the entrance and greeted us in the traditional Buddhist manner, slightly bowing their heads and putting hands together, as if in prayer. We acknowledged the greeting in the same way.

"This is Kham, the Headman," said Toby, "He welcomes you to his village.

We were invited to sit on some wooden chairs that had been placed in a circle. The two of us sat together while the three tribal men were seated opposite. No one spoke until tea arrived.

A very attractive Shan girl poured green tea into small thick glasses. Still nobody talked. It was nearly dusk and the numerous jungle bugs had started their evening chorus. I was now feeling tired after the long journey from Dhaka.

"Ask Kham what time the mule train is leaving" I asked Toby, breaking the silence.

I listened to Toby translate the question, wait for a reply and then speak again, how can such a simple question require so many words?

After a few minutes the three men suddenly stood up. Toby turned to me, "Kham say please follow"

We walked through the village to a small wooden shack with no windows.

"Kham say, please enter. You relax inside" translated Toby.

As I entered the hut, lit by a hurricane light, I was hit by a distinct smell.

"Fuck, that's opium" I said to myself.

The hut was Kham's opium den. The smiling headman beckoned us to sit on rugs on the floor, opposite him. The other two men settled down adjusting their rugs and a couple of dirty looking cushions for comfort.

The pretty Shan girl glided into the hut, the way oriental women do so well, and in one motion slid to her knees very gracefully. In her hand were opium instruments which she placed before the headman. He then offered myself and Toby a pair of pipes.

It was now obvious that the time had come to abandon this place. I did not want to offend my host by refusing his offer in the wrong manner. Using a variety of facial gestures and chest banging with my fist, I had hoped to convey that smoking would be bad for me.

It seemed to work. Kham smiled, maybe to acknowledge my good acting, and then speaking, through Toby, with a concerned look on his face.

"Do not confuse opium with tobacco smoking. Opium good for you, like medicine" translated Toby.

I smiled and nodded my head, further declining his invitation.

It was fascinating to watch the headman prepare his pipe. Using a knife, he scraped the remnants of opium from the pipe onto a flat piece of wood and ground them to a dark brown powder, which he then poured into a small wooden bowl. A small amount of fresh opium was added and the whole mixture, augmented with an occasional gob of spit, was stirred patiently. Once satisfied with the final product he rolled it with the palm of his hand into a ball.

Taking a long needle, he pierced the ball of opium holding it over the flame of an oil lamp. The opium swelled in the heat of the flame. When he felt it was ready, he placed the opium over the pipe bowl and pressed the mixture tightly into place and pulled the needle out revealing a small air hole.

Lying on his side, Kham bought the pipe to his lips, while making sure the opium ball was just over the flame. He inhaled deeply, drawing continuously on the opium. The pungent smoke filled the hut pretty quickly and my eyes were beginning to sting. Kham, already in a haze, obviously didn't run a mule train, so there was no benefit in staying.

"Lets go" I said to Toby.

We left the hut quickly, heading for the Toytota. Before the drive back to Mae Hong Son, I nipped behind a bush to relieve myself, when a loud rustle startled me. I looked down to see a pair of eyes staring at me in the half light. I was desperately trying to stop the flow of liquid when a giant rat, the size of a terrier, I kid you not, bolted out of the grass. I zipped up and hurried back to the vehicle.

Toby was sitting at the steering wheel looking glum. He had set his sights on one of the village girls and was trying to dissuade me from leaving. I was now very tired and rattled at the way things had gone. I was certainly in no mood for Toby's antics, opium dens and giant rodents were not part of my plan, nor my budget.

"Listen you dopey smuggler ....," I said very irritably but thought better of insulting him. "Don't worry about the girl or anything else, worry about getting me to the right place tomorrow."

In Mae Hong Son we checked into a local rest house. This time I stood over Toby as he telephoned the Shan contact. He looked sheepish as he spoke on the phone. There was a message for him to take me, before first light, to the mule staging post on the border.

Apparently, Toby had not listened to the original instructions carefully, the mule staging post at Mae Suya had been waiting for us. Because we failed to arrive, they had become concerned and left the message in case we returned. They had not realised that Toby had taken me to another village. In Toby, I had obviously chosen the 'wrong smuggler', but it was too late to shout at him, so I went straight to bed.

The next morning, feeling reasonably refreshed, I had a good breakfast of steaming hot noodles. I noticed Toby was very quiet. He was worried about Khun Sa and begged me not to tell the warlord about his mistake.

It was just before sunrise when we arrived at the Mae Suya, the Chinese Haw village. The buck-tooth headman from my last visit was there to greet us. I think he even remembered me. However, he seemed nervous and ushered us quickly into his hut. There had been a lot of military activity over the past 72 hours, and Tiger Camp was on full alert.

"Does he know the cause of the problem?" I asked.

The headman told Toby what he knew. The Burmese Army had laid new minefields along the border, to block Shan smuggling routes, and three cattle smugglers had been killed only yesterday. That was serious, I was aware how the tax on cattle smuggling was an important source of revenue for Khun Sa.

"Thai Rangers arrived just a few hours ago and are all over the border area" said Toby looking concerned.

The headman explained that Tiger Camp strongly advised against crossing the border now and that I should cancel my trip for a few days. Landmines were a serious problem, an average of five people a week had been killed and this would continue until the minefields were properly identified. The recent deaths had made the border area very tense and the whole region could easily be plunged into turmoil.

With my filming obligations to the Bangladesh government to be considered, I could not afford to sit around in Mae Hong Son waiting for the border tension to ease. I realised my mistake in trying to push the time frame along with the minimum of preparation, the first trip with Gritz had, after all, taken several weeks to organise. The lesson learnt was that travelling to the Golden Triangle was a risk, a serious venture that should not be treated like a stopover or weekend break!

The aborted trip had been costly and with nothing to show. I made a conscious effort to keep in contact with the two key people in Khun Sa's inner circle: Kernsai Jaiyane and Dr Sai. With their guidance any future trips to Tiger Camp would have a better chance of success.

Then by good fortune another opportunity presented itself.

22

The Cook Report

In July 1990, two young British girls, Patricia Cahill and Karen Smith, were arrested at Bangkok Airport by Thai customs officers. In their luggage was 67 pounds of pure heroin, hidden in tins of condensed milk and packets of sweets, one of the largest hauls ever taken from an airline passenger and valued at over 8 million US dollars. They were couriers of a smart Asian drugs dealer based in Birmingham, England. The girls proclaimed their innocence. It was a big story.

Because of my knowledge of the Golden Triangle and access to Khun Sa, I decided to act quickly and contact Mike Townson, at that time editor of *The Cook Report*, a high ratings, popular current affairs programme made by Central Television, a major British broadcaster. I had already been in touch with Townson a few weeks before with the idea of doing something on Khun Sa, using the footage I had previously shot in the Shan states. The arrest of the two girls was an ideal peg on which to hang the story since the heroin they had in their possession undoubtedly emanated from the Golden Triangle and from territory probably controlled by Khun Sa. Townson liked the idea and put his senior producer, Clive Entwistle, in contact with me. Entwistle was a fast talking Lancashire man, a no-nonsense journalist who had come up the hard way from newsroom to current affairs producer. He either liked you or he didn't!

"I hear you got something for us …. we'll see," he said gruffly on the telephone. "Come to our office in Birmingham tomorrow and prove it."

The following day at the Central Television studios I met Townson, Entwistle and Roger Cook, whose show it was, and pitched my plan of taking Roger and his crew deep into the jungle to meet the infamous Khun Sa. They listened politely about my previous visits and the possible dangers involved in such a venture. Danger however was nothing new to the Cook Report. The show had achieved its huge popularity with the viewing public because nearly every story was dangerous. Roger had earned a reputation for bravery and being the people's champion. His format was to expose crime and corruption by companies and individuals. His speciality was the 'doorstep', where he would confront villains when they least expected it and with cameras rolling. The result often ended with him being hit many times, with a variety of objects, by shocked and angry wrongdoers.

My trump card in negotiations with Mike Townson was having two hours of Super 16mm film footage of Khun Sa and his men which I had shot with the Italian crew the previous year. This superb footage could be used if Rogers's trek to the jungle camp failed, an insurance policy if you like. They agreed my involvement would lift the story of the local girl smugglers into potentially a great television investigation. Townson, nicknamed 'Tiger', was a chain-smoking Fleet Street journalist of the old school and hard as nails when it came to negotiations. He 'ummmed' and 'errred' about my demands. But I did have another card up my sleeve, or under it to be exact. I had with me a copy of the London Evening Standard which that day published my article on Khun Sa. What Luck! There it was nearly a whole page plus a photo of the warlord and my byline boldly staring up at Mike Townson. Are we going to do the deal or not? We agreed terms and I was taken on not only as a producer but with my company getting a credit as well.

The idea was to tackle the story in two stages. The first being to obtain an interview with the two girls in the notorious Lard Yao women's prison, dubbed the 'Bangkok Hilton'. Roger and Clive flew to Thailand that night and I was to follow the next day with the film crew: Grahame Wickings on camera and Keith Conlon on sound.

In Bangkok I teamed up with Clive and we tried everything possible to obtain permits to visit the prison for a filmed interview of the girls. Cahill and Smith were technically on trial for their lives, as drug smuggling still carried the death penalty in Thailand. What we wanted was for them to tell us who in Britain had set them up so we could investigate. But the Thai authorities would have none of it. Finally, we decided to just go to the prison and knock on the gates. To our amazement they let us in. While waiting in the courtyard for an official to come and talk to us, Clive spotted Patricia Cahill in amongst a group of women prisoners entering an outbuilding. We rushed across the yard to the building and as I stuck my camera through the bars of a window, pressing the shutter continuously, Clive shouted questions. The commotion of course attracted the guards who promptly frogged marched us out of the prison grounds.

That night Roger Cook called me to his room. He was worried that we were wasting time chasing the two girls and getting nowhere. We should

Roger Cook inspecting MTA troops

now implement stage two, in other words take the risk and trek into the jungle to see Khun Sa and I was to make all the necessary arrangements.

As Roger wrote in his book afterwards "Patrick immediately switched into military mode" and flew to northern Thailand to make preparations. I contacted Som Suk, my Shan friend from the previous visits, who would be our guide. Twenty-four hours later I met Roger and the crew in Chiang Mai, where we gathered supplies for the long trek, my third, into the Burmese jungle.

Som Suk explained that due to the monsoon season the terrain had become treacherous, so night trekking was definitely out, and we would have to trek by daylight. This meant leaving Chiang Mai by 11pm, travelling by minibus along winding roads to the border region and arriving at the mule staging post in Mae Suya before dawn.

My friend the buck-tooth headman at Mae Suya who, with a beaming smile, now greeted me as a regular. He remembered how I had enjoyed his wife's cooking on previous visits and insisted we all breakfasted on a cauldron of noodle soup. Then came the moment of truth, meeting the mules!

"Which poor beast is going to get Roger?" asked Entwistle with a wicked glint in his eye.

Roger, a big man, although glaring at Clive, took the joke well. Fortunately the mule, although unusually small, was sturdy.

Although the Shan horses are good for riding, it is the mule who is the real master of the mountains. These sure-footed beasts can carry tremendous loads over the worst terrain imaginable. From the outset of his rule, Khun Sa adopted a policy which ensured there were enough mules and staging posts all over his territory. The warlord had once read about the size of the Royal Navy and how Britain's policy in the 18th century, had been to have more warships than their two greatest rivals combined. The Shans estimated they had twice as many mules as all their enemies put together, which gave them the ability to move large quantities of supplies across inhospitable terrain in a very short time. It was without doubt one of the factors contributing to the Mong Tai Army's success against the Burmese military.

I certainly appreciated the ability of these beasts of burden on this particular trek to Tiger Valley, which turned out to be even more hazardous than the previous year when I had gone there with Bo Gritz. Heavy rains had washed away the dirt road that was usually used for the last stage of the journey, so no truck was available. Instead, our television crew had to ride on the mules for twelve solid hours before they arrived at Homong.

The crew were great fun and the banter about blistered arses continued all day long. Even the hardiest of them had never been on a trip quite like this. Nobody complained on the gruelling twelve-hour trek and by the time we reached Tiger Camp we had been travelling twenty-one hours nonstop.

The Shan officer who greeted us seemed mystified at our presence. He told us to wait while he sought a senior officer.

"Well I hope things are alright now we've come this far," remarked a tetchy Clive Entwistle.

The crew were apprehensive and extremely tired, understandably after such an arduous trek. Within five minutes three figures came running towards us. Thankfully one of them was Seng Jo, who greeted me warmly clasping my hands in both of his and refusing to let go.

"Welcome Mr Patrick, welcome."

The crew looked on in amazement, especially Clive. I introduced each member in turn.

"My Commander-in-Chief welcomes you all. Friends of Mr Patrick are friends of the Shan."

Clive was impressed. I must admit to feeling pretty pleased with the welcome. If any of the crew had doubted my claims before, then it was certainly dispelled in those first few minutes.

We enjoyed a hearty meal of wok-fried jungle greens and rice, topped with hard-boiled eggs, before collapsing on our makeshift straw beds, ready to sleep the sleep of the dead!

From the outset, though interested in the project and prepared to go ahead with it, Roger Cook and the whole crew disliked the idea of giving publicity to Khun Sa, whom they saw as a notorious drugs dealer, pure and simple. Their view did not change until they reached Homong, where they saw how the Shans lived and realised that these were human beings and not bandits who were only concerned with selling drugs. Maybe these people might have a legitimate case after all!

Khun Sa was very cooperative allowing Roger to see whatever he wanted and to ask as many questions as he needed. There was no doubt that Khun Sa was charismatic but nevertheless he was still an opium warlord, who held the power of life and death over many people. But did his claim of being oppressed by the Burmese military regime and used by the CIA to promote the growth of opium for their own ends have any validity. We had a lot to think about after our short visit to Tiger Camp.

Immensely sceptical at first, Central Television funded their own investigations, not only in Britain but also in Thailand, Australia and the United States before they accepted there was, as it were, a case to answer.

What this proved, to me as well as to them, was that the allegations made by both Khun Sa and Bo Gritz did, at the very least, have some foundation, and that the CIA and the DEA, or some local elements of these bodies, were, or certainly had been, involved in drugs smuggling on a grand scale. What we could not be sure of was the identity of some of the main culprits who were still active in political life. We decided to continue with our investigation.

Accusations of CIA involvement in the drugs business in Southeast Asia was looking more probable, every stone turned revealed new facts. It was decided that Roger Cook should fly to Australia. We needed verification that the CIA had used a private bank, called Nugen Hand, in Sydney as a money-laundering facility. The bank had once had a branch in Chiang Mai. Roger interviewed the Attorney General for New South Wales, who did verify the official Australian view, which was the CIA were involved in drug smuggling.

In the meantime, the rest of us flew to the United States where we talked to Victor Marchetti, a former CIA executive. He verified that CIA funds reserved for covert operations in Southeast Asia had been supplemented by drugs money.

I also suggested we meet Richard Thornburgh, the US Attorney General, who had recently indicted Khun Sa. However, he evaded us for the four days we were in Washington DC. Not a friendly gesture for an official to make towards a British television crew.

Mike Townson had sent a message that we should target Richard Armitage, former first secretary of the army. His name had cropped up constantly during our investigation. Khun Sa had mentioned him. Ross Perot, the American billionaire, had instigated a congressional hearing on the man and Time magazine ran a full page about it. Roger had already interviewed Colonel Bo Gritz and lawyer Danial Sheehan of the Christic Institute, both mentioned Armitage. But Armitage declined to be interviewed. Further, his lawyer indicated that legal action might be taken if we pursued the line on drug involvement. A strange reaction to have when a foreign television crew simply requests an interview with a public figure.

We returned to Britain and the story was transmitted, attracting the largest viewing figures of the series. Through the vast resources of the Cook Report, I learned that there had definitely been sinister activities within the CIA. The broadcaster may have lacked evidence to prove the case conclusively, but our research on some of the Agency's operatives had uncovered years of complicity in the drugs trade, on a global scale.

My research into Khun Sa's life, however, was going well. Every trip to Homomg revealed another extraordinary story.

23

Kidnapped

I had mixed feelings about Khun Sa: was he a misunderstood patriot or a cunning bandit. He was, after all, one of the players responsible for the world plague of narcotics. On the other hand, I was drawn by his determination to win freedom for his people. Does the end justify the means?

Of the many memories I bore back from Homong, the most abiding was that of the refugees brutalised by the Burmese army. I was moved by their gratitude, even love, for Khun Sa, who helped them, not with words but deeds, when no one else would. For those wretched people he was a patriot, a father figure, the only leader that ever gained their respect and devotion.

There was no doubt that Khun Sa was an important warlord and had, over the years, made many enemies. The Burmese military feared him as the man who could unite the Shan resistance, others because of his success as a drugs kingpin. He did not fear his enemies and was courageous enough to take risks most other leaders would not. The one major event, during his rise to power, that interested me the most happened in 1969. It illustrates his prowess as the supreme survivor. At 35 years old, he had survived many battles, as well as attempts of assassination and capture, you could say his instincts had served him well. Until, on one occasion, he let his guard down. Whether it was misguided trust, or being too self-assured didn't matter, it was an error that was going to change his life.

Through the extraordinary web of political intrigue that existed in Burma, the Kuomintang, encouraged by the CIA, conceived a different strategy to destroy the man that their armies had failed to put down. Using informants they had planted in Burmese government circles, they released news of a plan of Khun Sa's Army to combine with other insurgents and throw the Burmese out of the Shan States by force.

In October 1969, Khun Sa was invited to a special meeting at Taunggyi, the Burmese controlled Shan capital, to discuss the Kuomintang problem.

Since Khun Sa was doing rather better than the government in fighting their foreign opponents, he felt confident about the meeting. He certainly did not expect even the Burmese to be so treacherous. No sooner had he arrived in the capital he was arrested and thrown in prison, indefinitely and in solitary confinement.

Khun Sa was detained in a cell at the headquarters of the Burmese Army's Eastern Command in Taunggyi and was subjected to frequent and brutal questioning. Had he not been such an important player he would doubtless have been killed there and then. However, first of all, the Burmese were nervous of what reaction might be triggered off by such an act, possibly a full-scale Shan uprising, and secondly, Khun Sa was a valuable bargaining chip, someone who could be used to hold the Shans to ransom. In more ways than one.

Needless to say, Khun Sa was always planning to escape, and his captors were aware of this and kept him on the move. For safety's sake, they decided to transfer him south, to Mandalay, where he was placed in a small cell and was only allowed to see people twice a day. He was given one small bowl of rice mixed with a spoonful of fish sauce to eat each day, which over five years of incarceration began to affect his health. He was not physically tortured, though he would later describe feeling "spiritually tortured".

As the years in solitary confinement rolled by he became sullen, knowing that he had to come to terms with his predicament. During this difficult period he learned the art of meditation, which helped him survive acute bouts of depression. He was also allowed to cultivate a small plot of land within the prison and became a gardener. In later years he continued this hobby and would cultivate a garden wherever he went. He told me "Gardening is therapeutic, good for the spirit. Contact with the soil brings you back to reality and cleans the system."

All the time though, unknown to his Burmese captors, Khun Sa was still able secretly to send messages to his loyal Shan United Army and receive word back from them. One of the prison guards was a Shan spy and through this covert means of communication, Khun Sa became aware of what was happening in the troubled world outside. He learnt that Korn Zurng was encountering immense difficulties. The Chinese backed BCP had cynically infiltrated several northern units of the new Shan State Army, offering 'free' arms in return for an acknowledgement that Shanland was an integral part of Burma.

Not wanting to take part in yet another internecine struggle, Korn

Zurng and his followers moved south to the Thai border where, on 25 January 1969, he founded, yet another armed freedom movement, the Shan United Revolutionary Army (SURA).

The Maoist inspired Burmese Communist Party was of course the deadly enemy of the Kuomintang and General Li, commander of the 3rd Army, agreed to co-operate with Korn Zurng's SURA in fighting against them.

It was an uneasy alliance between the Kuomintang and the Shan's, and one which Khun Sa had warned Korn Zurng about. Furthermore, Khun Sa, still languishing in a Burmese jail, was about to make a spectacular leap back onto the political scene, just when his enemies had hoped he had left it forever.

In 1973, working to a master plan conceived by Khun Sa in his two-metre square prison cell, his Shan United Army embarked upon a rescue mission. Khun Sa's loyal chief of staff, Falang, was in charge of the operation. The warlord had met Falang, or Chang Hsu-chuen (his Chinese name), together with another top aide, Liang Chung-ying, when they were both Kuomintang officers, in Laos, at the time when the Kuomintang troops were being ordered to Taiwan. Many did not want to go and chose, instead, to join up with Khun Sa. Years later Khun Sa explained the relationship to me. "For one thing, we had a natural liking for each other, from our very first meeting. For another, they had no future ahead of them in Taiwan. There no one would notice them. In the Shan state, they had a future. The sky was the limit!"

There had been foreign doctors working in Taunggyi ever since the Soviet Union built the Zao Zarmhtun Hospital there, in 1960. Khun Sa's audacious plan was for his men to kidnap a Japanese doctor, in order to create an embarrassing international incident. The doctor would then be traded for the prisoner. It was a brilliantly simple strategy, typical of Khun Sa's fertile military mind, though the plan was not without inherent dangers.

Most of the foreign medical staff stayed at the Strand Hotel. One of the Shan United Army's dashing young officers, known only as Charlie, having found out the name of the Japanese doctor, who was the target, dressed himself up in a Burmese officer's uniform. He then strolled arrogantly into the hotel and asked to see his intended victim, only to find the Japanese doctor was out. Coming across two Russian doctors talking together, he decided they would probably do just as well, and he abducted both of them. They had some language problems but, since the personable young officer explained that they were required elsewhere, they went with him to a waiting jeep. Someone, somewhere, was obviously expecting

*Khun Sa being ordained
as a Monk*

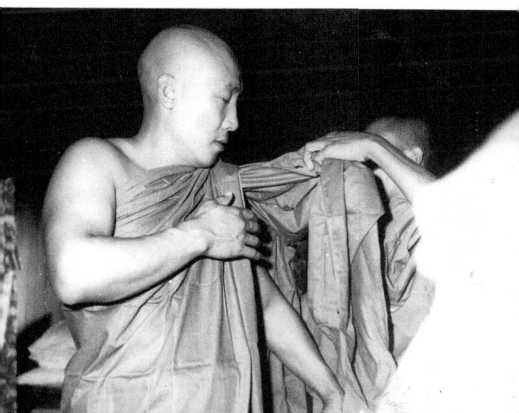

them.

Dazed by this unexpected hospitality, they were rushed through the city, passing numerous Burmese checkpoints. The swashbuckling Charlie just waved imperiously to the checkpoint guards who saluted respectfully as the jeep zoomed past. It was not until they reached the outskirts of the Shan capital, when the doctors were split up, each being under the care of a SUA officer, that they realised what had happened. While the Shan officers marched off their respective prisoners, Falang was carrying out the rest of the carefully devised operation.

Now there were two hostages, instead of one, a slight change of direction was needed. Falang ordered a search for two Palaungs of appropriate size and build, to pass as doubles for the Russian doctors. Members of the Palaung tribe have blue eyes and light blondish hair and can therefore pass at a distance as Caucasians. Having selected two suitable candidates for the task, Falang then dressed them up in foreign clothes, put them on horseback together with an armed guard, and then paraded them around several villages, set sufficiently far apart to create a major logistical problem for the Burmese, following up on reports of the prisoners being seen.

As soon as the doctors were discovered to be missing, all hell broke out. No less than six thousand troops were deployed by the Burmese to search for elusive Falang and his Russian prisoners. It was a massive hide-and-seek search which went on for several months, always miles away from where the doctors were really being held, during which time the Russian government became increasingly tetchy with the Burmese for their apparent blundering incompetence.

Khun Sa was able to say honestly that he did not know where the Russian doctors were hidden, and the Burmese realised there was no point in torturing him to elicit information he didn't have. It also started to become crystal clear to them that it might be prudent to get themselves on the good side of Khun Sa, for he would undoubtedly be a key figure in any future solution to the Shan independence problem.

The Shan United Army had named Zao Sarm as their representative and contacted the Burmese to negotiate for Khun Sa's release. To prove they had the doctors, and that they were safe and well, they invited a British documentary filmmaker Adrian Cowell and his crew to photograph them in their jungle prison, before quickly moving them on somewhere else. The embarrassed Burmese sent Thein Pe Myint, the well-known author of several memoirs and novels, to Mae Sai, to negotiate on their behalf. Thein

Pe Myint had been the Secretary General of the BCP when it was still a legal organisation and before it went underground in 1948.

He made several trips from Rangoon to Mae Sai, on each occasion increasing the offers of weapons and payment for the release of the Russian doctors. Every time, he went back to Rangoon with the reply that they would accept nothing less than the freedom of their leader in exchange for the Russians. Thein Pe Myint told the Burmese generals bluntly that he had totally failed in his mission to buy back the Russians. He also made it clear that he was deeply impressed by the obvious loyalty which Khun Sa's followers had for their leader. This was not what the Burmese wanted to hear, and he was dismissed from his assignment.

In fact, secret negotiations had already been started with a view to ending Khun Sa's term of imprisonment, with the ubiquitous General Kriangsak from Thailand acting as a supposedly impartial go-between. Many blustering threats were made but Khun Sa's emissaries remained unflustered. A successful conclusion was eventually reached and Khun Sa was exchanged for the Russian doctors in 1974.

Although released from prison, he was still not free. The Burmese were keeping him under close surveillance, doubtless hoping he would lead them to Falang and other parties in the kidnapping, on whom they still hoped to wreak revenge. But their hopes were in vain. When they followed Khun Sa the trail led only to a temple, where he went to study to be ordained as a monk.

The wily Khun Sa had guessed the Burmese would watch his every move and becoming a monk seemed to be the ideal cover. He was actually very convincing. He shaved his head, donned the robes of a novice, and studiously read the teachings of Buddha. "I actually enjoyed the idea of being a monk," he said to me, "but I couldn't imagine a life of celibacy!"

Although the Burmese began to be lulled into a false sense of security, the chances of Khun Sa escaping their clutches as a monk was looking less likely, so a change of plan was needed.

Khun Sa announced that he would no longer take holy orders and gave up his robe in order to get married, this time to a rich lady from Southern Burma, which further confused his adversaries. He was seeking to give the impression that he was not interested in going back to his men and that he had cut himself off from the past. When I asked him, "How did you meet Daw Htay Htay?" he replied, with a grin, "I didn't find her, she found me."

In Mandalay, on 7th February 1976, Shan National Day, Khun Sa offered to bury the hatchet with the Burmese intelligence officers shadowing him. He invited them to join him in a night of carousing to celebrate his Burmese marriage and renunciation of all things past. The wine, however, was doped and Khun Sa bid farewell to his sleeping guards before escaping in a waiting jeep which drove for a night and day back to the Shan hills. Although exhausted by the time he reached Tangyan he was also elated to rejoin his men.

At Hsenwi, the people held a ceremony to welcome him back. From there, he was escorted to the border, breaking through several envelopments by the angry Burmese Army, who were seeking to recapture him. Khun Sa was determined to get back to his base in Thailand and his waiting Shan wife, Nang Kay-Yun. In doing so, he had to survive no less than thirty skirmishes on the way to Bin Hin Taek, including the battle of Kawng-ai, in his home district. He lost in all twenty men, while thirty were wounded.

There was a loving reunion between Khun Sa and his wife, who had done much to hold the Shan United Army together during his incarceration. Falang had been the officer in charge of the army, but being Chinese, a foreigner in the eyes of the Shan, he was regarded with some suspicion until it became clear that he had the full support of Nang Kay-yun and therefore Khun Sa himself.

Three days after Khun Sa's return, he was visited by Falang, who transferred all the powers he had been given back to the warlord. He then left him to carry out whatever audits he wished and returned to the camp two days later, asking when he could be of service again. Khun Sa was deeply moved by this show of loyalty, and immediately reinstated Falang as his second-in-command. He could never have known then that one day the faithful Falang would seek to replace him.

24

The Mysterious Bank

It is said that if you ever have the misfortune of being shot at, you will experience one of three possible effects. The first is fear, combined with the instinct to make yourself as small as possible and hoping the moment will pass. The second is a feeling of elation and the inclination to do something positive, such as hitting back. The third is simply one of bewilderment.

It was this third effect that I felt on the day I was hauled off my mule and flung to the ground, after which a body collapsed on top of me.

"Ssssh" was all I heard from the body as it rolled off. Several other bodies, all dressed in jungle green uniforms, began crawling across the ground to take up firing positions. My first reaction was to look up. What's going on?

Moments before I had heard several cracks, similar to a whiplash. It took me a few seconds to realise that it was gunfire. An ambush, perhaps? It's not as if I hadn't heard guns firing before. Nevertheless, here in the jungle the gunfire sounded different.

The body that flung itself on top of me was in fact one of my bodyguards. It might sound like something more in common with presidents than with documentary filmmakers, but a squad of ten soldiers from the Mong Tai Army had been detailed to escort me through dense jungle, from the Thai border to the Na Mon mule station just inside Burma.

The route we had taken for my fourth trek to the area, seemed longer than usual. Previously there had been no need for armed escorts, but this visit coincided with an unusual amount of activity on the border. Independent bands of armed gangsters, mainly from the Wa tribe, had been ambushing mule led convoys transporting opium. As the warlord's personal guest it was felt there may be a need for protection.

Unfortunately, I could not communicate easily with any of my escorts as none of them spoke English, although the sergeant in charge knew one or two words, such as "stop" and "go". When we finally reached the Na Mon mule station a familiar face was there to greet me. Seng Jo explained that the shots we had heard earlier had come from across the valley, but the sound had been distorted by the dense vegetation, which could make it seem closer. My escort, under strict orders to look after me, had taken precautions in case of attack. Apparently, he assured me, there had been no danger. Despite my bruised arm, I was impressed at the diligence of the bodyguard.

Before continuing our journey by truck to Tiger Camp, we rested and ate a meal. Sitting in a circle, while our mules munched on the grass around us, we were each presented with a bowl of rice and jungle vegetables. It was good to talk to Seng Jo again, an amiable man who had learned English at a missionary school run by Roman Catholic nuns. Before long, a bottle of Mongtai whisky appeared.

"Let us toast" he said.

There now proceeded a few minutes of toasting everything that came to mind, a popular Shan pastime. We even raised our glasses to the mules. But I was now an old hand and fully aware of the potency of Mongtai whisky, or 'jungle juice' as we called it. With his tongue now sufficiently loosened, Seng Jo explained the real reason behind the bodyguard. The armed Wa gangsters were acting as a proxy force for Burmese Military Intelligence, who were feeding them information on the whereabouts of the opium caravans.

The author treks through a poppy field

Tracking the opium caravans had been done by the CIA. Their agents were planting covert signalling devices to locate the convoys either from a satellite or other systems. The devices were even being pushed up the anus of the mules so that they couldn't be found. Every mule that moved was being tracked, thereby getting instant intelligence to pass on to the Burmese army.

The irony was this intelligence gathering was not full proof. Once the ploy had been discovered, the Shans collected the devices from the mule dung and laid false trails in the jungle. For any unfortunate agent caught planting a device, by the smugglers, the end was inevitable. Considered to be spies, who ratted on their comrades, they were summarily executed.

Sipping my whisky slowly, I looked around at the smiling faces of these teenage soldiers. They looked so young, yet they were already battle-hardened. It was easy to forget that this region had been continuously at war for decades, fighting an insurgency campaign against a brutal Burmese military regime.

Few regions compare in beauty with the land of the Shan, but I hadn't made this long trek to admire the landscape, it was to find answers to some nagging questions. In particular, I wanted to know about General Kriangsak of Thailand, a leading figure in the Khun Sa story and the mysterious bank linked to the drugs trade. To understand how the CIA got involved with the bank, I needed to unravel a series of events that took place in the seventies.

Kriangsak

Thailand had a brief taste of democracy with the revolution of 1973. The problem for any elected administration that follows a military dictatorship is that the generals have usually made such a mess of the economy and the new government has no time to effect an improvement before the generals feel they must take over the reins again, in the national interest. In 1976, General Kriangsak led a successful coup in Thailand, following the shooting of some protesting students.

To give his actions the semblance of legitimacy, Kriangsak appointed a judge as Prime Minister. This was a serious error because Judge Thanin Kraiwichien turned out to be an honest man and even worse, immediately set about using his new position for an onslaught against corruption. Nobody batted an eyelid at first, it was the usual practise to commence with pious promises of this kind. But the military nearly had a collective heart attack when he ordered the execution of convicted drug smugglers and set light to a ton of confiscated narcotics himself.

There was nothing abnormal about ritual bonfires. The Americans found them particularly pleasing. But usually, the genuine narcotics were just on the surface, and the rest of the pile was a mass of rubbish. One famous incident occurred in 1972, when Kriangsak had ordered 26 tons of opium, seized from the Kuomintang, to be burned at a much publicised public bonfire. A few months later the *Washington Post* reported only 5 tons of the 21-ton pyre had been opium, the remainder being "plant fodder". But Thanin was burning the real stuff.

Although President Jimmy Carter may have been impressed by Thanin's war against narcotics, Kriangsak was not. They could bear a good man being in office, provided he was just a figurehead, but a good man who took decisive action was too much for the generals to bear. After a year, General Kriangsak acted again. This time he chose as Prime Minister the only man he could trust, himself.

General Kriangsak, needless to say, was well known to Khun Sa. Kriangsak had gained many useful contacts during his years as liaison officer to the Kuomintang in the north of Thailand. It was he who had attempted to play mediator when the Russian doctors were kidnapped. Among the contacts he made during that time was General Li, one of the Kuomintang commanders. In 1972, Kriangsak arranged a brilliant propaganda coup, in which Li handed over a caravan of a hundred mules, weighed down with opium. On behalf of a grateful government, the CIA parted with about two million dollars. According to the press, this quantity of the drug "could have supplied half the American market for one year."

It probably did, for this was a Kriangsak type bonfire, at least 80 per cent of what was burning was definitely not opium. It was Kriangsak who spread the fiction that General Li had repented of his involvement in the drugs trade and was now just a humble businessman earning an honest crust in the precious metals trade.

Kriangsak began to play a dangerous game. It was one thing to try to outflank his friend, Khun Sa, using another friend, General Li, but it was quite another to show hostility to the CIA, from whom he had gained much of his wealth. He had the audacity to question the morals of the agency publicly. "Those who criticise Thailand for corruption among officials concerned with drug enforcement," he is reported in the *Bangkok Post* as saying at the time, "should also look into the corruption in other official circles which has made it possible for the narcotics trade to flourish in many countries."

This criticism, undoubtedly levelled against the CIA and the DEA, was not appreciated in Washington.

Nugan Hand

In 1979, the year of the Goat, the world's attention focused on the Vietnamese Army's invasion of Cambodia to remove the cold-blooded Khmer Rouge. Attention was then diverted when Soviet Russia sent troops into Afghanistan to support the pro-Soviet government against the mujahideen guerrillas who were being trained by the CIA. Their ten-year occupation would not only involve the Russians heavily in the drugs scene but would also end with retreat, as the communist empire crumbled. For the CIA, it would also be a pointless campaign, one where victory had to be measured against the cost, both in terms of money and also of creating another monster in the drugs war.

That same year nobody hardly noticed an Australian bank with offices in Thailand had mysteriously collapsed.

When a major bank collapses, like the Bank of Credit and Commerce International (BCCI) with its worldwide branches, in the 1990s, it will certainly hit the headlines. When a small bank goes bust, it will hardly make a stir unless there is some other ingredient. This was the case with an Australian registered bank called Nugan Hand. The extra factor was the suicide of one of its founders, Frank Nugan.

Then again, there was a thought that it might not have been suicide? After all, small banks like this one were often used for their laundering capabilities. No small bank would ask too many questions about the source of deposits for fear of losing a major client. Khun Sa knew all about the Nugan Hand Bank, for it had opened a branch in Thailand's northern city of Chiang Mai. He also knew that a government agency, probably the CIA, was behind it. Who else would want to open a bank in a place which was then little more than a sleepy hollow? And for what reason except for the purpose of laundering drugs money?

The bank had been founded in Sydney by two friends, Frank Nugan, a lawyer, and Michael Hand, a former Green Beret and Vietnam veteran turned businessman. From the outset, the bank's practises varied from the dubious to the downright dishonest. It was financed initially with a million dollars that were obtained by misrepresentation. Frank Nugen wrote a personal cheque for $980,000 to buy 490,000 of shares in his own

Bank. He then covered his overdraft by writing a Bank's cheque for the same amount. Through this simple accounting fraud, the company had a paid-up capital of one million dollars.

Nevertheless, Nugan and Hand flourished, paying themselves enormous salaries, as the bank opened other branches in places conveniently close to where the action was. Glossy brochures gave glowing accounts of the bank's ever-increasing assets and turnover, and the drugs money was soon augmented by earnings from gun running. A branch was opened in Hong Kong, the world capital for the transfer of illicitly acquired money, and a subsidiary opened in South Africa for the sale of arms, at a time when such sales to that country were banned by the United Nations.

Whether or not these enterprising friends were themselves involved in drug trafficking had not been established, but addiction in Australia increased substantially after they began their operations, and their bank certainly benefited from the trade, merely by facilitating the flow of funds. At that time, Australia had very tight foreign currency controls.

By the end of the decade, Nugan Hand, which had by then opened a branch in the Caribbean, was the principal bank for the CIA, and many members of the bank's board were former agents. There were some straightforward deposits as well, from ordinary businessmen, and American expatriate workers, anyone who might be misled by the bank's flashy way of doing business.

The bank's collapse was inevitable, but what triggered it was the loan of twenty million dollars to Edwin Wilson, another former CIA agent who was operating as a gunrunner. Wilson was a supplier of arms to the leading friend of all terrorists, Colonel Muammar Gaddafi the ruler of Libya. Among Wilson's connections were Theodore Shackley, one time Deputy Director of the CIA, and Thomas Clines, a CIA covert agent in charge of their secret war in Laos, so it's unlikely the agency could not have known about his arms deals.

When the tax authorities announced an inquiry into the bank's operations, anxious depositors began a run on the bank and the shortfall soon became evident. When the investigating accountants refused to accept the bank's accounts, the total collapse occurred. Australian fraud squad investigators soon discovered the extensive links with the CIA and Frank Nugan died from a gunshot wound. Whether he knew the game was up and shot himself, or whether it was a contract killing is not known. Michael Hand flew back to Australia to try to sort things out, but the bank was beyond saving and with twenty-five million dollars unaccounted for.

The business was declared insolvent, and a full inquiry was launched. Naturally, the investigators wished to question Michael Hand, but he had disappeared, only to re-surface 35 years later in Idaho, using another name. Edwin Wilson went to prison in the United States, having said nothing for fear of being 'wiped out', his own words.

25

The Four Cuts

In 1993, Aung San Suu Kyi, leader of the National League of Democracy (NLD), was still under house arrest in Rangoon despite having been awarded the Nobel Peace Prize two years earlier. As Burma was attracting more media interest than ever before, I realised the time was right to approach Central Television with a proposal to update the Khun Sa story. It had been nearly two years since my last trip to Tiger Camp, although I was still in regular contact with both Kernsai and Dr Sai.

My new storyline was based on General Ne Win's bloody initiative 'The Four Cuts' and how Khun Sa's thirty thousand strong private army was defending refugees fleeing the brutality of the Burmese military, a twist on the usual drugs story. Central liked the idea and agreed to a small research and development budget which would finance my return to the Shan states.

To most observers, the attitude of the American, British and other European governments towards Burma was 'not to rock the boat'. But even they couldn't completely ignore the cold-bloodedness of the military regime. By the early 1990s, the Burmese population including many of the country's ethnic minorities were openly demonstrating against the military dictatorship. Burma had been totally misruled and now ranked as one of the poorest countries in the world.

In the capital city of Rangoon, the demonstrators protested peacefully. The military regime however, struck back hard. The world was taken aback by the brutality of the government troops. Tens of thousands of unarmed people were gunned down. Protestors throughout the country were put down with equal ferocity. Women, children and even Red Cross personnel were slaughtered.

The Burmese government's attitude to their country's ethnic minorities was best illustrated when they reactivated General Ne Win's infamous "Four Cuts" strategy. The term originally came from a speech given to his troops. "We cut off the rebels from the villages. We cut off the people from

Young Shan refugee

their country. We cut off their supplies and food. We cut off their heads".

The problem with this doctrine was it directly targeted civilians in war zones. Over a two-year period in the northern Shan state, the Burmese military destroyed over 1400 villages and more than 300,000 local people were displaced as a direct result of the policy. People were dying daily at the hands of the Burmese army and pleas for international humanitarian aid by the women, children and the aged went unheard.

Many thousands sought refuge in the mountainous frontier area. People were trekking in droves to Homong, the capital of the self-styled Free Shan State, for the security offered by Khun Sa and his army. It seemed the refugees would rather fight for the opium warlord than live with the atrocities inflicted upon them by the Burmese military, a regime supported by the West.

During my previous visits I would meet new arrivals, each refugee family with its own horrendous story of brutality to tell. Unfortunately, many bore not only the mental scars but the physical ones too. The most common atrocity was having a tongue cut off or the mouth slashed downwards, from nose to chin, inflicted on the unfortunates who the Burmese thought were lying when asked questions.

The Burmese military have consistently used the peasant population as slave labour. Forcefully taken from their homes these tribal people are put to work on airfield construction or other major projects. There is no choice. Those who do not obey to work can expect harsh treatment both for themselves and their families.

Crucifixion

A popular atrocity committed by the Burmese army on the Shans was to crucify the village headman as a warning to others. Some of those crucified survived. Others were not so lucky. A refugee family told me the following story which was interpreted by Dr Sai.

On the banks of the Salween River, a small village had just been celebrating a good crop of rice and vegetables that year. The wily headman ordered that the bumper harvest be kept secret and hidden from view. He knew that the various armed factions would be looking for supplies.

The Burmese army was supposed to protect the village but were not anywhere near the place the day twenty Wa rebels came. The Wa helped themselves to whatever they could find and then moved on.

The headman felt aggrieved and reported the incident to the nearest Burmese Army outpost. One week later a Burmese fighting patrol of about 80 men came to the village.

An arrogant young captain was in command of the patrol. He took an instant dislike to the headman who he blamed for making the report, which reflected badly on his unit, whose sector the village came under.

The captain insisted the rebels must have been Khun Sa's Mong Tai Army and not Wa. But the headman was adamant, they had been Wa. The captain would hear none of it and took his patrol into the jungle in search of the rebels.

The force had been patrolling for two days when they were ambushed by a fusillade of small arms fire. The surprised Burmese reeled at the onslaught and had little stomach to continue and so withdrew. As they slinked away the attackers' flung jeers, insults and taunts at them. The laughter resounded through the jungle. The humiliated Burmese were in an ugly mood as they retraced their steps to the village.

The captain had been brooding over the retreat. In his own mind he was convinced it was the villagers who had betrayed the patrol. On reaching the village he split his force. Using 50 soldiers to encircle the perimeter, he ordered the remainder to help themselves to whatever they could find in the dwellings, including the women. The men were bound, gagged and herded into a large hut, where they had to endure the screams and pleading of their women, as they were repeatedly raped by relays of soldiers.

After about twelve hours the ordeal stopped. The headman was bought to a clearing and forced to kneel before the captain. For the next hour he was interrogated and kicked. Nevertheless, the frightened headman kept his dignity.

The frustrated captain barked out orders to an ugly looking tribesman from the Arakan (now Rakhine State), who was a porter with the army patrol. The headman became hysterical as he watched his wife being dragged towards a hut. He pleaded desperately with the Burmese officer, but it made no difference. The sobbing headman, placed at the entrance of the hut, was forced to endure the spectacle of his pitiful wife being sodomised by the Arakanese tribesman. Her screams could be heard across the jungle.

That act was the gravest insult the captain could inflict on the village. He had already decided that the headman would die, but nobody had guessed in what manner. Turning to his executioners he instructed them to take the headman to the site where he would spend the last hours of his life.

At the opposite end of the clearing was a large tree, with a trunk as large as a car. At the foot of the tree was a wooden bench. The executioners lifted the ill-fated headman onto the bench, stretched out his arms and nailed his hands and wrists to the tree trunk. The bench was pulled away and the brave little headman was left to dangle, writhing in agony, until he was dead, thirty-six hours later. It was routine 'Four Cuts' terror.

Two months later the headman's wife, brother and three children trekked to Khun Sa's territory as refugees. The brother joined the Mong Tai Army.

26

Return to Tiger Camp

My story update required an independent assessment on the effectiveness of Khun Sa's army and so I decided to take Mike Borlace, a former major in the Rhodesian (now Zimbabwe) special forces, with me. He was a man fast gaining an international reputation as a private military advisor.

Mike and I were old friends and had over the years shared several adventures together. Apart from the fact I enjoyed his sense of humour, it was never wise trekking to Khun Sa's camp solo, although some foreigners had. The main concern had nothing to do about being caught by the Thai Rangers or Burmese army, or even the independent gangs of bandits, it was in case you had an accident and broke a limb. The smuggler guides are more likely to leave you, not out of malice but when they go for help it could be days before they return – the jungle can be a lonely and hazardous place, especially at night.

My other reason for enlisting Mike Borlace was his knowledge of how covert operations work. Mike had led an action-packed life. As a combat helicopter pilot, he had won the Silver Cross for bravery, been shot down five times, and wounded twice. As a special forces soldier and undercover agent, he had been betrayed and then put on trial for his life in Zambia. His operational experience included wars in Africa, Asia and Central America. In 1986 he had been running a team for the Americans flying into Nicaragua, supplying arms to the anti-Communist Contra organisation. It was a mission controlled by Lieutenant Colonel Oliver North and the CIA, one that eventually led to the Irangate scandal. So he understood how the CIA worked and they of course were inseparable from the Khun Sa story.

On arriving at Tiger Valley we were greeted by Khun Sa, who had no hesitation in allowing us to inspect and talk to members of the Mong Tai Army. After our initial tour of the camp, Mike was impressed with the size and efficiency of the warlord's army and also with its equipment, particularly the SAM-7 missiles which, if the Burmese did attack, could be used with devastating effect, to shoot down planes paid for by the

The author, Khun Sa and Mike Borlace

American taxpayer. Mike did not dismiss the statement made to him by Khun Sa that, if necessary, he had armaments to launch a missile attack on the military headquarters in Rangoon.

"If the Burmese attack us here in Homong then we will retaliate with a bombing campaign in Rangoon, Mandalay and other big towns," said the warlord. "We have a complete sabotage plan ready."

At this stage in their short history had the Mong Tai Army been commanded by a general less capable than Khun Sa, they might well have followed the pattern of so many insurgent groups and sunk out of existence. Fearing that his troops would become indolent, Khun Sa insisted that not only they train hard but also undertake regular and aggressive patrols into the neighbouring territories. He knew the importance of having the enemy think his army was a much larger and dangerous force than it really was.

The first change I noticed in Tiger Camp was the new guest quarters adjacent to the Liaison Office. The old rickety wooden shack, with corrugated iron roof, had been replaced with a new brick and cement building. The interior consisted of two long dormitory style rooms, furnished with a couple of lockers and six beds in each. At the end of each dormitory was a washroom housing a shower and toilet, although not western style. To a new arrival it could easily be considered as spartan, but to me, who had been before, it was luxury.

Homong had also grown. Since my last visit a basic telephone service had been installed to satisfy the growing need for communications among the ever-increasing population. The main street had new wooden buildings, which reminded me of a movie set for Westerns. There was still a thriving market selling all types of goods but now I counted four hotels as well as bars and food stalls. A taxi service, using light 100cc Suzuki motorbikes, took individuals from place to place. The taxi drivers wore red helmets and waistcoats with a number on the back and the name of their company.

Another remarkable feature has been the introduction of satellite television. Homong didn't have twenty-four-hour electricity, the main generators only operated in the evenings. But you could catch *BBC World News* on television or switch over and watch the end of *Gunsmoke*. One night Mike and I watched the American television police series *Hill Street Blues* which, ironically, was about a heroin bust!

The picture was a very different one from other towns along the border region and the main reason given was the atmosphere of freedom. People felt secure under the protection of Khun Sa and the Mong Tai Army, knowing the Burmese army would never be able to take Homong by force.

Many of the ethnic minorities, such as the Karen, Karenni, Mon

and Shan, escaping Burmese persecution, sought refuge in Thailand. Many ending up in a special camp, though little was known about it, for 'displaced Shans', a phrase coined by the Thai authorities. The Thais did their best for these people but at that time there was also a refugee crisis from Cambodia to deal with and they were unable to stretch their limited resources.

During the nineties, the Thais were pleased that Khun Sa administered a relatively stable territory, where most of the Shans wanted to go. After all, Homong was only twelve miles from the Thai border. The population of the town had multiplied several times over in ten years, from four thousand when it was carved out of the mountains in 1985, to a staggering sprawl of about 30,000.

With so many people now entering Homong, the ever careful, Khun Sa had given strict instructions to his officers to take precautions and increase internal security. For instance, businessmen were never allowed to travel out of the immediate area and journalists rarely. If you came for a particular reason, for example to trade in gems, or as a journalist to get a story, then you were given every assistance. If you did something wrong or they perceived you were doing as such, then it could become very dangerous. If you crossed the line, or upset a senior Shan, by asking the wrong questions, then you would be instantly deported.

Naturally, they expected journalists to ask questions about narcotics and the drugs trade, but it wouldn't be wise to ask, more than once, where a heroin refinery was located. If you started to seek the sort of information the DEA would want, or persisted in asking sensitive questions that could, in their minds, lead to raids on refineries or the arrest of people, then you could even be killed.

Every day more refugees arrived in Homong causing a severe strain on the Shan administration. Like the rest of the population, the new refugees were required to abide by the strict laws. Theft and rape were practically unknown in the region. There was a strict morality among the people and rapists, for instance, were considered lower than vermin. If proved guilty, they were executed without delay.

All the Shans I spoke to were determined to see their children reach adulthood as free people. With a strong emphasis on education every child attended school. At that time there were twenty-four schools in Homong and learning English, from the age of five, was considered a priority in the curriculum. To Khun Sa religion and education were one, and so he decreed that for every fifty families there should be a school and a monastery. All religions were tolerated, and little wooden churches could be seen dotted around free Shan land, unlike Burma where all non-Buddhists were mistrusted, and Christianity was seen as a colonialist religion.

Once a monastery was established in a new community the Monks arranged cultural events for the local people. The idea was to preserve the rich musical culture of the various tribes. The Burmese government were not keen for the country's ethnic minorities to perform singing and dancing shows. The main reason was that many of the songs and dances often commemorated some ancient victory over the Burmese.

Every day in Tiger Valley you could hear music of some kind. The local bards were not only the custodians of the ancient songs, but also the creators of new heroic verses about recent Shan victories. Khun Sa provided a reasonable budget to the Cultural Department for the upkeep of a seventy-strong troupe of performers, drawn from the various hill tribes. The troupe's priority was to entertain the frontline soldiers, not only to boost their morale but to enforce national identity.

The Monks also set about teaching the people the importance of respecting the environment when it was discovered that the refugee farmers from the lowlands were indiscriminately burning large areas of forest to cultivate. They explained that thick forests were for their own security as a protection against attack from enemies. By using Buddhism they were able to prevent the wanton destruction of thousands of trees, many of them valuable teak. To the simple villager it made sense for if he chopped down all the trees then the Burmese army will get to him quicker.

Khun Sa, with the help of the monks, had tried to maintain a balance between nature and the needs of his 250,000 people. The wildlife was rich and varied and included Elephants, bears, tigers, deer and many smaller mammals and birds. All the forests, including teak, were strictly controlled. One of the most important conservation measures implemented by the warlord was to set up a ministry of resources which he oversaw.

What the Shans lacked, because of the Burmese siege, was medicine and medical facilities with trained doctors and nurses. I remember well a particular smiling fifteen-year-old Lahu girl I spoke to at a school in Homong. She was typical of the bright Shan youth who were determined to succeed. Like the other eighteen hundred volunteers, all aged between thirteen and sixteen, she was receiving medical training. She told me her father had been killed by the Burmese army seven years before, after which she and the rest of the family fled to Homong. Her ambition now was to help the Shan cause by becoming a medic.

Dr Sai was running the medical course, which lasted about five months. The most important lessons were dealing with traumatic gunshot wounds, basic first aid and minor surgery. The students were keen and learned quickly. When they returned to their villages, they would be required to deal with all the minor ailments brought to them. In times of emergency, they would report to the frontline units as army medics.

Most operations such as appendicitis, bone surgery, hernia and amputations were carried out by doctors at the one hundred bed Homong hospital. I was told how hard it was to transport medicines and drugs to Homong, that even the doctors have trouble getting it past the Thai border guards, who often take supplies away. The only way to get them through is to offer bribes, which means the medicines end up costing twice or even three times as much.

Modern hospital equipment was unavailable so many amputations had to be carried out under local anaesthetic, or even acupuncture. Land mines were a real problem and the cause of many casualties, particularly amongst young children. During one of my visits, I witnessed a nine-year-old boy having his leg amputated below the knee after stepping on a Burmese land-mine. The operation was carried out under local anaesthetic,

Shan school children in Homong

given in the thigh. The boy was wide awake as the surgeon sawed through his leg bone. He survived.

That young wounded boy made a lasting impression on me and I wondered why international medical organisations, supposedly above politics, were not helping these refugees.

One Shan army officer explained: "I know it is difficult for the West to believe us, but our people are dying. The Burmese army nail people to trees and blow children up. We have no alternative but to defend ourselves by whatever means."

27

A Gift for Princess Diana

Just outside the town of Homong, on the edge of the jungle, two factories had been built as part of an effort to create new industries. The factories were manufacturing jewellery and garments which the Shans hoped would generate funds to lessen the dependence on opium.

What impressed both myself and Mike was the support given to wounded soldiers. Workrooms had been established where disabled veterans made small pieces of furniture out of bamboo, or other kinds of wood. With Seng Jo translating, we talked to the former soldiers at some length, and they in turn asked us several questions. They seemed fascinated by all things western.

It wasn't only the Tiger Camp that had grown, Khun Sa now had three houses and, for security reasons, alternated his sleeping arrangements daily. Next to his main house there was a badminton court where his family, friends and close associates came to play. Nearby was a magnificent guest house made entirely of stone and teak. Like all the houses, it was designed by Khun Sa himself, who was an accomplished amateur architect. On this visit I noticed that one of the properties had a zoo which housed sun bears and monkeys. For house pets, the general kept a pair of Rhodesian ridgeback dogs.

Over my several visits I became aware of the general's many habits. Although he liked brandy, he did not drink regularly to excess, as opposed to his heavy smoking. He enjoyed his food and his Chinese cooks could produce one of the best banquets in the East. Because he never left his territory, he loved to watch travel films and had an impressive library of Readers Digest and Time Life titles.

Khun Sa had a sizeable gun collection and particularly liked American Wild West memorabilia. If he saw something new on television, or in a magazine, he would order it and, a few weeks later, the goods will have crossed the world to appear at his jungle retreat. Once during a meeting Khun Sa asked if I could obtain three saddles for him. The interpreter tried to explain exactly what the general wanted; an elaborate Western saddle from Texas; a smaller quarter-horse saddle; and, finally, a fine English dressage saddle. I sent him some brochures and a few months later all the items appeared in Homong.

While Mike and I were sipping our drinks on the new verandah, Khun Sa jumped up and disappeared, reappearing a few minutes later with a book under his arms. He had seen the fuss that was being made on television about the American pop singer Madonna and her famous suggestive picture book Sex, and sent off for it. When it arrived, it was a bit more than he had envisaged.

"Do all American women behave like this?" he asked me, showing us the book. "Americans worry so much about foreign influences, yet seemingly like decadence at home," he mused.

On my visits to Tiger Camp, I would bring a selection of personal photographs, often of stories I was currently working on. The Shans always had an interest in what was going on in the wider world. On this occasion I showed Dr Sai and Khernsai a photograph of myself, standing in a palatial reception room next to Princess Diana of Great Britain and an old veteran soldier. I had just finished making a wartime documentary when, during my research, I discovered George Ives, the last survivor of the Boer War (1899-1902), who was the veteran in the photograph. I had arranged for George, who was 111 years old and living in Canada, to be flown to London for the Remembrance Day commemorations, during which we met Princess Diana. The Shans were impressed, and the photograph immediately found its way to Khun Sa, after which the following incident happened.

During our meeting Khun Sa explained how he considered me to be a true friend of the Shan. I had after all delivered letters on behalf of the Shan Council to the British Prime Ministers, Margret Thatcher and John Major respectively. He had therefore decided I would be suitable to write his authorised biography. Both Mike and I were bewildered at this unexpected declaration. I smiled and nodded, well I couldn't very well refuse, certainly not there and then. Khernsai, who had been translating, concluded the meeting by handing me a pre-prepared letter to this effect, already signed by the warlord. After a quick round of smiles and more head-nodding, Khun Sa stood up, shook our hands and left.

It seemed the Princess Diana photograph had had an effect on Khun Sa, and it also prompted another amusing incident.

With an ever-increasing refugee population into the Free Shan State

Khun Sa's main jungle residence

meant more animals were being slaughtered for food and therefore there was an abundance of hides. Khun Sa got the idea to profit from this by starting a shoe industry. Most of the output was intended for women and, because of the availability of gems, many were adorned with semi-precious stones. These styles did not really appeal to Western women and so the Middle East and Africa had become the main markets.

Khun Sa had watched a show on satellite television that depicted Princess Diana as a fashion icon and reasoned that if he could get the Princess to wear a pair of Shan shoes, then it would boost sales enormously. He instructed his people to find out what Diana's shoe size was and then ordered a special pair to be made, encrusted with semi-precious stones around the edge. Because of the photograph of myself and Diana, I was then asked to deliver the shoes personally to her at Kensington Palace, London, much to the amusement of Mike Borlace. Needless to say, that on my return to London I did not have the nerve to follow their request and knock on the palace door with a parcel in my hand and sent the shoes by post instead. Whether the princess ever received them, or tried them on, is unknown.

Most people in the West will find the incident laughable but from Khun Sa's point of view, although naive, it was a calculated move to get

Sharing a joke with the warlord

publicity for the Shan shoe business. He took the new industries very seriously indeed.

Because the businesses were labour intensive, they employed many young Shan girls. The real significance of employment for these girls was that without it, they would be condemned to a life of slavery in the brothels of Southeast Asia.

Prostitution was, and remains, a major problem in poor countries and the hill tribes of the region, notwithstanding the fabulous profits made by those who exploit their labours, are poor. With no education and experience, they are particularly vulnerable to smart talking brothel agents who search for fresh girls among the isolated mountain communities. The peasant families in the outlying villages often sell their girls, some as young as six, to these unscrupulous entrepreneurs, who often pretend to be officials, taking the girls to special government schools. Unfortunately, they end up in brothels throughout Asia – with no chance of escape.

To help stop the trade in children, Khun Sa had implemented a policy of creating employment for young girls. He had warned all refugees entering the Shan Free State not to sell their children but to ask his councillors for assistance. Sadly, there was an inexhaustible demand and the numbers that went missing every year ran into thousands. Since Khun Sa's intervention, the brothel agents became wary of dealing in the Free Shan State for they knew, if they were caught, they would be quickly dispatched from this earth with a bamboo club.

Thailand at that time was one of the worst affected areas in the world for the AIDS virus. Many of the infected prostitutes originally come from the hill tribes and the Frontier Area. Proper education and checks could have prevented thousands falling victim to the dreaded disease. Even today these young attractive girls are very tempting to young, and not so young, Western males who go to the Far East on cheap package holidays. They visit the brothels, many not having bothered with precautions, and fly back with a new souvenir of their trip – AIDS. The price of a good time may well be an early death.

Probably the most important construction in Homong was the dam. This quite magnificent engineering feat had been completed in less than six months. Homong, which was literally carved out of the jungle, lacked a regular supply of electricity, a real problem for an ever-growing population. The dam was essential to support the ambitious plans of creating new industries. The hydroelectric power produced by the dam was only 30 kw, but it was a start and improvements were going on all the time. The project began in 1992 when a valley was selected, and two

Mealtime with Khernsai Jaiyane (right)

small fast-flowing streams were diverted to flood an area approximately three-square kilometre. Once completed, the lake was stocked with fish and used as a recreational area for the community.

The task of overseeing the construction was given to a Shan engineer, another refugee from Rangoon. Labour of course was readily available, but the badly needed machinery was not. The trucks, excavating equipment and grading machines had somehow to be obtained from Thailand.

Logging companies in Thailand were anxious to get hold of the valuable teak in the Shan states. Allowing the timber concession was important to the Shans politically, so a quick deal was negotiated and the Thai companies were given access to log the trees in return for the machinery. The Burmese government strongly objected, of course. The teak, they said, was on their land and, in effect, the Thais were doing business with their enemy. However, the objections were soon dropped once a secret tripartite agreement was concluded. The Burmese, of course, were given a share of the profit.

You have to live there to understand it!

28

The Mad Hatter's Tea Party

The following year, in 1994, I made my sixth trip to Tiger Camp, this time accompanied by Pamela Martin from Dallas, Texas. A long-time friend she had managed to persuade me to take her along. Although I was now considered a friend of the Shans, which made treks to Tiger Camp easier, the journey was still an arduous one and with an element of danger. Pamela, however, was a keep-fit enthusiast and managed the ordeal extremely well.

From the moment of our arrival in Homong I was amused at the way Pamela, an attractive petite blonde who made men turn their heads, was welcomed by the Shans. They couldn't do enough to make her comfortable. Silk cushions, a small dressing table and even curtains appeared, as if by magic, in her sleeping quarters. The local kids couldn't help staring at her, their heads bobbing up and down, desperate to catch a glimpse of blonde hair. When I introduced Pamela to Khun Sa, as the first genuine American tourist to Homong, he insisted on showing her around personally — all day long!

Homong had grown yet again. In fact, it was also changing from the place I once knew. Strangers were arriving daily, attracted by the opportunity to trade and make money. I likened it to the Yukon gold rush of the 19th century, where prospectors and opportunists arrived in droves hoping to make their fortune.

The atmosphere was now surreal. This was probably because the place existed on the edge of the legal world, that most of us lived in. For example, there were all sorts of deals being negotiated that had nothing to do with narcotics, such as trading in gems, or arms. Imagine attending the 'Mad Hatters Tea Party' with bizarre characters coming and going all day long. In one area there would be a group of people huddled over a table of precious stones and on another would be a spread of semi-precious stones. A few paces away a bunch of oriental men would be arguing, in a multitude of dialects, over heavy lumps of jade, while across the road a couple of peasants tilled a small patch of earth. In the bars, menacing looking strangers sat silently drinking Mong Tai whisky, waiting for an appointment to sell some outlandish new weapon to the army. Amongst all this commotion were children running around in bare feet playing football, while off-duty mules ambled around looking for tasty morsels.

Staying at the liaison office was very informative — we got to hear the local gossip first — although one's reaction to any news had to be carefully judged. So you can imagine that our first reaction on hearing that an elephant had been stolen, was to laugh. In our society irony is considered funny and someone stealing a big pachyderm is funny. Well, the Shans didn't find it amusing at all. Very rarely was there elephant theft. It happened when Thai bandits crossed into Burma and stole an elephant, a domesticated not a wild one, from one of the logging camps. The thieves then vanished, undetected through Shan territory. Worse still, it had happened several times over the past few months. The Shans did not find it funny because of the security implication; how had bandits been allowed to pass through a Mong Tai Army sector, unseen, and with such conspicuous booty in tow?

Once I enquired about a photograph of Khun Sa standing next to distinguished looking man. I was informed the other man was none other than Prince Puren, half-brother of Puyi, the last Manchu Emperor of

Homong High Street

China. He had become a close friend and admirer of Khun Sa and had visited Tiger Camp twice. It was just another amazing story from this bizarre place.

Travelling in and out of Homong could potentially cause me serious problems with various authorities. For example, I could easily be accused of being a drug dealer myself and using journalism or filmmaking as a cover. As a precaution against false accusations and before every trip, I would write a synopsis stating my reasons for going to Homong and what I hoped to achieve. I would then file the document with my film union, a broadcaster and a newspaper. On occasion, I notified Margaret Thatcher, my member of Parliament, with an update of the project, knowing she was interested in the Shan story. I still have her replies. The most important person on my list, however, was my friend Jeff Maxwell, who was also my lawyer. We had an agreement that if I didn't telephone him at an allotted time, give or take a day, then he would immediately make enquiries as to my whereabouts. These simple procedures were an essential safety net, as well as affording me some degree of comfort.

The importance of this particular trip was to update the story by filling in some obvious gaps. My relationship with Khun Sa and his advisors had strengthened considerably over the years and having been given permission to write his official biography, I felt confident in asking more searching questions.

He would rarely speak about his children and never about their whereabouts, although there was a slip on one occasion. It happened when Khun Sa asked me to deliver a personal letter to Lord Bottomley, who had been the British Government observer at the Panglong Agreement, in 1947. I thought the last paragraph Khun Sa wrote was very interesting:

"My son has also been to school in Britain. So, unlike his father, he thinks and acts like a Britisher except for the fact that he's not. With your permission, I would like him to visit you and pay respects on my behalf."

One important question I wanted answered was how the Shans felt about Bo Gritz, now that his promise to take Khun Sa's offer, to eradicate opium, to the White House had amounted to nothing.

"Colonel Gritz proved he is full of hot air", was Dr Sai's blunt reply.

From the start, Dr Sai had never been convinced that Bo had the contacts he claimed to have had in the American administration. Khun Sa, on the other hand, liked the Green Beret colonel and was greatly disappointed he never came through, just as he had been with the other American officials many years before.

The one person Khun Sa was never keen to mention was Lo Hsing-han, the Chinese warlord from Kokang state and one of his main rivals. Lo came to prominence during the 1970s, a decade that saw an explosion of narcotics across the world.

Lo Hsing-han

During this decade China began to show a friendlier face to the world. In Burma, they withdrew their support from a number of revolutionary communist movements, including the anti-Rangoon Burmese Communist Party. Until this point BCP involvement in the drugs trade had been small but without the support of China, it was forced to make other financial arrangements and there was only one source available to them, the opium trade.

With the BCP fast taking over the domain that had once been the Kuomintang's, the only armed groups opposing them were the various Shan resistance movements. There was Khun Sa of course and his Shan United Army. After his escape from the Burmese, Khun Sa, now a respected warlord, had rapidly regained all his old territories.

Then there was a group under the Chinese warlord Lo Hsing-han. A contemporary of Khun Sa, Lo Hsing-han had begun his career as an officer in the resistance group in Kokang headed by Olive Yang. It was a group which allied itself with the Kuomintang but when the Burmese invaded Kokang in 1962, Lo chose to ally himself with the victors. The Burmese put him in charge of a Ka Kwe Ye (KKY) unit which, as happened with others, including Khun Sa, was built into a private army for the purpose of drug trading.

Lo Hsing-han was a secondary figure to Khun Sa and his fortunes improved only when Khun Sa's decreased. Lo was neither a great warrior nor an outstanding leader, but, typical of authoritarians, he was a bearer of grudges. In his paranoia he wanted to rid his domain of any person who might be tempted to challenge his position of 'top drug lord'.

Khun Sa's reported defeat in the Opium War gave Lo the chance to expand his operations, when both Khun Sa and the Kuomintang took a pause to reconsider their operations. By employing his forces to fight alongside the Burmese against the BCP, Lo ingratiated himself with the Military government who then afforded his opium caravans a measure of protection.

Lo got really lucky after Khun Sa's arrest and imprisonment. This, during the several years of his rival's captivity, enabled Lo to earn the title, "heroin kingpin of Southeast Asia" bestowed on him by Nelson Gross, President Nixon's co-ordinator for international narcotics matters. When the KKY were abolished, the wily Lo severed his ties with Rangoon in 1973. He adopted the title of a Shan resistance leader somewhat to the irritation of Khun Sa, who knew him to be very much a Yunnanese from China and patron of the local Chinese temple in Lashio, his headquarters.

Lo Hsing-han allied himself with the Shan State Army to validate his conversion and to use their strength and reputation. He went on to be the dominant force in the area except that, even working from a prison cell, Khun Sa was able to frustrate his ambitions.

Embarrassed by all the publicity surrounding the kidnapping of the two Russian doctors, the Burmese, while raiding rebel encampments throughout the Shan states in their futile search, hit Lo's headquarters. He managed to escape across the border into Thailand, only to be arrested by Thai border police. In 1973, he was extradited to Rangoon where he was charged, for internal political reasons, not with drug-smuggling but with high treason and sentenced to death. The sentence was commuted to imprisonment and that put Lo out of action until 1980, when the Burmese would eventually befriend him again.

Fortune certainly smiled on him, and he was reputed to be one of the richest men in Burma. He died in Rangoon in July 2013, aged 80, a short distance from the five-star hotel he owned.

Collecting the family rice ration

29

The Congressman who wanted to buy Opium

The massive increase in drug addiction throughout America after the Vietnam war was at last being taken seriously by few senior American politicians and officials. They were also willing to take a more enlightened approach to solving the problem.

In 1977, members of the House of Representatives select narcotics committee, of which Joseph L. Nellis was chief counsel, made a fact-finding visit to the Far East to investigate the flow of heroin from the Golden Triangle to the American mainland. Asian heroin, usually very pure and comparatively cheap, then represented about 35 per cent of the heroin available in the United States.

The DEA had stated publicly that they wanted to end the opium traffic in Burma, but Nellis understood that arresting people at the bottom end of trafficking, was not the solution. He knew that if anyone wanted to solve the opium problem, they had to deal with the people who were growing it.

Nellis and his committee wanted to find out more about Khun Sa. They knew that a previous delegation led by Representative Lester Wolff, in 1975, had met with officers sent by the warlord. On that occasion, the offer had been made to sell the entire Shan opium crop to avoid it ending up on the streets of American cities, but that offer had been rejected by the State Department in Washington. Nevertheless, Nellis was interested in meeting Khun Sa and possibly purchasing the crop if the offer was genuine.

This was not an unprecedented offer. In the early 1970s the United States had persuaded the Turkish government to restrict the poppy fields in their country to 'sufficient only for medical requirements', and the scheme was extremely successful. However, there were differences. That was an approach to a legitimate, recognised government. Also, the CIA had no great stake in that area, which was the famed 'French Connection'. That fabled French bust, incidentally, amounted to only 110 kilos. Khun Sa was involved in the traffic of almost as many tons!

During this period Khun Sa controlled 80 per cent of the opium trade in the Golden Triangle and making a lot of money. He only had about three thousand troops under his command, so his overheads were reasonable. But he knew that opium was not a solution to the political problems facing the Shan independence movement. But if the United States could be convinced to help their political aspirations, so much the better.

Khun Sa was contacted and expressed a willingness to meet the delegates, so they made the journey to the Golden Triangle. The meeting coincided with a visit by the distinguished British documentary filmmaker, Adrian Cowell, which meant there would be a filmed record of this important meeting. Cowell had been making a film about the opium warlords for some years and had previously been involved with the Shan State Army making a similar offer, one which had also been received with indifference by the United States. The cameraman was Chris Menges, who would subsequently earn distinction both as cameraman and director on Oscar-winning feature films.

Nellis had planned to remain behind and see what information could be gained by his associates. Unfortunately, the intended Chairman was taken ill and Nellis had to substitute for him. He was quite astounded to find that his transport to Chiang Mai was provided by the Thai Border Police, who were supposed to be hunting down the evil drugs baron. Khun

Shan guard of honour

Sa had a surprisingly large amount of control over the arrangements. He insisted that the number of helicopters be restricted, probably to prevent any surprise attack.

It is difficult to say exactly what Nellis expected? Whatever his expectations, he must have been surprised to find himself in a quiet restaurant, discreetly set in a quiet side street. Nor were the Shan delegates either primitive aboriginals or scowling cut-throats. They were just well-groomed, softly spoken men led by a polite colonel, representing Khun Sa.

From what Nellis heard, it seemed clear that Khun Sa was eager to leave behind his 'opium warlord' image and to be accepted as a statesman, a bona fide representative of his people's aspirations. This was why he was prepared to forego the profits from opium.

Nellis was certainly attracted to any scheme that could help solve this terrible blight of drugs on his own people. In spite of the attempts by the representatives of the State Department to dissuade him, he undertook the hazardous journey.

He was certainly a man of admirable fortitude and he needed to be. If he had expected that he would be met at the end of his flight by the general in his camp, he was in for a shock. After the helicopters touched down, there was a tortuous four-mile trek on foot through dense Burmese jungle. Nothing in his previous experience could have prepared him for the pain and exhaustion of that journey. To his credit, he struggled on manfully. He was rewarded at the end of the journey by a Shan guard of honour, accompanied by a band of fifes and drums.

Honoured by this advance guard, the visitors were escorted into camp, where they were greeted by the colonel who had met them in Chiang Mai. Then a Chinese looking man wearing a faded jungle green army combat shirt and trousers appeared – it was Khun Sa, Lord of the Golden Triangle. Nothing of the general's infamy, though, was obvious from the smiling welcome with which he greeted Nellis. When the American delegates were suitably refreshed, Khun Sa led them into a long hut where the negotiations were to take place.

Khun Sa spoke only a word or two of English but told Nellis, through an interpreter, that he had written to the President but had received no reply. "Opium is only a means to an end," he told Nellis. "The end is freedom for the Shans and all the hill tribes of the north."

The Americans had come expecting to find a less than civilised person with a total disregard for moral values and human life, certainly after the stories the Thai authorities had told them about him. He was alleged to have treated the peasants with the utmost brutality. If he took a fancy to any of the women, he was said to have had no hesitation in kidnapping them. They also knew of the kidnapping of the Russian doctors, was there a danger that Khun Sa would seek to pull off another coup, by taking them hostage? Instead, they found an articulate man who lived in modest comfort, surprising perhaps for the location but was far from the splendid luxury to be expected from anyone interested only in money and his own welfare. Khun Sa was well able to present a reasoned argument.

He pointed out the folly of the United States in trying to counter the spread of communism by giving aid to oppressive governments. All that happened, he said, was that the rulers creamed off the lion's share of the aid for their own secret bank accounts and used the rest to purchase weapons for the suppression of legitimate protest. The result was that the downtrodden peoples were attracted to the communists, who promised freedom and independence. In Burma, American support for the administration had led to an increase in the strength of the BCP.

He was also able to give them detailed calculations of the figures involved in opium production and the cost of eradicating it, though his only computer was an aide with an abacus, who rapidly flicked the beads in response to Khun Sa's figures. He estimated that five hundred tons of opium was produced annually in the Golden Triangle with roughly half of it coming from the Shan States. This meant that some fifty tons of heroin went onto the streets every year. Tons, not kilos!

The general claimed to be no lover of the drugs trade and also shared the American dislike of communism. He feared that, if the United States continued its support for the repugnant regime in Rangoon, the 40 per cent of the population involved in the growing of poppies would increase. Furthermore, he predicted, the spread of communism would be total.

In spite of his hatred of the Burmese government, Khun Sa said that he was prepared to sit down with them to discuss their differences, but only under the auspices of the United Nations or the Americans and only provided Shan independence was on the agenda.

Nellis was sympathetic to the plight of the Shan nation, though he was interested to know how Khun Sa could deliver on his promise to eradicate opium production in the region. Khun Sa had already thought out his strategy.

"If you trust me, then I would co-operate by collecting the opium for you. Then you can either burn it or make it into medicine."

Khun Sa went to explain that without help for the tribes people, who grow opium, to substitute other crops, they would starve. Therefore, success can only come through a whole process of re-education with new schools opened, so they can learn to read and write, and learn other trades. "What will not succeed, I can tell you for certain," continued the warlord, "is using your wealth and power to try and suppress them, by giving the Burmese money and weapons of war. That will get you nothing."

After the meeting, Nellis and his companions, including the Thais who had escorted them, were treated to a most lavish banquet. It seemed that, far from being sworn enemies, Khun Sa and his Shan officers were on the most friendly terms with the Thai army, even though they were supposed to be working day and night to bring about his destruction. If further proof were needed of the lack of hostility between the groups, the general permitted the helicopters to land on the parade ground, much to the relief of the Americans who were not relishing the arduous journey back. When Nellis asked if this were not a risk, he was assured that the Shans had excellent defences against air attack, including the very latest weaponry.

The Americans were given a send-off worthy of their status. The Shans retained a great affection for Americans because they had fought gallantly on the side of the Allies against the Japanese in Burma during the Second World War. Many British and American servicemen owed their lives to the help that had been given to them by the Shans, while so many of the Burmese, like Aung San, found it more expedient to co-operate with the invaders.

As the helicopters took off, Khun Sa stood at the head of a guard of honour. However optimistic he may have felt, his hopes were to be dashed. A decade later, reflecting on his experience, Nellis outlined how the innovative scheme he and Khun Sa had dreamed up had been ridiculed, and subsequently rejected, on his return home. In the same period, the Golden Triangle's exports of opium, had roughly quadrupled.

A series of meetings took place with President Carter, attended by Peter Bourne, the president's special assistant on drug abuse, and Mathea Falco, the assistant secretary of state for narcotics affairs. Adrian Cowell, and the British film crew which had accompanied Nellis to Khun Sa's camp, filmed many of the meetings held with Nellis in Washington. There was a widely publicised public hearing, when the idea of a pre-emptive purchase of the Shan opium crop was buried by the executive. The usual arguments were given. How could the United States deal directly with Burmese rebels? How could they ever trust someone like Khun Sa? And suppose it was all a big scam, designed for the general to pocket thirty-six million dollars?

Looking back, Nellis was certain, in spite of the rejection, that his journey to the Golden Triangle had been worthwhile. He was sure he knew now what the elements of any successful government attack on the traffic and abuse of drugs had to be.

First of all, there had to be effective controls to prevent the drugs from entering the country, which would require an increase in the number of customs officers to check the ports and airfields, as well as an expansion in the border patrols. It would, however, be far more effective to eliminate the source of illegal narcotics.

Nellis favoured an emphasis on assisting the governments of those countries which produced the drugs, where poverty drove the farmers into the relatively simple and regular supply of opium. However, he had seen too clearly the abuse that some governments had made of the massive American handouts. Nellis wanted a DEA with teeth, that would ensure such funds were used for their intended purpose. While he was eager to offer these countries the help they needed, he was also convinced that pressure should be brought to bear on them through the United Nations, by means of sanctions, if they continued to flood the markets with drugs. He wanted the government to begin an intensive campaign of education to warn of the dangers, and he supported calls for heavier jail sentences for drug dealers and their masters.

Khun Sa had not misplaced his faith in Joseph Nellis, who firmly believed that it would pay dividends if the United States government were to buy up the harvest of peoples like the Shan, and encourage them to grow more wholesome crops instead.

The three successive years of drought that followed Nellis's visit to the Golden Triangle increased the price of opium and its derivatives, and concentrated production in the hands of the most powerful operators. As the Kuomintang weakened and the BCP came under severe pressure, the splintering of the other Shan resistance groups left one influential force, Khun Sa.

Still a controversial figure, Khun Sa's principal reputation at that time was as a local warlord. But Korn Zurng, a tireless worker for Shan unity, realised Khun Sa's potential and hoped to take him under his wing.

Khun Sa however was worried about finances to pay for his growing army. But always ready to co-operate rather than confront, he faced the problems posed by the great drought at the end of the seventies by making some imaginative, if unlikely, alliances. The communists, with their control of so many outlying areas, were still able to gather opium from some regions unaffected by the drought, but at that time they could not process it. The laboratories and storehouses were mainly in Khun Sa's territory.

To the horror of the CIA, they began to receive reports about this new activity and even heard about communist accountants visiting Khun Sa's region to audit deliveries and revenues. The monstrous trade which the CIA had helped to create was not only thriving, but in enemy hands!

The United States government reacted, as part of its worldwide crackdown on the drugs trade, by giving massive financial and material support to the military controlled governments of both Burma and Thailand to help wipe out the source. On the face of it, this move looked to be another attempt to help defend the region from the communists but, in practice, there was no question as to who the main targets were – Khun Sa and his army.

30

The Battle for Ban Hin Taek

Apart from the political changes in Southeast Asia, there were also big changes in the commercial world. Asian states like Singapore and Hong Kong, even if they had a large share in the drugs market, were also achieving prosperity by means of legitimate business enterprises, becoming what were known as the 'Tiger Economies'. Furthermore, this success was being achieved not by the few, while the majority of people struggled in abject poverty, but by large sections of the population. There was a whole new cake and ordinary people in Thailand also wanted a bigger share of it and no longer wanted to know about General Kriangsak and his army friends. Big business had also become disenchanted with the generals and felt it was time for a change.

So, facing up to the inevitable, Kriangsak reluctantly resigned in 1980. He had enjoyed a good run and had saved huge sums for himself and his family. A new coalition was formed, though the military still had a major presence. To appease them, the Thai parliament chose a general, Prem Tinsulanan, to be the new prime minister. They had chosen surprisingly well and Thailand began to enjoy a new period of prosperity.

General Prem was a man with no interest in drugs, which was very rare in the politics of the time. From the outset, he determined to eliminate the trade in Thailand and to develop the economy on a legitimate commercial footing. In attempting to do this, he had to come into conflict with Khun Sa. Prem wanted to bring his country into the twentieth century. For his part, Khun Sa considered that he too was a patriot with his nation's interests at heart.

In 1981, reports that the Burmese Army's arsenal had been replenished with modern weapons, including the horrific chemical 'Agent Orange', had reached Khun Sa. He, like the leaders of the other resistance movements, were well aware that it was the United States who were supplying the aid and chemicals to the Burmese. That same year Khun Sa wrote a letter to Ronald Reagan, the newly elected President of the United States, which said in part:

Battle hardened Shan soldiers

"By pointing the accusing finger at us and other minority groups as the only opium trafficking groups, the Burmese have attempted to hide their oppression behind a cloud of opium smoke. Actually, the Burmese are using this opportunity and international aid to build up their army to encroach on the Shan soil forever and to rob her natural resources."

Khun Sa's point about the misuse of aid that had been given by the United States to Burma, for the furtherance of that country's political aims, and the pointlessness of that policy, are borne out by a letter in the American publication *Cultural Survival Quarterly* in 1985, which used these words:

"Hill tribes are dependent on opium as their primary source of cash and more than six hundred tons were produced in Burma last year. Thailand has had a great deal of success in providing the tribes with alternative crops, but similar programs do not exist in Burma. Hill tribes in the north have been adversely affected by the aerial spraying of 2,4-D herbicide (an Agent Orange component) over their land by the Burmese government. Provided by the U.S. for opium eradication, 2,4-D may produce such long-term effects as cancer and birth defects. In the Shan state, the spraying of 2,4-D is said to have ruined non-narcotic crops and caused medical problems in animals

and humans. Fear of the spraying is said to be causing migration of the hill tribes, and the ruined crops are causing economic hardship and further political destabilization in the area. Hill tribes may be seeking the protection of the insurgent groups."

Khun Sa was at this point maintaining a permanent headquarters on Thai soil at Ban Hin Taek, a few miles from the main Kuomintang base at Mae Salong, and had been there since his escape from the Burmese authorities. In July 1980, a warrant was issued against him by the Thai authorities, and he personally made a prudent withdrawal across the border. Despite this, Prem ordered the Thai air force to bomb Ban Hin Taek, but still failed to budge forces loyal to Khun Sa.

Next, the Thai government offered half a million baht for the general's capture, dead or alive. Given Khun Sa's reputation there were, unsurprisingly, no takers. He himself modestly asserts this was because no one wanted to kill the goose that laid the golden egg, meaning presumably the robust local economy.

Although Khun Sa always denied it, there was a persistent story that knowing the bounty offered by the DEA, he responded by announcing his own reward for the death of any DEA agent operating on behalf of the Burmese and Thai governments. The story may not be true, but within six months eight people connected with the DEA had been assassinated, and there were an awful lot of resignations by local agents.

The wonderful thing about democracy is that anyone can run for office. In Thailand, in the 1981 Parliamentary elections, it was the comeback star himself, General Kriangsak. It reputedly cost him half a million dollars, but he was helped by his friends in the Kuomintang, who also showed their gratitude by building him a luxury holiday home near their camp at Mae Salong.

When stories about this got into the press, Kriangsak denied that he had any connection whatsoever with drugs. Asked about his dealings with Khun Sa, the General had no knowledge of him either. The truth about that would soon come out.

In 1982, the United States, through the DEA, persuaded the Thai government to make a decisive move against Khun Sa. They partially funded the attack by the para-military Thai Border Police, backed by units of the Thai army, as well as an airstrike by aircraft and helicopter gunships. Complete secrecy prior to the operation was essential, or Khun Sa and his men would simply vanish into the jungle. The problem with this was that the majority of the senior officers had had dealings with the warlord and therefore a leak was likely. So, the troops were dispatched in the belief that they were going on manoeuvres near the border.

The elite Thai Rangers that were to be the spearhead of the attack were under the command of General Chawalit Yongjaiyut. They made their way to Khun Sa's headquarters at Ban Hin Taek, close to the border with Burma. They arrived at night time and awaited the opening assault from the Thai Air Force. By the time the sun rose, no planes had yet arrived.

This was not the only blip in the operation. In spite of all the precautions, someone, somehow, had got word to Khun Sa of the impending attack. General Chawalit was in a quandary. He had to decide whether to go for glory and risk a mauling or play for time. Given the reputation of Khun Sa and his Shan warriors, he decided on caution, inviting the rebel leader to parley. The trouble was, Khun Sa was not even there, contrary to popular legend, and his commander on the spot had absolutely no desire to negotiate with such a formidable force. Indeed, to make his intentions clear, when a motor-cycle cavalcade from Sector 6 of the Border Patrol Police approached the Shans' fortress village, he ordered his troops to open fire on them.

The Thai's responded immediately but their fierce attack was eventually repelled by Bin Han Taek's spirited defenders. The number of Shan soldiers defending the headquarters, Khun Sa told me, regardless of the many inaccurate accounts since published, was only a handful. Other Shans confirmed there could not have been more than fifteen at the most, which considering the number of opposing forces, did seem like only a 'handful'. Therefore, it seemed it would be only a matter of time before they were overwhelmed, especially when Chawalit's urgent calls were finally answered with the arrival of the promised airstrike.

Khun Sa's men, led by the redoubtable Falang, still managed to keep the battle raging all day. The Shans courage was resolute. One particular skirmish was remembered with pride by Khun Sa. A Shan fighting patrol was sent to scout an escape route by a slope, with long grass, rising from a muddy ditch beside a dirt road. As the Shans mounted the slope, a body of Thai Rangers appeared on its crest and opened a heavy fire which drove them back to the shelter of the ditch. As they retreated three of the Shans were hit, two were killed and the third badly wounded.

The Rangers began sniping at the helpless wounded Shan. Suddenly from the ditch leapt a lone Shan soldier and, rushing up the slope, threw himself between his comrade and the firing guns of the Rangers and pushed the spreadeagled man down the slope to shelter. This sudden act of gallantry was admired by both sides. The Thais stopped firing for a few seconds to allow the hero to escape. The heroic soldier was never identified at the time, nor did he come forward afterwards, even though Khun Sa, when he heard about the incident, offered to reward the brave Shan.

When night fell, sixty crack Shan troops crossed the border from Burma to give cover while their brave comrades retreated in comparative safety, though not without first putting a torch to their own arsenal. The fire raged for two days and, at the end of it, much had been destroyed.

Although Khun Sa, having advance knowledge of the operation, ordered the removal of most of their material before the attack, the Thais still managed to salvage some 15 tons of arms and ammunition. The official report admitted that seventeen Thai soldiers lost their lives in the skirmish. The Thai claim that a hundred and thirty rebels died is rejected with contempt by Khun Sa and others to whom I spoke. It was a botched operation and the Thais had to make such a claim to save face.

A survey of the site found what remained of a one hundred-bed hospital, a 'guest house' for the soldiers' entertainment and some luxurious holiday villas with swimming pools, one of which had been a vacation residence for the omnipresent General Kriangsak. Khun Sa's soldiers, however, had escaped, slipping across the border into Burma and leaving behind what was left of the only village in Northern Thailand that possessed, in addition to its other amenities, its own ice-making machine.

After the battle of Ban Hin Taek, almost a hundred attacks were launched against Khun Sa, many of these in Shan territory, by Thai police, military, or special forces, all of which were instigated by the DEA. They had killed and wounded more than a hundred Shans and burned many villages but even so had failed to produce any concrete results to justify the subsequent losses, and the cost, mainly to the American taxpayer.

31

Two Patriots

Talking advantage of the turmoil in the region the ever treacherous Kuomintang broke their pact with Korn Zurng and invited the BCP to help take the old warlord's opium areas. Time had proved Korn Zurng right about the BCP. Over the years the Shan people had become disillusioned with the communist organisation. They objected to its anti-religious stance and perceived that it was constantly inciting Shan against Shan.

However, a patriotic hero was at hand to save the Shans and ready to take on both the BCP and the Kuomintang. The man Korn Zurng had always seen as a future leader of the Shan nation was going to join him again. When on 16 June 1983, Korn Zurng made yet another appeal for national unification, it was enthusiastically welcomed by almost every section of Shan society, including Khun Sa, although at first his membership of the new body was kept secret. Their enemies were worried enough as it was, why worry them even more?

After the Battle of Ban Hin Taek, it did not take Khun Sa long to re-establish a power base. He engaged in a series of military operations, by which he managed to settle some old scores. He stationed himself in Burma, to the north of the border with Thailand, to the annoyance of the BCP forces who had also settled in the area.

Khun Sa hoped a period of comparative peace had set in while he reorganised his forces and built new camps. On one long reconnaissance, searching for a temporary hideout for his headquarters, his keen eye noticed a densely forested mountain top. On reaching the summit and deciding the site was ideal, Khun Sa and the 50 men accompanying him, made camp. Whether it was either by luck or good intelligence gathering, the BCP had somehow got wind of Khun Sa's whereabouts and sent a fighting patrol to capture him. The patrol proved far too small and the assault was repulsed.

Khun Sa knew the BCP would soon return with a much larger force. Realising his own reinforcements were too far away for a speedy rescue,

Khun Sa began fortifying his new camp. He immediately set his men building mounds of earth supported by large, freshly cut, logs with a glacis - a bank sloping down from a fortification. A fast-flowing stream was diverted, by using giant bamboo logs split in two, like rain gutters, allowing the water to flow downwards and soak the slopes in front of the mounds. At each side of the perimeter camouflaged booby traps were prepared: deep pits, armed with long Punji sticks, spikes made from bamboo, ready to impale any victim who fell in. Being short of ammunition, the warlord's plan was to repulse the enemy with weapons other than guns.

Two days later, a force of about 200 BCP troops appeared and began to climb the steep slopes of the hill. They crawled up slowly, carefully hacking the entanglement of undergrowth. They were within a few metres of the precipice when suddenly, to their dismay, they heard the Shans shouting above them and a multitude of logs descended from above. Panic-stricken the troops turned to flee, but so treacherous was the water-soaked terrain, that the troops could hardly keep their footing in the sticky mud. The logs fell violently into their midst cracking some so hard on the head that their skulls burst open. Others were bowled over like skittles, breaking limbs against the trees. Some ran the wrong way and fell into the pits, to be impaled on the Punji sticks. Only a handful escaped while the rest lay helpless and in agony waiting for the Shan marksmen to pick them off. It was another example of Khun Sa's resourcefulness and tactical genius.

Defeat of the Kuomintang

Khun Sa began to take control of the entire southern Shan lands and soon dominated the principal supply routes into Thailand, which meant that any movement of opium had to pass through his territory. He also seized an opportunity to strike at his old adversaries the Kuomintang and in particular General Li. Ever the pragmatist, Khun Sa chose to ally himself with the Burmese, if only for the time being. Being equally pragmatic, the Burmese were willing to engage with him in attacking the irritating Kuomintang.

Far from retiring from the narcotics trade, General Li's business had been booming. So, Khun Sa began by cutting the Kuomintang's supply routes. Then the alliance of Shan and Burmese troops made an all-out attack on Li's installations and destroyed nine of his refineries. 1984, was not an auspicious year for poor General Li. Not only did he lose those refineries, but his former Thai friends turned on him and destroyed

several more.

The old general was, of course, seriously rich and commanded his operations from the comfort of his mansion in Chiang Mai, Thailand, but even his home was a target. Khun Sa's forces planted a truck loaded with seven thousand sticks of dynamite in his driveway, which they then detonated. General Li was fortunately away at the time, in Bangkok. When he arrived home, it wasn't there anymore, with some bits scattered up to a mile away.

When I asked Khun Sa about this assassination attempt, he recalled the occasion when General Li had sent a killer to despatch Khun Sa, who at that time considered himself no more than a merchant. He was living in Ban Tham with his wife and children when the would-be assassin, one Lai Kuo-hua, called on him, pretending to want 'a chat'. They sat facing each other, a table between them, and Khun Sa became aware that Lai was holding a drawn pistol. Khun Sa continued talking, waiting for the visitor to make a move. Eventually Lai gave up, laid his pistol on the table, and told Khun Sa what the real purpose of his visit had been. But Khun Sa had so impressed him, as a man with a sincere and genuine mission to free the Shan state, that he could not rob him of his destiny. Lai Kuo-Hua could not, of course, return to General Li. Instead, he fled to Taiwan where it is believed he lived for many years.

Khun Sa's actions had secured a final divorce between the Kuomintang and Korn Zurng's SURA. The Kuomintang was still there to be reckoned with, but Khun Sa had appropriated General Li's properties. The ground was clear for a genuinely united Shan army and in April 1984 the Shan State Army and the SURA joined forces.

These two groups had been waging separate wars against the Burmese and financing their armed struggle by trafficking in drugs, the only way they could survive. Now the trafficking stopped, a move as dramatic as it was sudden. The long battle for independence was being prejudiced, Korn Zurng realised, by the contempt with which they were held in the outside world because of their drug trafficking activities. It was necessary for the secession movement and the insurgency groups at large to improve their image in the eyes of the world.

To show it meant business, the new Shan Army now turned on their other enemy, ambushing a BCP convoy that was carrying drugs through their territory. Along with 47 kilograms of raw opium and 22 kilograms of refined heroin, they seized weapons, Chinese banknotes, a copy of Mao Tse-Tung's Little Red Book and some traditional Chinese army green forage caps.

At the Shan Army headquarters in Maisung, about 250 kilometres northwest of Chiang Mai, a bonfire party was held. Official guests included representatives of the Thai armed forces stationed along the border, who also saw a number of BCP prisoners put on parade - a mixed bag of Wa, Chin, Kachin, Chinese and Shan nationalities, part of the hundred-man convoy of soldiers and porters, most of them being civilians hired by the BCP commander, each one to carry five to seven viss of opium - one viss is the equivalent of 1.6 kilograms - to the Thai border. They were shackled with chains around their ankles and ropes around their necks.

Then the visitors saw Korn Zurng put a match to the bonfire and they watched incredulously as the drug haul went up in flames. On this occasion, the fuel was actually opium, and a haul that was said to have a New York street value of about $7 million US dollars.

In Shan mythology there is the story of the White Tiger who united and led a streak of striped tigers who normally preferred to hunt alone. The white tiger is depicted on the congressional flag as a symbol of Shan unity and, as a result of his actions, Korn Zurng became known as the White Tiger of Shanland.

Of all the allies he joined together in his unceasing struggle for Shan unity, perhaps the most valuable alliance he formed was that with Khun Sa, in whom he found not only a nationalist as fervent as himself, but a potential leader of the Shan nation.

From the beginning, the Shan people believed they were the ideal combination — an alliance of 'Two Patriots'. Those of Chinese origin liked to compare Khun Sa as the yang and Korn Zurng as the yin of the partnership. For half a century, the Shans had talked about freedom and independence as a kind of dream, but the prospect had at last become a reality.

Khun Sa told Korn Zurng how he was reluctant to take on the mantle of Shan leadership although he felt it was his destiny to be part of that fight. The White Tiger laughed, "So you are a reluctant warlord?

32

The Piper of Homong

The Khun Sa story was certainly taking shape, albeit rather slowly due to constant interruptions of me having to earn a living. Apart from developing projects for my own company I would accept paid commissions from newspapers and broadcasters.

In June 1994, I was on assignment for Central Television in Calcutta, India, investigating a rather gruesome story about street kids being killed for their spare body parts, a report guaranteed to dampen anybody's spirits. However, I used the opportunity of being in Calcutta, which is reasonably close to Burma, to organise a side trip to Tiger Camp. This was my seventh trek to Khun Sa's camp and like previous visits the experience proved fascinating and, on this occasion, rather sobering.

The first strange encounter occurred as I neared Homong. Straining my ears, I could hear the unmistakable sound of bagpipes. At first I thought it was my imagination, after all I had been researching the history of the bagpipes as an instrument of war for a future television series, so the music was often in my mind. Well this sound wasn't in my head, it was here in the war-torn jungles of Burma. Even my mule pricked its ears and stared in the direction of the sound.

Behind a jungle thicket was a small hamlet and standing in front of a hut was the piper, an old man with a deeply wrinkled face, probably in his eighties. Unfortunately, his bagpipes sounded dreadful and the tune unrecognisable, although one or two phrases seemed familiar. The old piper was actually a Kachin, not a Shan. He had served under the British during the second world war, but his knowledge of English was limited. With the help of my guide, Seng Jo, I discovered that he had learned to play the bagpipes in the Assam Rifles, a regiment of the British Indian Army, in 1938. When war was declared he transferred to the Burma Rifles to fight the Japanese and continued to play his pipes.

On leaving the army, and despite his best efforts, poverty had prevented the old piper from buying the necessary parts needed to maintain his instrument, the most important being the reeds which he had to continually replace with homemade samples. I now understood why the sound was so bad and promised the old piper that on my return to Britain I would send him a box of the best reeds available. The proud-looking piper, whose face, betrayed a lifetime of war and violence, broke into a wide toothless grin and he saluted smartly in the style of the British Army. It was a touching sight, and I did keep my promise.

Shan Commandos

The first thing that caught my eye on entering Homong, was the sight of an elderly man laying on a stretcher, his shirt covered in blood from a deep cut inflicted by a Dha, a long Burmese knife. The man wasn't going to survive and Dr Sai had to take down his dying statement as to what happened. It was a tragic business as the man was obviously in great pain. He had been stabbed by a stranger who had wandered into his jungle village 3 days previously and then had to travel about 30 miles, with his wound undressed, to seek medical aid. He died thirty minutes after my arrival, another victim to violence in the Shan lands.

It was during this visit that a short lull in the fighting occurred, which

The author's bodyguard

gave me the opportunity to seek Khun Sa's permission to travel to the front line to witness the Mong Tai Army in operation. I thought this would make a good feature for one of the newspapers back home. At first the warlord was reluctant, but after a bit of persuasion, regarding the benefits of the publicity, I was allowed to accompany a re-supply caravan destined for one of the forward positions. A bodyguard consisting of three soldiers and a sergeant, Jon Suk, who spoke passable English, was assigned for my protection.

After a day's trek we arrived at the headquarters of a frontline battalion where I was met by the fierce looking Colonel Seng, a stocky well-built Kachin. Seng was a Christian who had fought with the Kachin Independence Army (KIA) before marrying a Shan woman and joining Khun Sa's force. His fighting and leadership qualities were soon recognised, and he rose rapidly through the ranks to command his own Mong Tai Army battalion of four hundred men.

I was particularly interested in learning how the Shan's operated in the jungle. I was told that their tactics were essentially evasive, with the soldiers being trained to melt into the jungle and to only attack when it was to their advantage. The Shans learned how to lure a pursuing enemy into the dense jungle and to slip away only to re-emerge at a different spot and hit them when and where they least expected.

Colonel Seng, who had been instructed to show me around the sector, was showing concern at the timing of my arrival, which coincided with some new local intelligence. A recently arrived Burmese army unit had become active the previous night. From a fortified position located about 500 metres away, they had randomly fired mortar bombs into the forward Shan positions.

Barely an hour after my arrival at the battalion headquarters there was a sudden flurry of activity. My chat with Seng was interrupted by a signaller who handed him a two-way radio. The gist of the Colonel's radio conversation was translated to me by Sergeant Jon Suk. A Shan patrol had pinpointed the exact location of the Burmese mortar and the colonel had now given the order for the position to be captured.

Within minutes more than 50 tough-looking fully armed Shans appeared and began moving forward in small groups. Jon Suk explained they were commandos. Most of the frontline battalions had a small commando unit attached, men specially selected for their fortitude and cunning, expert in setting boobytraps and skilled in surprise attacks. Their other speciality was in hit and run tactics where they not only killed the enemy but captured weapons, ammunition and general supplies intact.

I watched Colonel Seng grab his automatic rifle and hurry after his men, stopping briefly to yell something at us. But in the confusion Jon Suk was unsure of what the colonel had shouted so we just trailed the main column of troops at a reasonable distance.

On reaching higher ground we were ordered to lie flat before crawling towards a grassy mound, where a Shan machine gun team were dug in. Somewhere below was Colonel Seng's main force. Jon Suk pointed to what he thought was the Burmese positions but, with an untrained eye, it was hard for me to make out, especially in the dense jungle vegetation.

Ten minutes later we heard a fusillade of gunfire in the distance. Then, in the direction of where Jon Suk had been pointing, the Burmese opened up in all directions with small-arms fire, hoping to flush out and then engage the Shans in a firefight. The Shans, well trained as they were, did not respond. Instead they crept, expertly, towards the Burmese positions. The colonel, so I was told, did not want to hurl ordnance at the mortar pit for fear of damaging the mortar itself, which he wanted to capture undamaged. While the main body of Shans launched a diversionary assault on a neighbouring Burmese position, the commando crept stealthily to within meters of the mortar pit before rushing the defenders. A series of ferocious bursts of fire from the Shans and all was quiet. Five of the seven Burmese were dead, one was mortally wounded, and one taken prisoner.

Quietly we made our way down the hill to the captured mortar pit, where I took a few photographs. It wasn't a pleasant sight. As for the Shan commandos, there was no outward display of elation. While some gathered the abandoned mortar and munitions, others went through the pockets of the dead, looking for scraps of information that could be useful. They then walked back in silence and in single file to their lines. The enemy corpses were left for their comrades to deal with.

33

The Drug Czar who changed his mind

It was late January 1995, when Danny Buckland, a journalist friend, rang to ask if I could take him into the Golden Triangle to meet Khun Sa. He was currently working on a story for The *People,* a London based tabloid newspaper, about the heroin epidemic sweeping Britain. I accepted the commission as it was an opportunity to visit Tiger Camp at someone else's expense. Within four weeks of the call, we were at Mae Suya mule station about to set off for my eighth visit. Pamela from Dallas was with us again, her second visit. She obviously didn't mind the attention.

I was amazed to find Adrian Cowell at Tiger Camp. It was a wonderful piece of luck to be under the same roof as the celebrated British filmmaker, who had known Khun Sa longer than any other journalist. He and cameraman Chris Menges had first ventured into the Shan States in 1972, and his fund of knowledge about the Frontier Area was second to none. I had been told that Khun Sa regarded him as the most trusted journalist and true friend of the Shans. This fact alone, together with the experience of his numerous visits over the years, meant we could talk for hours about the whole Shan and drug issue, and we did.

One thing we were both agreed upon was the importance of Peter Bourne to the story. Both of us had already met Peter and knew that his time as drug czar to American President Jimmy Carter meant his opinion, gained from years of experience in a position of the highest authority, was a vital piece in completing this extraordinary jigsaw.

I first met Peter Bourne in Washington DC and then later in London. We had long and interesting discussions about Khun Sa and the Shan resistance movement. He had been helping The Shan State Association in the United States, which had formed itself into a strong organisation designed to lobby politicians. He counselled them about trying to establish the Shans as a political entity in America, making it quite separate from the drug issue. Most of the Shans lived in the New York area but the Shan State Association was legally incorporated in Washington. The man who was in charge lived in Maryland and was called Sao Khun Pha. He was not a professional politician but worked in the construction business.

Various groups of exiles from Burma resident in the United States had periodically met together but had never in the past included the Shan, mainly because the Shans were disorganised. Now the Shans were becoming major players within the expatriate groups. There was a problem in that the exiles were very committed to Aung San Suy Kyi and the restoration of full democracy and not particularly interested in the Shan states becoming independent. So they were not too sure how much the other groups such as the Mon, Karen, and Karenni wanted to support the Shan agenda. In addition, there was the drug issue, in that they didn't want to be contaminated by association. Nevertheless, Bourne believed that, as the groups became more confident, and as the Shans became a more significant political force, they would see the positive advantages that such a course might outweigh the negative ones.

Congressman Bill Richards was an influential figure on the Burma scene. He went to Rangoon and met Aung San Suy Kyi and had taken a real interest. Khernsai Jayane, Khun Sa's interpreter, had also met with him. However, like most politicians, although interested in the Shans, he was more interested in the big picture. Nobody wanted to end up being identified with the Shan cause, not because they didn't support it, but because they didn't want to be seen as being partisan.

As a former presidential special advisor and director of the Office of Drug Abuse Policy, Peter Bourne still had access to Jimmy Carter. The former president was interested in the Shan problem and because he had helped other similar groups, saw himself as perhaps being an honest broker when the time was right. He was not out on a limb for any group and supported Aung San Suy Kyi because she stood for democracy. He knew that she would, if allowed to take her rightful place, be an important figure but was concerned about being seen as solely for her. Khernsai was taken to meet the Carter Foundation staff in Atlanta by Bourne, who had talked at great length with Carter about the Shan problem. Carter sent Bourne a handwritten note saying he was very interested and asked to be kept informed. The former President had slipped naturally into being a world peacemaker and observer, especially in the Palestinian elections.

Bourne realised Khun Sa's indictment by the New York District Attorney's Office was a matter of real contention. Khun Sa himself realised the image problem he had in the United States and asked Bourne for advice, whether he should pay lawyers to try and fight the case for him. Bourne

US Drug Czar Peter Bourne visits Khun Sa. Seen here with Seng Jo

advised him against it as this was a political indictment, not a criminal one. It came out of the period when the George Bush (senior) people were all flushed with the Noriega success, and they were just looking around for somebody else from whom they could get political mileage. The moment lawyers are hired to go to court to deal specifically with the indictment, the clear indication would be that it is a legitimate criminal charge. What was required was to keep the matter in a political context. Then, if the political problems were resolved in some way, the indictment would be taken care of automatically. Khun Sa greatly appreciated the advice.

Bourne believed the indictment was actually a conspiracy. One of the men arrested was a Chinese who supposedly had dealings with Khun Sa and fell out with him. In order to save his own skin, he agreed to inform on Khun Sa and explain that the trail of drugs led back to the general. Lawyers, though, said the whole statement was so tenuous it would more than likely be thrown out of court. Bourne believed the government was actually horrified at the thought of going to trial and having to present evidence. But they had to leave it on file to keep public opinion on the boil about the drug barons of the world.

Bourne had corresponded with Khun Sa since 1977, when both Congressmen Lester Wolff and Joe Nellis were also in regular contact, but he did not meet face to face with the general until 1994, though this was not in any sense an official visit. He had asked Adrian Cowell, the British documentary filmmaker, to arrange the visit.

It was then that he made up his mind that Khun Sa was in fact a genuine freedom fighter. As he said, however, this being more an assessment of personality than anything else: "You make your money, you reach that point in life when you ask what is it all about...? If I make more money what do I do with it...?" He was convinced that for a man who had always been driven to be a leader, maybe to play some kind of historic role who was now in his sixties, that must be the continuing driving force in his life, the idea of becoming a legitimate statesman.

Bourne saw a very close parallel to Yasser Arafat, the Palestinian leader. Arafat reached a point in his life when he said in effect, "I can't go on fighting the terrorist route anymore, otherwise I shall just die as a terrorist, maybe revered, but only as a terrorist who never quite made it." So he decided that he wasn't going to die without having some sort of territory to preside over. Then he was willing to begin a dialogue and make concessions to get something before he died and where he could say he was president of a free Palestine, which his election, overseen by neutral observers, was then confirmed.

In the same way, Khun Sa had reached the point in his life where he wanted that kind of recognition. It must be remembered that the Shan nation would not have flocked to him unless they saw some legitimacy in him. These people had spent their whole lives in a struggle for Shan independence. They were not involved because they got a huge cut from the drugs trade or they had some extraordinary living standard. They didn't. They were only attracted to him because they felt he was the best route to political freedom.

Bourne quoted to me what he was told in Thailand about the Shan character, that the Shans never like doing anything themselves but were masters at getting other people to do it for them. This epitomises the argument about whether the Shans who supported Khun Sa were part of the 'actual' drugs scene. It was the Chinese and Taiwanese traders who were principally involved in the trade and all the Shans had to do was turn a blind eye and tax it. Let someone else do the work was the Shan philosophy, which is why they had brought in a former Kuomintang officer to be the Chief of Staff in the military, why they brought in Koreans to manage the gems trade and other Taiwanese to farm mushrooms. This was the great skill that the Shans had and it paid dividends. Because the Chief of Staff was ex-Kuomintang, they had an excellent connection with the Taiwanese. It seems astonishing now to think Khun Sa had been able to send all his top people to be trained at the Taiwan military academy.

I should make it clear that the Kuomintang, also known locally as the KMT, in Burma, during the drugs wars of the fifties through to the eighties, was not the same political Kuomintang ruling Taiwan. However, having said that, there was a kind of bond between the various Kuomintang groups. It is this bond that allowed economic aid from Taiwan to exist. By the mid-eighties, the Golden Triangle Kuomintang were being disowned by the Taiwanese. Khun Sa however, had cultivated a few highly placed people in Taiwan. They obviously saw he was determined to build up a strong military force backed by an effective political wing.

During the nineties, the Taiwanese offered economic help and allowed a few businessmen to go, discreetly, to Homong. Because the crop substitution programme had worked in Thailand, and this was looked on by the United Nations as a step forward, Khun Sa realised he had to have one of his own. The first crop substitution project was given to a group of Taiwanese businessmen who set up mushroom farms, exporting millions of them. Khun Sa certainly wasn't going to be able to maintain an army from the proceeds of mushrooms, but it was a start. But what would help the army was good training and his Mong Tai Army officers were sent to Taiwan for that reason.

The Shans' relationship with the Thais is too strange for Westerners to comprehend. Peter Bourne on one occasion asked Khernsai whether there was anything he wanted him to say to the Thai Ambassador in Washington. Khernsai replied that they would like to have an office in Bangkok, to deal with various international agencies. He also said they would like a bunch of passports for their use. The Ambassador told Bourne that this was not possible, there were too many problems involved. A few weeks later when he relayed this information to Khernsai, the nonchalant reply was, thanks very much but they had already been given the passports. There are always wheels within wheels. It was not so long ago that the DEA in Washington was most upset when the word went around, after Colombian drug baron Pablo Escobar's death and Noriega's imprisonment, that the drugs problem was being solved. They quickly created scenarios so they could keep their budgets intact.

When Bourne came back from his visit to Khun Sa, the Burmese reacted in a very strange way. For some reason they translated and printed his letter to the Bangkok Post in their national newspaper. The President of Burma made a speech attacking Khun Sa and mentioning Bourne, implying that Khun Sa had penetrated the corridors of Washington. The whole affair certainly rattled the Burmese.

It was a difficult problem for Bourne as he could see, quite clearly, the dilemma when attempting to solve the Khun Sa puzzle. When the United States argued it could not countenance negotiating with a drugs dealer, it should be remembered that it could not justify its dealings with the Burmese government and their appalling human rights record. The justification of it being a trade-off in exchange for an attempt to deal with drugs, made it an even bigger risk. This was an artificial argument because it is not an either-or situation. It was possible to be tough on human rights while dealing with drugs as a separate issue. It was certainly wrong to allow the Burmese government military aid which was then employed to violate human rights.

It was Bourne's decision, when he served under President Carter, to give the Burmese helicopters and two fixed-wing aircraft. It was a fifty-million-dollar aid package and designed to help them attack the drug smugglers' caravans. Yet, to the best of Bourne's knowledge, they only ever intercepted one. The Burmese were afraid of losing their prestigious helicopters. Indeed, it appeared from reports later that the aircraft were sometimes grounded for as long as three months, so as not to risk them!

When the US military authorities delivered the helicopters, they put radio transmitters in them in order to track their whereabouts, the idea being that they could hold the Burmese accountable for any misuse of the aircraft. Ninety percent of the time, they were kept parked on an airfield at Taunggji, in the Central Shan States. What was more important, though, was the involvement of elements of the Burmese ruling council in the drugs trade, and the American authorities were either totally in the dark or keeping very quiet about it.

When Bourne came back from his visit to Tiger Camp, he went to see the CIA and found it very different from Capitol Hill, he could at least converse with people who knew where Burma was. The CIA actually had people whose sole job was to work out the political balance of the Wa, the warlike Northern tribe, which was very impressive. Bourne's reason for contacting the CIA was to convince them to send people into the Shan State to start a peaceful dialogue. At the end of the meeting, he told them it had been a real pleasure to find somebody in this government to talk to, and somewhere one could have a serious conversation.

Bourne told the CIA that in his view the Shans had made good progress. The trouble was their naivety, in the political sense. They thought they only had to see the right person and all their problems would be solved. Bourne told Khernsai when he was in Washington that you can never meet the right person, there are many steps that need to be climbed first and, even then, the top may never be reached. Foundation building and relationships were the important things at that stage.

Whether the Shans could ever overcome this political naivety, whether the Burmese could ever conquer their own duplicity, whether the CIA could ever get to grips with its own treasonous and disruptive elements, were all questions that needed to be answered before there was ever a solution to the Shan's problems of independence and the West's problems of deadly drugs flowing out of the Golden Triangle.

The one question I was most commonly asked while researching this story was why the CIA hadn't assassinated Khun Sa. After many hours of discussion with various Americans they, more or less, came to the same conclusion about the CIA. There was a time once, perhaps, when the CIA might have solved its own problems with Khun Sa in a forthright fashion. But since the attempts on Fidel Castro were made public, there is a law in the United States which expressly forbids agents of the government assassinating foreign nationals. The Agency has a contradictory character. Part of it is essentially law-abiding. Other parts, though it may not be their intention, serve only to undermine the government.

34

A Service to the Crown

In 1995, I was again asked to work with Central Television, whose Cook Report episode about Khun Sa six years earlier had proved extremely popular. The programme's investigation team, led by producers Clive Entwistle and Sylvia Jones were inquiring into the activities of organised crime syndicates which were engaged in laundering 'funny money', especially that derived from drugs trading. They asked if I could help.

Their principal target was a man called John Palmer, a notorious British criminal. He had been part of one of Britain's most spectacular crimes, known as the Brinksmat Robbery when a huge gold shipment was stolen, spirited away and never recovered. Palmer was found guilty of melting down a portion of the gold as part of a tax fraud and received nine months in prison. The time he spent in prison must have seemed well worth it to Palmer because his various activities over the years, whatever they may have been, had netted him a sum reputed to be in the region of half a billion dollars. He also owned a great deal of property on the Spanish island of Tenerife.

Because Palmer was super-rich, it would not be easy to bait him. He would only be interested in dealing with people he thought were on the same financial level as he was, like the infamous Khun Sa, for example. Because of my connections, I was asked to find out if the warlord would co-operate in helping to catch this criminal while being filmed by Central Television's secret cameras. I was told by Clive and Sylvia that my job was to convince him. Not easy I thought!

Two Honorary Colonels

I agreed to make yet another trek to Tiger Valley, by now my ninth, it would also be my final visit.

My friend Mike Borlace was also keen to return to Homong with me. On reaching Tiger Camp we were welcomed by Khun Sa who, probably because of his isolation, greatly enjoyed seeing visitors and was particularly pleased to see Mike again.

On this visit both Mike and I noticed how unwell Khun Sa was. I mentioned it to Kernsai Jaiyane, who dismissed our observation by stating the general only had a cold. However, we were convinced it was more than that. Later we found out that this was the beginning of a long period of ill-health, culminating with a diagnosis of possible lung cancer.

In Homong itself there were a considerable number of new faces on view, especially South Koreans who had come to run the jewel factories Khun Sa had set up. Like the Taiwanese, the Koreans believed that the Shans would eventually win independence for their fantastically rich land and wanted to be remembered as friends and helpers of the Shans when that happened. The situation reminded me of Vietnam, now a booming country but one from which the Americans had excluded themselves. The Japanese, on the other hand, as well as the Koreans and the Taiwanese, have been cleaning up.

For our second meeting Khun Sa arrived wearing a thick leather jacket with the collar turned up, as if he was cold. Though he still had an unhealthy pallor, he seemed more cheerful as he beckoned me to sit beside him. He then addressed the thirty people sitting around us. In recognition of my many visits to Tiger Camp and the support both Mike and I had given to the Shan cause, he was awarding us the titles of Honorary Colonels of the Mong Tai Army. We all drank a toast with some fine French cognac which suddenly appeared on the table. I have had much amusement at my own regimental dinners and other functions referring to my rank as a 'colonel' in the Mong Tai Amy!

During our meeting I put forward the proposition made to him by Central Television, emphasising the fact that this would be an opportunity for his close aides to visit Britain and make some government contacts while they were there. The general was not too sure about this request, and we all fell silent as he considered it.

On previous visits it had been my habit to bring a small gift for the warlord. The items were never expensive or ostentatious, more of a personal token. One gift was a wooden plaque bearing my regimental badge, another time, as I was in a Scottish regiment, a Skean Dhu, which is a small knife that a Scotsman places in his hose top when wearing a kilt. On this occasion I bought another wooden plaque, but now emblazoned with a beautifully painted Scotland Yard badge on a blue background. Khun Sa's face lit up when I explained the gift was from the world-famous

The warlord agrees that two of his men can go to the UK

police force. I noticed Mike rolled his eyes, but it did the trick.

Together with Kernsai's excellent translation, I managed to persuade the warlord that it was a good move and he had nothing to lose. It was on this basis that Khun Sa allowed his name to be used and for two of his close associates, Dr Sai and Mr Mook, both excellent English speakers, to travel to London to help catch a crook — the irony!

Mike and I took our two Shan 'tourists' to the British Embassy in Bangkok to collect their special visas which had been hurriedly arranged by the authorities back in Britain. Central Television organised their stay in London, and we also kept our end of the bargain with Khun Sa by arranging for the two Shans to meet a variety of important people and organisations. These included visits to Jim Lester, Member of Parliament and Chairman of the Foreign Affairs Committee on Burma, Amnesty International and the Campaign Against Torture. Unofficially, we arranged further meetings both with Scotland Yard detectives and with officers of the heroin squad of Her Majesty's Customs and Excise.

It had been arranged for Dr Sai and Mr Mook, acting under-cover for Central Television, to take tea at the famous Ritz Hotel with the arch-criminal, John Palmer. They were wonderful actors, totally convincing, and he fell for the bait, that Khun Sa wanted a few hundred million dollars of drugs money laundered for him, hook, line, and sinker. To be fair to Palmer, if he had checked out the two Shans, and he probably had, they were the real thing and not actors, they really were Khun Sa's men!

Ten million viewers saw Palmer eagerly assent to being involved in this proposition, giving full details as to how he would go about the task. His sales patter was interrupted by the appearance of the fearless television investigator, Roger Cook, when a shocked Palmer beat a hasty retreat in the usual manner of Cook's victims. The result, which achieved high ratings, was marvellous for the broadcaster and justified the expense.

Mr Mook and Dr Sai, armed with a number of large medical books we bought for him in Foyles Bookshop, returned to Tiger Camp. No doubt Khun Sa hoped that his service to the Crown on that occasion would not go entirely unnoticed.

With Dr. Sai at Tiger Camp

35

The Brockets of Brocket Hall

There is an amusing side story of the visit to Britain by Khun Sa's men. Dr Sai and Mook were invited to Brocket Hall, a five-thousand-acre Hertfordshire estate, to meet Lord Brocket the old Etonian third Baron. The dashing former cavalry officer was also a polo-playing friend of the Prince of Wales which greatly impressed the Shans.

Lady Brocket (Isa Lorenzo) was an American heiress and former Vogue cover girl. A few years earlier the Brockets were on holiday in Thailand at Chiang Mai, where they were guests at a dinner which included the local Chief of Police and an emissary from Khun Sa. The Brockets gave their host a brochure of Brocket Hall, a lavish fifty-bedroom mansion which operated as a conference centre, and a photograph of themselves. Both these gifts found their way to Khun Sa.

The warlord was much impressed with Brocket Hall and, then in the process of building his guest house, amended his plans to include a marble bathroom, chandeliers, deep-pile carpets, and a king-size double bed. Ever a brilliant propagandist, and doubtless confusing nobility with influence and power, he then invited the Brockets to visit Tiger Camp.

Sadly, his invitation to the Brockets was never to be taken up. But the warlord's representatives did enjoy the hospitality of Brocket Hall and no doubt reported their impressions to him. I was told that the general had Brocket Hall in mind as a suitable and neutral setting for a peace conference, if ever he could get the Burmese officially around a negotiating table. After all, Prime Minister Margaret Thatcher and Presidents Gorbachev, Reagan and Bush all had meetings there. As for Lord Brocket himself, well, he ended up serving a jail sentence of five years for insurance fraud. He claimed he was shopped by his wife, who had by then divorced him.

The unfortunate peer also took part, though at arm's length, in one of the most fascinating stories to emerge from Khun Sa's dealings with foreigners. This occurred between 1992 and 1993, instigated in part by Bo Gritz's old contact, Barry Flynn.

It all started with the US Attorney's indictment of Khun Sa in March 1990. At first, news of the indictment had little effect on the warlord, who had never seriously anticipated law enforcement officers coming to arrest him in his jungle stronghold. What did start to trouble him though was the effect on his political ambitions. As long as the indictment lasted it would be very difficult for him to negotiate as a political leader, since he would always be officially classified as a criminal. If the indictment did one thing, it brought home to him the fact that the United States government saw him as a criminal, plain and simple. He was not even classified as a terrorist, who might be allowed to have political motives. Yasser Arafat, for example, was vilified daily in the American media for years, for being a terrorist but he never had an indictment slapped on him and he was then elected President of a free Palestine. In fact, very few terrorists ever get indicted by the Americans, or the West for that matter, just in case a deal is needed.

So, with his political aspirations somewhat impeded, Khun Sa set about planning on how to rid himself of the indictment. In an extraordinary example of ambulance chasing, as soon as the indictment was announced, a New York lawyer had taken the trouble of finding out how to send Khun Sa a letter, in which he offered to get this quashed for a million dollars. He wanted the money upfront however!

The general sought and received some serious advice. He was told the indictment could be fought in the courts but, in order to do this, he would have to obtain the services of a top lawyer. The snag was that Khun Sa's money was tainted by the drugs trade and he would have to prove legitimate funds before an attorney of real substance would take the case. "Would a deal involving legitimate gems suffice?" asked the Shans and, after a while, they were told this would definitely circumnavigate the problem.

While this was happening, and completely unrelated, Barry Flynn, who had been out of favour with the warlord, returned to Thailand. In need of money, he was hoping to tap into the gem wealth of the Shans. When he heard on the grapevine about Khun Sa's problem, he decided to get involved.

Flynn was a small-time hustler, handling anything that would earn him a buck. The Shans had little time for him as they knew he was a security risk who enjoyed getting drunk in Bangkok bars, where he would pull out photos of his "great buddy" Khun Sa to impress the tourists. However, he had his uses, and on this occasion, Flynn actually had something to offer. He explained that he had a cousin, Rick Furtado, who worked for the famous Lord Brocket, and he would be able to use his cousin's base in

England to arrange for gem sales in Europe.

By a fortunate coincidence, this was at the time when Lord Brocket and his American wife were visiting Thailand. Although they met with the general's representatives, the meeting was only a social one and no business was concluded. However, a few months later, Brocket's brother and Rick Furtado paid a visit to the gem factory in Homong.

Khun Sa now hatched a plan to raise money for his indictment fight. He had in his possession a ruby of great value, possibly worth as much as fifty million dollars. It had been with the Shans for many years and its exact history was not known but it was one of the largest stones ever found. What was needed were customers who could afford the price, probably only a handful in the whole world, and a smart agent to broker the deal.

The Lady from New York

Lord Brocket, of course, had many connections, and so did his American born wife. Lady Brocket's family were very wealthy Cubans and socialites who moved around in New York's affluent circles. Presumably through contacts, a suitable broker was eventually found, who turned out to be Mrs Shirley Sachs, a rich American woman.

Mrs Sachs came highly recommended but, if she was going to act as his agent, then Khun Sa wanted to meet her and, since he couldn't leave Homong, then she would have to come to him.

The deal was big enough for most mortals to endure a certain amount of hardship, but not for Mrs Sachs. This American bleached blonde, in her late fifties, was a pampered woman who had no intention of riding on the back of a mule through the jungle. Because she came by way of his new aristocratic connections, Khun Sa ordered that all stops be pulled out to get her to the Free Shan State. In order for her to travel by vehicle, on the dirt road all the way to Homong, special arrangements had to be made. This involved bribing the Thai military so that the guards would turn a blind eye at the border post. Favours are not cheap in that part of the world.

A special guest house was made ready for the honoured guest. As the immaculately clean jungle vehicle pulled into the compound Khun Sa, dressed in a very smart grey suit, crisp white shirt, and silk tie, stepped forward to receive her. Mrs Sachs' appearance was spectacular. Overdressed in a blue designer suit, with a large pink hat, and matching white gloves and shoes, she looked like she was on her way to the races at Royal Ascot. Like many middle-aged American women, she wore heavy make-up and,

The Lady from New York

although she carried it off well, she was something of a comical figure to the Shan onlookers in the jungle camp of an opium warlord.

Khun Sa loved it. He was impressed by the fact that Mrs Sachs had a list of potential buyers for the ruby. The name of the Sultan of Brunei was bandied about. Her fee would be 20 per cent of the deal, which she justified by claiming she had already broken international laws, crossing the border illegally, and defying her own State Department in dealing with a wanted man. Although that part didn't go down too well, her reasoning was accepted. The deal was struck, and the rules were agreed. First the ruby had to be valued and the examination would take place in the vault of a bank in Hong Kong.

The ruby duly found its way to Hong Kong and a small group from each side, including British filmmaker Adrian Cowell, witnessed the independent expert valuation. Then came the shock! The ruby had a small but critical flaw. The expert even doubted that it originated from the Shan state. The value, instead of being in millions, was only in thousands.

The Shans were deeply shocked at this revelation. They certainly had not intended to trick anybody because they would obviously have been found out. The whole elaborate exercise had been a waste of time. The other side however did suspect there might have been a set-up. In the circumstances, they were glad to get out with only the loss of some expenses.

36

Beginning of the End Game

When the student uprising, in 1988, was brutally crushed by the army, leaving the streets of Rangoon littered with hundreds of dead civilians, the ruling Junta felt secure again. The military government's tight grip on a frightened population had been achieved, as usual, by the spilling of innocent blood. To them, the everlasting insurgency wars being waged in the Frontier Area seemed too far away to be considered a serious threat. But one man knew better.

Lieutenant General Khin Nyunt, the Military Intelligence chief, knew that the ever-growing Mong Tai Army and its leader posed a significant threat to the country. The Americans may have thought of Khun Sa as nothing but a drug lord, but to Khin Nyunt he was a dangerous nationalist aiming for an independent Shan state. If the present regime was going to survive and indeed if Burma was not to fragment into smaller states, then the warlord had to be defeated.

Khin Nyunt was undoubtedly a unique figure among his fellow generals. Like Khun Sa, he was half Chinese and possessed a brain that was precise, using logic instead of emotion. As a keen chess player, he was aware that any end game is usually won with a strategy your opponent did not expect.

His rise to prominence began when he was appointed personal aide to the notorious dictator, General Ne Win. He quickly gained promotion and was eventually appointed Chief of Intelligence, presiding over the development of a large and powerful security apparatus that underpinned military rule for the country. Khin Nyunt knew that military force alone could not defeat Khun Sa, only guile could. The Junta had to hit the warlord where it hurt most, in his pocket.

The huge income Khun Sa derived from opium had to be diverted, so the effectiveness of the Mong Tai Army would suffer. He already knew, through reliable intelligence, that the warlord was spending large sums of money importing huge quantities of rice from Thailand, to feed his army. The Burmese were never quite sure of the exact size of the Mong Tai Army.

Only Khun Sa and his senior commanders knew the truth. They were happy to let the world's press continue with their wild guesses, ranging from 5,000 to 30,000, figures that kept everyone on their toes.

A few years later Khernsai Jaiyane told me the true figure. The regular army had 22,000 fully trained soldiers available for frontline duties. In addition, there were 12,000 officers and men assigned other duties, such as instructors, technicians, office, and headquarters personnel. Also in that number were about 3000 young men and boys on recruit training. Finally, there was a trained Militia of 15,000, consisting of former soldiers and civilians. In total, 49,000 fully armed troops could, at a pinch, be mobilised for emergencies.

Khin Nyunt's plan, therefore, was to immobilise any potential allies Khun Sa had or may seek in the future, not by force but by offering them a truce. The benefits to the insurgent groups of a ceasefire with the Burmese army would mean they would be allowed to increase their opium income unhindered and at the expense of Khun Sa.

The only other fighting force to compare with the Mong Tai Army was in the Wa territory. Khin Nyunt was aware that the Wa, and their opium dealing associates, would be a key element of the end game.

The fearsome Wa

The Wa, who were once known as headhunters, have always had a fearsome reputation. These ruthless fighters are of Chinese origin whose homeland, in north-east Burma, bordering the Yunnan province of China, has been off-limits to foreigners for over seventy years.

Originally the Wa were split into two groups. The smaller Weng Lin group joined the Shan back in the eighties. The main group, called the United Wa State Army (UWSA), used to be the old Burmese Communist Party (BCP). Their political aim was to have an independent Wa state. Traditionally the Wa and Khun Sa were bitter enemies as they had fought for control of the opium, although periodic truces were called when it suited both sides.

Like the other ethnic groups of the Frontier Area, the Wa depended on local resources to finance their political aim. Not much grew in the Wa hills except opium. During the early seventies, the communists attempted to implement crop substitution by introducing wheat. A plague of rats wiped out the new crop and the Wa soon went back to opium. In the early eighties when aid from Red China stopped there was a boom in opium

MTA troops reinforce the Doi Larng front

production. It was the only reliable crop to support the Wa army.

During my visits to the Frontier Area, the Wa told pretty much the same story as the Shans, namely, that the reason for growing opium is to survive. To Western leaders it was always the same lame excuse. But most political analysts I had spoken to, certainly in the United States, agree that it was almost impossible to eradicate opium from Burma while such strongly nationalistic sentiments existed. The political aspirations of these groups had to be addressed first. It is still pretty much the case today.

Reaction amongst the ethnic groups to the West's support for Aung San Suy Kyi stretched to mere politeness. "Yes, she is a fine woman," the Wa leaders would say, "and possibly we could work with her, but not under her, for she is not Wa." The Shan, Karen and other groups had similar sentiments.

Shan intelligence officers explained to me, "Since the Wa don't have the brains for politics, they depend on the Burmese government for their propaganda. It was the Burmese General Khin Nyunt who put to them the idea that Shan land is actually part of the Wa state. He encouraged the Wa by saying that, as the Wa were good fighters, they should take the state back."

It seemed fairly clear to me that the Wa drug business, controlled by the

Wei brothers, operated with Burmese consent. The Wa were considered to be major heroin producers by the Western press. The Burmese denied any involvement.

I was told of an amusing event that occurred on 7th March 1994, at the Wa headquarters in Pangsang, a town near the Sino-Burmese border. In order to improve their international image, the Rangoon government, at the instigation of Khin Nyunt, had arranged a heroin burning spectacle and promised the Wa leadership financial aid in return for this propaganda exercise. They brought with them representatives from the United Nations along with DEA and American embassy officials. Many in the crowd laughed at the spectacle of the Rangoon generals trying to detach themselves from the narcotics business. The giant bonfire was set alight although only the top layer contained heroin, the rest being made up of compost more suitable for a country garden. The presence of the DEA caused further laughter.

Were the Burmese involved in drug dealing on a massive scale? The Shans said Mandalay was a main route for opium and maintained the Burmese could not cast off responsibility just by saying they "only make treaties with the Wa". The fact is that Burmese drug agents never arrested the Wa, who were actively involved in the opium trade, often on behalf of their Burmese masters.

The Shans had a joke about the Burmese and their involvement with drugs. It was about a senior secretary in Rangoon, named Po Bwa, who often called Khun Sa "the Prince of Death". Po was not his real name but a nickname which meant Number 4. Bwa meant inflated or rich. So the nickname meant inflated with the best grade 4 heroin and that's just how greedy he was.

There was never any love lost between the Wa and the Shan. Over the years the two sides fought numerous battles and quarter was seldom, if ever, given. Atrocities were commonplace. Whether the soldiers were called BCP, or later the Wa Army, the change of name did not mean a change of attitude.

It was the villages, often caught in the middle of two warring factions, that experienced horrendous brutality. If a village was suspected of favouring one side more than the other, retribution was swift.

The old BCP could be particularly ruthless. Villages were often plundered to feed the "People's Party". One incident I was told about exemplifies this. A group of BCP soldiers surrounded the sleeping inhabitants of a small hamlet, outside Mai Haw, whom they suspected of fraternising with the enemy. They set fire to the thatched roofs of the bamboo houses and butchered the villagers, including women and children as they ran out panic-stricken from their burning homes. Any of the men who attempted to defend their families were caught and disembowelled.

The BCP also killed a Kuomintang soldier, a prisoner from a previous engagement, and left his body behind in order to fuel a rumour that it was Kuomintang soldiers who had committed the atrocity.

The next few weeks saw many revenge attacks against the BCP who, in turn, burned down more villages. A large number of the peasants appealed to Khun Sa to send troops to their area as protection.

By chance Khun Sa's troops stumbled onto a group of BCP renegades. Whether these were the same troops who committed the massacre was never established but the Shans like to think it was. The Shan commander pushed his scouts forward to the edge of the BCP camp, where they stealthily crept up on the guards and slit their throats. They then stampeded the cattle and, as the rest of the camp woke up to total confusion, the main body of the Shans attacked. Startled by the ferocity of the Shan attack, the BCP survivors fled into the jungle.

Between 1989 and 1992, in the mountainous and strategically important Doi Lang Range, many minor battles were fought between

Elephants transport Shan military supplies

Khun Sa's MTA, the Burmese army, the Wa and even remnants of the Kuomintang. The fighting was callous. Unless prisoners served a useful purpose, they were killed. The Wa in particular preferred to execute with the blade rather than the bullet.

Fewer captives were executed by MTA soldiers, not because they were by nature more merciful but because of orders from Khun Sa. He had decreed that all prisoners should have the option of joining the independence struggle. Like Genghis Khan of old, the general was a shrewd man, and he knew that a peasant soldier, appreciating the gift of life, would serve him loyally.

The entire Frontier Area had, over the years, been a scene of incredible brutality, with each group outdoing the other with more horrific atrocities. One favourite game of the Wa was to separate their captives and silently cut the throat of each terrified victim, leaving just one alive. The next morning the stunned survivor, who had been spared in order to tell the tale, would be released.

The Kuomintang, on the other hand, were more businesslike. They preferred torturing prisoners for any useful information. Execution would follow, either by beheading or clubbing, depending on the whim of the Kuomintang commander.

The Wa were probably the most fearsome of all the tribes in Northern Burma. Not so long ago, they were still spiking human heads to plant in their fields, to impress the gods. The heads were usually those of unwelcome visitors.

They were the BCP's best fighters, paid from the proceeds of opium farming. In 1989, the Wa turned on their masters and took over the business, which they have ruthlessly expanded ever since. Their most famous sons were the Wei brothers, who once served under Khun Sa but became one of his principal competitors. They bankrolled the 20,000 strong United Wa State Army, who protected them against any incursion into their territory.

Their own claims for independence were not so vociferous as the Shans', mainly because the Burmese allowed them to do pretty much as they willed within their own state. Rangoon, as always, had a good reason for this. Once it would have been just to topple Khun Sa, but now it was to keep the pro-democracy movement in check.

In 1989, the artful General Khin Nyunt, put into action the first part of his long-term plan to defeat Khun Sa. He agreed a cease-fire with the Wa and Kokang (ethnic Chinese) insurgents in the northern Shan states.

The intermediary in this unholy alliance, between Rangoon and the Wa, was Lo Hsin Han, the former 'kingpin' of opium. Lo, the great survivor who was once sentenced to death by the military junta, was now back in favour. He would be allowed to rebuild his drug empire but this time for the benefit of the Burmese generals.

Khun Sa, at that time, controlled 80 per cent of the Golden Triangle's opium harvest. On top of that, the warlord taxed most of the gem trade passing through his territory to Thailand, a trade to Burma worth a billion dollars a year. Khin Nyunt realised he had a trump card in Lo Hsin Han and had decided to revive his 'lucky star' by making him, once again, the 'kingpin' of the northern Shan state.

With Khin Nyunt's blessing Lo, the Wa and Kokang opened 17 new heroin refineries, challenging Khun Sa's monopoly. Lo's new coalition then launched trafficking routes across southern China to Hong Kong, thus bypassing the Burma Thai border, controlled by the Mong Tai Army.

War between Khun Sa and the Wa for control of the opium was inevitable. The warlord still had a booming opium economy and together with the merger of his Shan fighters and Korn Zurng's army, to create the powerful Mong Tai Army, had given him confidence to take on the Burmese government head-on. In 1993, Khun Sa's new coalition declared an independent Free Shan State, much to the annoyance of the Burmese generals.

Khin Nyunt however, was a patient man and believed his inventive plan would eventually pay off. All that had been happening in the Shan states would take time to impact on Khun Sa. But the wily intelligence chief also knew that eventually he would have to deal directly with the warlord, a formidable adversary.

37

The End Game

The Shans open declaration of independence could not be tolerated by the Burmese generals. Apart from losing face, they could, potentially, lose control of all the Frontier Area as each insurgent group attempted to emulate Khun Sa. Fortunately for the Junta, they had General Khin Nyunt on their side, a planner of high calibre.

The first military offensive was launched early in 1994, when 10,000 Burmese troops took the Mong Tai Army by surprise, pushing them back towards the border. The MTA regrouped and with determination, backed by their formidable firepower, slowed the Burmese advance. With the monsoon season about to begin both sides accepted the stale-mate and dug-in.

Khin Nyunt had been pleased with the outcome of phase one. The Burmese Army campaign had not only gained territory from Khun Sa but they had forced his opium caravans to be diverted and some refineries to close, inflicting a large dent in his income. To make matters worse Homong was virtually blockaded, which meant provisions would cost twice as much to smuggle over the Thai border, especially the all important bags of rice, needed to feed his army.

No sooner had the monsoon season ended when the Burmese Army launched a two-pronged offensive. One force attacked Homong itself, while another hit the southern border sectors. The Mong Tai Army resisted ferociously, fighting for every inch of ground, taking a heavy toll on the enemy.

It was now time for the machiavellian Khin Nyunt to make his next ingenious move. Khun Sa had been engaged in secret talks with the Wa about ending their conflict with the Shans. The Burmese intelligence chief had also been having talks with the Wa but holding back from making them an 'irresistible offer' that would turn the tide in his favour.

In return for sending their troops to fight alongside the Burmese army, the Wa would be given state protection for their heroin shipments.

Khin Nyunt was right, the Wa couldn't resist this extraordinary offer and immediately broke off their talks with Khun Sa.

Khun Sa's position was becoming untenable, or so it seemed. Despite the huge military pressures on the Mong Tai Army and with the finances drying up fast, the Shans, who fought like tigers, would not be budged.

While the Shans were holding their own against enemies on two fronts, the senior commanders could not fail to notice the change that had come over their General. For some time, they had been concerned about the decline in Khun Sa's health. Dr Sai in particularly was worried. The sudden change in the warlord's nature, his moodiness, his despondency and ultimately, his irrational decisions had alerted the medical man.

Mutiny

In July 1995, Major Kornyard, commanding the 16th Brigade of the Mong Tai Army and one of Khun Sa's bravest and most trusted officers, mutinied. The two principal reasons he cited for his action were Khun Sa's absolute dictatorship and racial discrimination in favour of those with Chinese blood, for example, Falang, Khun Sa's Chief of Staff.

It has not been possible for me to judge, with any precision, the truth of those charges, there are too many conflicting stories. What is important, is that the troops in Kornyard's command believed them, and they in turn influenced others. In this way, yet another small army was formed, this one named the Shan State National Army.

I believe it when they said Khun Sa was truly shocked. He immediately sent one of his closest aides, Sao Gunjade, to try and recover the position. He could not have sent a better envoy since Gunjade was held in the highest regard by Karnyord. There was no going back for the dissident major, though Gunjade did manage to prevent the mutiny spreading like wildfire to the rest of Khun Sa's troops in the western war zone. Furthermore, he elicited a promise from Karnyord not to turn his men against their old comrades, unless they were fired on themselves.

News of the mutiny spread like wildfire and could not have occurred at a better time for General Khin Nyunt's master plan. The Wa and the Shans were already engaged in a bitter struggle along the strategically important Doi Lang Range. Reports of the insurrection were beginning to filter through to the Shan troops fighting at the front, resulting in a growing number of deserters. The Wa, once they realised what was happening, made full use of the mutiny for propaganda purposes, while driving their forces on.

There was consternation among the Mong Tai Army leadership. Chief-of-Staff Falang was adamant, their forces would be overrun by the Wa unless something was done quickly. They had, in some way or the other, to change their strategy or even cut their losses.

Khwanmong, Khun Sa's chief political officer, was insistent that the style of the general's leadership had to be addressed: it was this that had led to the mutiny. After talking to Falang, they both put to Khun Sa the idea of a new form of 'collective leadership'.

At first, Khun Sa would not even consider it. His own highly personalised methods had certainly served the Mong Tai Army well, building it up into a genuine cohesive force with the single aim of Shan independence. He poured scorn on Kornyard and his new 'army', viewing it as a return to the fragmentation of the past. The Burmese, he added, would be rubbing their hands in delight. 'Divide and rule' had always been an essential strategy for them.

Worst of all, his senior advisers proposed that the principle of independence should be replaced by 'the right of autonomy under a single government'. This, they insisted, was the only way to appease the government, and only the Burmese Army could stop the rampant advance of the Wa.

Unexpectedly, and surprisingly, Khun Sa conceded the point made about his dictatorial leadership and allowed a new Central Executive Committee to be set up, consisting of Gunjade, Khwanmong and Falang,

with Khun Sa remaining as Chairman of the Shan State Restoration Council.

Then in November, Khun Sa resigned from the Executive, citing poor health and the wish for a quiet life, in tea cultivation. It was a shrewd move. By this one action, he officially cut off all his political ties and had given himself room to manoeuvre.

In the meantime, Major Kornyard, who had started it all, and his new army had been shabbily treated by the Burmese who, when approached, had refused to deal with him unless he mounted an attack on his former comrades in the MTA. This, Kornyard was not prepared to do and, consequently, his troops went unpaid and must have had definite second thoughts about their rejection of Khun Sa.

The newly formed Central Executive, under pressure from the advancing Wa, sent a letter to the Burmese Military Government, or 'Tatmadaw', as it was known, in Rangoon, proposing peace talks. The new leaders waited anxiously for a reply.

On the evening of 31 December 1995, the people of Homong and members of the Mong Tai Army, gathered on the large football pitch, waiting for midnight to signal in the new year. Many were scared for their future, so the mood was muted and the celebrations low key. What no one could have guessed on that cold night, high in the mountains, was how their lives were about to change forever. That is, no one except Khun Sa, who was already ahead of them.

Khun Sa's winning hand

In the east, there are always wheels within wheels, within wheels. Khun Sa's great talent was the ability to read the game well ahead of all the other players. While his senior officers had been nervously discussing how they might respond to any Burmese proposal, he had already been in touch with his own secret government contacts.

On New Year's Day, Khun Sa, still feeling unwell was given an energy boosting injection by Dr Sai, before leaving his quarters for Tiger Camp. Waiting for him on the parade ground were his commanders, soldiers, and recruits, eager to hear an uplifting message. To everyone's astonishment, he told them that he had agreed to the Burmese demands. Rather than be overwhelmed by the forces of the ever-treacherous Wa, he had invited the Burmese to enter Homong. Further, in an act of reconciliation, he asked all the MTA soldiers present to lay down their weapons.

With perfect timing, Burmese Army helicopters flew into view, landing noisily on the camp's open spaces. As the senior Burmese General stepped out of his aircraft, he was greeted by a smiling Khun Sa, bearing gifts of Scotch Whisky. The landings had coincided with a fleet of army trucks, carrying 1500 crack Burmese troops, driving into Homong, sealing off the town from the outside world. The surrender was complete.

The next day, Burmese troops also entered the Doi Lang Range and fighting ceased between the Shan and the Wa.

The stunned Shans had not expected this. The general, playing his own game, had secretly sent his only remaining uncle, Khun Seng, as a token of good faith to Rangoon. Khun Seng, who was actually six years younger than his famous nephew, remained there as a hostage while the Burmese generals sent a team of nine negotiators to meet secretly with Khun Sa, headed by Lieutenant Colonel San Pwint, representing General Khin Nyunt.

It was true that Khun Sa had surrendered. However, he had also paid the senior generals millions of dollars to secure favourable terms in return for ending his insurgency and surrendering his weaponry. Of all the conditions agreed the most important were: Khun Sa would be allowed to live in Rangoon with the freedom to engage in legal business and he would not face extradition to the United States.

The astute Khin Nyunt had selected New Year's Day as the date of surrender, calculating the Americans would not notice any land and air movements as being very significant. The last thing Rangoon wanted was for the Americans to interfere and jeopardise their plans with Khun Sa. It worked. The first significant US government reaction came five days later, with the release of a statement condemning Rangoon for its lenient attitude towards one of America's most-wanted drug barons. The non-extradition of Khun Sa to the United States, they concluded, would constitute a major setback. But it was an extremely weak response. There was no threat of sanctions and no discouragement of investment or tourism in Burma.

While the New Year's Day surrender had been kept relatively quiet, the official public one, on 18 January, was heavily publicised. In front of a large press corps, Khun Sa together with 4,000 Mong Tai Army troops officially surrendered to General Tin Htut, chief officer of the Burmese Eastern Command. He told Burmese television "Let us forget the undesirable deeds of the past." The Burmese responded by welcoming Khun Sa and his army as "Blood Brothers."

If anyone thought this was an ignominious end for such a flamboyant character, they were wrong. I have good information that Khun Sa was cheerfulness itself at the ceremony, watching television afterwards as he drank whisky with his newfound Burmese allies.

Following the voluntary disbandment of the Mong Tai Army, many of the troops joined local militias controlled by the Burmese army, including the Homong Local Defence Force based at the Mong Tai's old headquarters in Tiger Camp. Others, who had believed that Khun Sa was a Shan patriot, were devastated by his actions and refused to accept the surrender. They couldn't understand why he hadn't followed the usual custom among insurgent groups, especially the opium forces such as the Wa and Kokang, to seek a ceasefire with the Burmese and continue to hold the area. Instead, Khun Sa took the arbitrary decision to surrender, for his personal advantage, without telling his subordinates until it was too late. Those true believers in the Shan cause had no alternative but to go underground and continue to fight the Burmese army.

The question was why did Khun Sa do what he did? At the time one of his close associates explained to me that the warlord was not the sort of captain who would go down with his ship, at least, not without taking the rest of the crew with him.

Certainly, it was a mistake on the part of the others ever to propose

The Chinese New Year

the idea of a collective leadership to him. To use a film making analogy, I recognised in Khun Sa, from the first time I met him, that he was the star, the producer and the director all rolled into one. Only the late Korn Zurng might have persuaded him otherwise.

So was all this no more than an elaborate defensive ploy on the part of Khun Sa? It may well have been. I found another piece of the puzzle, five years after the mutiny, when I managed to contact Dr Sai again. He told me that Khun Sa had been suffering from deteriorating health for at least two years before the mutiny. He had developed diabetes accompanied by extremely high blood pressure and his immune system had suffered. I remembered that on my last two visits to Tiger Camp, during 1995, the general had been unwell on both occasions. That same year he had also been diagnosed with heart disease. I would guess his ill-health was a major contributing factor on his decision to make a deal with the Burmese.

Exile

After the official surrender Khun Sa moved to Rangoon, where the junta had provided him with a large mansion on Inya Road, an upmarket area near the capital and not very far from the residences of General Ne Win and Aung San Suu Kyi. The secure compound, guarded by Burmese Intelligence, also housed his immediate family and twenty close friends and aides, including Dr Sai, who had been allowed to accompany him.

Over the next two years, Khun Sa kept a low profile. His movements had been restricted by the government and all contact with the outside world was monitored by Burmese intelligence. These hindrances, however, did not stop the former warlord from initiating a new business empire.

One benefit of relocating to Rangoon was that Khun Sa's family had been allowed to operate business interests in Burma. Khun Sa took full advantage and began financing large projects to be run by his children. One son became boss of a hotel and casino in the border town of Tachilek, another managed a transport company operating lucrative air and bus routes, while a daughter controlled a large ruby mine.

Many believe that Khun Sa kept his drug business going, though on a slimmed down scale, sharing his profits with some members of Burma's military regime. But there is no concrete evidence to support that belief. Much of his former drug empire had been taken over by other drug lords and groups, in particular the Wa.

For the most part his ten years in exile had been spent supervising his business empire between bouts of poor health, due to his many ailments. During 2007, already diagnosed with heart disease and partial paralysis, probably due to a stroke, his condition was deteriorating fast. His lungs were only working at 30 per cent capacity, due to a lifetime of chain-smoking. Dr Sai called it the '555' malady, named after Khun Sa's favourite brand.

By October, Khun Sa lay struggling with death. Close friends and family had gathered in his house. Doctors and specialists had been administering medicines to keep the old warlord going, using the correct balance of opioid painkillers to make him comfortable until his last breath. He died, aged 73, on 26 October 2007.

Khun Sa's funeral, 4 days later, was attended by relatives and close friends. The men who had known him for most of his life and had served him loyally were overcome with grief and openly wept. Some of his ashes were later scattered on his beloved Salween River, in the Shan states, in accordance with his wishes. The rest of his remains, however, were buried at Yayway Cemetery, near Rangoon. Khun Sa had decided not to be buried in the Shan lands for fear his tomb would be vandalised.

Khun Sa knew that many of his former comrades in the Shan resistance movement and the Mong Tai Army had never forgiven him for the surrender ten years previously. Maybe he had a conscience after all, and it still troubled him to the end.

POSTSCRIPT

Today, Ban Toed Thai is a Shan-Lahu village in Chiang Rai province, Thailand, close to the border with Burma, but in 1982, it was known as Ban Hin Taek, site of Khun Sa's base. It is where he fought the famous battle against the Thai Rangers sent to displace him. In Ban Toed Thai the warlord is also remembered not as a notorious 'drug kingpin', but fondly as a patriotic and charismatic leader. The locals recall how he built the first school, the first hospital, a monastery, paved the roads and put in place a functional water and electrical infrastructure.

On the village outskirts is a small compound with a sign 'Khun Sa Old Camp'. Inside is a Khun Sa museum displaying mementoes of his life, and nearby is an impressive life-size statue of the warlord on his horse. What I found remarkable was that Khun Sa was not even from Thailand, yet he is commemorated by the Shans living there.

This respect for a man who supported the people with actions, rather than words, is not shared by everyone. Most non-Shans maintain his generosity was simply because the warlord used the village as his base for an immensely profitable drug business. But let's not get side-tracked by the predictable official mantra, 'Khun Sa is just a plain old drug dealer'. He clearly was not.

Even in death Khun Sa was controversial. The Mong Tai Army veterans, who blamed their own officers for not backing the warlord in his time of need, certainly mourned his passing. But a few die-hard nationalists saw the warlord as a traitor. My old friend Khernsai Jaiyane, a fervent nationalist, maintains that Khun Sa could have been the great liberator of the Shans, but his dictatorial style of leadership wasn't accepted by the people and instead of changing, he turned his back on them. Many Shans would disagree.

Whatever people thought of Khun Sa, he has certainly left his mark on history. He was always a controversial figure, so where did his strength lie? He had a good brain, a sense of humour and like a seasoned politician he knew how to charm an audience. He also possessed the power to draw the hearts of people to him.

The old saying of 'you make your own luck' definitely applied to Khun Sa. His adventures, deeds and audaciousness drew respect, even from his enemies. He had the ability to bounce back from every mishap, time and time again. In the early days he had to rebuild his army several times over. In the 1967 Opium War, the attack by the Kuomintang on his force was intended to crush him. But he saw off the Kuomintang and even retrieved the position after his defeat by the Laotian forces, demanding and getting compensation from General Rattikone.

He was written off almost entirely when he was captured by the Burmese. They locked him up and were probably prepared to throw away the key, until the kidnap of the Russian doctors forced them to reconsider. The plan Khun Sa devised in his cell, orchestrated by the faithful Falang, almost caused an international incident, and secured him a dramatic release.

In 1982, at Ban Hin Taek, a determined attack by the Thai army forced him to move his headquarters back to the Golden Triangle. He survived and went on to merge all the Shan insurgents into a single and united force.

Khun Sa was the supreme manipulator, constantly playing personalities and groups against each other. He knew money was power and he kept control by distributing it wherever it was needed, in carefully calculated doses.

The mutiny in 1996, and the events that stemmed from it, may have been the biggest reverse Khun Sa had ever suffered. Well, to the outside world that is. There was no trial. He was not imprisoned. There was no talk of him being extradited to the United States of America, to answer the indictment against him. And not surprisingly, nobody ever came forward to claim the two-million-dollar bounty on the old warlord's head.

This half Shan, half Chinese Houdini, had secretly negotiated with the Burmese military another of his incredible escapes. Despite the ceremonial handover of power to the other Shans leaders, it must have been obvious to anyone with half an eye that Khun Sa would never really give up his power – that was just not his style. It was still Khun Sa who had been pulling the strings. Before the official agreement was announced Khun Sa had secretly negotiated his own comfortable retirement in Rangoon.

The Burmese Generals, however, knew Khun Sa was still the only man who could unite the great majority of the Shan insurgents. Their plan was to convert the former warlord into a business magnate by publicly honouring him and granting profitable concessions. Interestingly, this red-carpet treatment for the most wanted drug kingpin in the world had escaped criticism from any international body. Occasionally the DEA or US State Department would spout-off some meaningless slogan about the war on drugs or berate the Burmese government about them refusing to extradite Khun Sa. Then it would all simmer down.

Aung San Suu Kyi

Khun Sa's predictions were also uncanny. He told me back in 1993, that if Aung San Suu Kyi, leader of Burma's pro-democracy movement and Nobel Peace Prize winner, ever gained power she would never back the country's ethnic minorities. And especially not their struggle for the Right of Self Determination. "She is first of all Burmese and the daughter of her father", he would say.

In 2017, Aung San Suu Kyi, and now one of Burma's leaders, was globally vilified when she stood by as the Burmese military killed and raped thousands of Rohingya people, forcing more than 700,000 to flee into neighbouring Bangladesh. She claimed the accusations were unfair and that her hands had been tied by the military, who would not listen to her pleas. Despite this defence, the International Court of Justice in the Hague, Netherlands, in 2020, condemned her and her fellow leaders, for their treatment of the Royingya minority. It seems Khun Sa's prediction was correct!

Despite this setback Aung San Suu Kyi and her National League for Democracy party won the Myanmar general election, in November 2020, with a huge majority. The military however refused to accept the result and a few months later staged a coup, triggering widespread protests throughout the country. The coup quickly led to economic collapse and renewed civil conflict. Predictably, the army reacted violently killing hundreds of demonstrators and making more than 10,000 arrests, including the pro-democracy leaders.

In December 2021, Aung San Suu Kyi was found guilty in Myanmar of various bogus crimes, in a politically motivated trial, and imprisoned. Realistically, she remains the best hope for the Burmese people to achieve some form of democracy, if she's ever released by the military. In spite of the Rohingya crisis Aung San Suu Kyi still has strong international support, but the hill tribes and other ethnic groups of Burma simply do not trust her.

The new opium!

If this book goes some way in resolving the enigma of Khun Sa, it does little to solve the drug problem. The war on drugs is a ceaseless merry-go-round and as Khun Sa used to say, "to the immense profit of everyone on board and to the intense suffering of the addicts".

I wonder what he would have made of the proliferation of synthetic drugs now dominating his homeland. It was reported in 2021 that the Shan State had become the hub for methamphetamine, the commonly used illicit drug. The United Nations Office on Drugs and Crime (UNODC) claim that modern-day Myanmar (Burma) is probably the biggest meth producer in the world.

The seventy years of conflict between the ethnic insurgent groups and the Burmese army have left the Shan lands extremely poor. For generations, the hill tribes have relied on opium growing as their main source of income, and swathes of land covered with opium poppies can be seen by aerial surveillance, especially from satellites. Synthetic drugs, such as methamphetamine, are less challenging to hide, thus making it easier for the authorities to turn a blind eye. The new, up and coming drug lords are now switching to methamphetamine, which is cheaper to produce and easier to transport. It is the new opium!

The Myanmar government claim that the rebel armies are financing their organisations with the money from drug trafficking, which includes methamphetamine. Following Khun Sa's surrender in 1997, the Wa took control of the bulk of the opium trade in the Golden Triangle. The United Wa State Army is still the largest ethnic force in the region and financed from drug trafficking. However, the Wa do not use their army to fight the Myanmar military, who lost control of the region years ago, they use it to guard their drug empire.

A former Khun Sa aide laughs at the periodic anti-drug police raids, arranged by the Myanmar government, to demonstrate to the world how the problem is being confronted. He insists it is just a publicity gimmick. Organised crime and drug syndicates rarely invest large sums of money in production and smuggling unless they have guarantees. This illicit trade could never flourish without the vast network created by the local warlords and the official complicity of governments. Nobody is clean. Khun Sa may be gone, but it's business as usual.

The total number of people who die around the world from regional wars and natural disasters such as hurricanes, tsunamis, and earthquakes, is less than the 700,000 who die annually from drug abuse. This huge figure makes you wonder if any Western governments and their ineffective enforcement agencies are taking the problem seriously. Drug gangs now operate on a global scale using their immense fortunes and power, in the corruption and control of politicians and law enforcement.

The problem for the ordinary folk is that if the judiciary is ever truly compromised, as it is in many countries, then it's all over for society as we know it.

But that is another debate.

Conclusion

I am often asked about my opinion of Khun Sa and strangely, I still find it difficult to answer. He undoubtedly possessed many qualities, though they were not, by any means, all good. To get to the truth, or as near to it as possible, I have searched out Khun Sa's life wherever a lead took me. I have found his character to be stronger than I would have ever imagined. Looking me straight in the eye, he once told me that he was a reluctant warlord, but I was never quite sure if he truly was the statesman-in-waiting he hoped to be.

My view tends to follow that of former US drug czar Peter Bourne and filmmaker Adrian Cowell. Khun Sa grew up in a troubled land, where opium was part of the way of life and where he skilfully managed to become a leading player. In later life he desired legitimacy and took up the banner of Shan resistance. If only the US had listened to Congressman Lester Woolf and Joseph Nellis and given Khun Sa's offer a chance, things may have been different.

Khun Sa was an intelligent man and must have eventually realised that efforts to win Shan independence were looking less likely as the years went by. I believe he was reluctant to push the resistance movement to one side, but his personal circumstances had changed. I would say, knowing the man, that once he knew his health was deteriorating, he began formulating a long-term strategy to secure a safe retirement for himself, his family and close friends. Bo Gritz once told me that time is usually a fair assessor and will no doubt assign Khun Sa his proper place in history.

Shan Nurse and entertainer

Akha family in traditional dress

Last word

I have been very fortunate throughout my life, having travelled to unusual places and seen many sights, some good and some grim. After a lifetime of adventures meeting and dealing with an amazing mix of people, including: Royalty, Prime Ministers, Presidents, as well as African despots, drug barons, mercenaries and great train robbers, I can confirm that real life is more extraordinary than the wildest fiction. At the end of this long trail of discovery, I have learnt much that I did not know before. One day my grandson asked out of the blue, which experience of my life I found the most exciting. Without hesitation, I heard my voice answering, "meeting the Shan people". If there had been a week's warning, I could have given no other answer.

APPENDIX A

Two letters written by Khun Sa for author Patrick King to deliver to British
Prime Minster Margaret Thatcher.
   (Letters in date order)

Right Hon. Margret Thatcher M.P
Prime Minister
10, Downing Street,
London

August 3, 1990,

Dear Prime Minister,

Further to the visit of Mr.Patrick King to the Shan States with the Central
Television crew from England, I would like to make the following proposal,
to you;

The Shan Council of the TRC has always had great respect for you, your
leadership and your achievements. Historically Great Britain has been linked
to the destiny of the Shan States and indeed the rest of Burma. It is our
sincere wish that you consider sending an envoy to see us, and then to discuss
ways in which Great Britain could play a part in ending our dispute with the
Burmese. The way to do this is for your country to act as a mediator as
your judgement would be respected.

We understand there would be very difficult political problems, but the final
objective would be the complete eradication of the opium crop from the Shan States.

The Panlong Agreement signed in 1947 by your country did give us the right of
self determination. We are asking for your help infinding ways to stop the
fighting and oppression of our eight million people.

Our promise to stop the opium trade will be kept and we need the help of your
good office to succeed. It is our intention to keep all communications between
us confidential so as not to compromise your position.

We eagerly await your reply and of seeing your envoy. Please assist in this
Worthwhile objective which will benefit the entire world.

                    I remain yours faithfully,

                    Khun Sa
                    Representitive of the
                    Tai Revolutionary Council

General Headquarters,
Mong Tai Army,
SHAN STATE.
May 30, 1989.

Right Honorable Margaret Thatcher
10 DOWNING STREET
LONDON W.1

Dear Mrs. Thatcher:

I have the honor to send you this letter through the goodwill of
Mr. Patrick King who visited me in May of this year.

The Shan State , as a Protectorate of the British Crown, from 1887
to 1947 enjoyed one of the rarest periods in Shan history of peace
and tranquility, if not progress and prosperity,under your humane
rule.

After World War II, with your voluntary support, we could   have
achieved separate independence like other peoples once under your
protection. But our foregoing leaders, hoping to shorten the duration of the struggle, decided to join Burma - which had already won
approval from the post war Labour government to be   independent
within a year - on the Burmese promise that we should enjoy equal
rights and full autonomy of our own internal affairs in the Union,
and that we could withdraw from it if we were dissatisfied   with
treatment.

As it turned out that was a serious mistake, and the Shan people
have been suffering the consequence for more than 40 years now.Our
life under Burmese oppression is unbearable. Older people,whenever
I meet them, ask me whether the British will be coming back. They
cheered you when you courageously fought and preserved sovereignty
for the people of the Falklands. And my people say if there is one
British politician alive that can help us obtain what's rightfully
ours, it is Margaret Thatcher. I sincerely echo their faith.

With your interest we can focus the attention of other world
leaders on our plight. We can eliminate opium and establish a legitimate prosper.ous FREE NATION STATE.

Thank you for reading my letter. I am prepared to act immediately
on any positive suggestion with the mutual welfare of my   people
and the world in mind.

Most respectfully,

Khun Sa
Commander-in-Chief
Shan State

247

APPENDIX B

A note from Margaret Thatcher to Patrick King, as his Member of Parliament, regarding his report on nationalist groups and drug trafficking in Burma. The reply to the report from the British Foreign Office is from the Secretary of State, Douglas Hurd. It is interesting to note that the comments from the British authorities on this subject are in line with those usually made by the Americans, French, Germans etc. With this unwillingness by the West to look for real solutions it is no wonder that Burma (Myanmar) remains a country divided by hatred and at war with its own people. In the meantime the narcotics keep flowing.

THE RT. HON. MARGARET THATCHER, O.M., F.R.S.

27 March 1992

Dear Mr. King.

        Thank you for your further letter of
the 12 March to Joy Robilliard.

        I have now received this reply from the
Foreign Secretary about nationalist groups involved
in drug trafficking in Northern Burma.   I am
afraid there has been some delay in sending this
to you since the enclosure - the Panglong text -
was missing and I have now obtained a copy.

        By all means let me have any further
comments.

Yours sincerely

Margaret Thatcher

Mr Patrick King

35 Chesham Place SW1X 8HB

16 March 1992

Dear Margaret.

Thank you for your letter of 11 February enclosing a memorandum
from your constituent, Mr Patrick King, about nationalist groups
involved in drug trafficking in Northern Burma.

Officials here were interested to read Mr King's comprehensive
memorandum. His ideas for stemming the drugs trade are
superficially attractive, but flawed. First, Khun Sa's reliance on
income from narcotics is a major stumbling block. We would no more
do a deal with self-confessed major drug traffickers than we would
with terrorists. Secondly, however much we dislike the military
regime (the SLORC) it is not in western interests to be involved
actively in destabilizing the integrity of Burma by supporting
Khun Sa, even if we believed that he would deliver on his promise to
end the drugs trade - a claim he has made many times to western
journalists. He is only one of many involved in the drugs trade.

This does not, however, detract from our serious concern about
Burmese heroin production. Mr King is right in asserting that the
Golden Triangle (Burma in particular) is the world's major source of
illicit opium. The inaccessibility of the area, the unsuitability
of most of the terrain for ordinary agriculture and the fact that no
central administration in Burma has ever been able to exercise
effective authority and control, have all contributed to the
growth of drug production and trafficking there. We are committed
to tackling the global problems of drug production and trafficking
wherever and whenever possible. As there is justifiable and

The Rt Hon Margaret Thatcher OM FRS MP

widespread scepticism about the willingness of the Burmese regime to tackle the narcotics problem in Burma, we believe the most hopeful approach lies in multilateral action through the UN International Drug Control Programme (UNDCP) sub-regional strategy for South East Asia, which we and other major donors, including the US and our EC partners, have endorsed. This aims to promote dialogue and joint action between countries in the Golden Triangle (Burma, Thailand, Laos and China). Talks about improving cross-border cooperation and interdiction of heroin in transit have already begun.

As for the political situation in Burma, we have been at the forefront of international criticism of the SLORC's appalling human rights record and their failure to respect the democratic process since their assumption of power in 1988. The SLORC's priorities appear to be the repression of all sources of opposition and the expansion of the military as the dominant force in Burmese society. We were delighted by the outcome last week of the UN Commission on Human Rights on Burma, roundly condemning the SLORC and instituting a public scrutiny procedure, including the appointment of a special rapporteur.

Misrule and ethnic strife are sadly not new to post-independence Burma. But until the authorities in Burma are prepared to work constructively towards a resolution of national minority issues, the prospects for peace are bleak. The Shans are only one of many ethnic groups resisting control by the central authorities in Rangoon; but Khun Sa is on weak ground in calling in aid the Panglong Agreement to support his contention that we have let the Shan down.

First, we did not sign the Agreement; it was the product of essentially intra-Burmese negotiations at Panglong on 7 February 1947, about a year before Burmese independence. Lord Bottomley, then Under Secretary of State for Dominion Affairs, attended the discussions which were designed to establish the basis for political cooperation between the hill peoples including the Shan, who were administered separately as the Frontier Areas under colonial rule, and the central interim government (led at that time by Aung San, father of the 1991 Nobel Peace Prize winner, Aung San Suu Kyi).

British approval for the agreement was needed, and Lord Bottomley recommended this as he regarded it as a "satisfactory compromise". I enclose a copy of the Panglong text. The spirit of the agreement was incorporated in the Independence Constitution adopted by the interim government in September 1947, which envisaged a federal system with significant local autonomy. By then, however, Aung San had been assassinated, and the Burmese leadership which took over on 4 January 1948 reneged on the commitments made to the national minorities.

We have noted what Mr King says about a possible Irish connection. We have passed this on to the experts in this field.

Yours

Douglas

DOUGLAS HURD

APPENDIX C

An interesting letter from Khun Sa to Patrick King.

SHAN STATE RESTORATION COUNCIL
General Headquarters : Ho Mong, Shan State (Mong Tai)

Mr Patrick King
Westminster King Productions Ltd.
Impact House
20 Accommodation Road
London NW11 2EP
United Kingdom

July 8, 1993

Dear Mr King,

I have known you since 1989 when you first came to the Free Shan
Territory to make a film about our struggle for the Right of Self-
Determination.

You have since made many trips and I believe you are a film producer who has listened to our side and your opinion is neutral
and unbiased.

I believe you are the right person to produce an authorised biography of my life.

Yours truly,

Khun Sa

President

APPENDIX D

The letter written by Khun Sa for Patrick King to deliver to British Prime Minster John Major, who succeeded Margaret Thatcher.

4 March 1994

The Right Honorable John Major,M.P.
Prime Minister
10 Downing Street
London
THE UNITED KINGDOM

Dear Mr Prime Minister:

We are writing this letter to ask you to help the Shan people
in their struggle against oppression.

We have asked documentary film producer,Mr Patrick King,who
has seen for himself the plight of the Shans,to convey this
appeal to you.

Although we realize that there may be some difficulty in
achieving full recognition of Shan Independence,we also think
that the issue of human rights or lack of them in the once
British Protectorate Shan State is still something worth considering seriously.

We know that you,as Prime Minister of the United Kingdom,have
personally striven for world peace. Great Britain is respected
by all Shans and still has an historic and important role to
play in this region. We ask you not only as a leader but also
as an Englishman to help.

Besides moral and and human rights,the Shans most of whom are
refugees from Burmese atrocities,have basic needs-- items
that your own people have taken for granted,such as medicines,
are practically unavailable here.

We therefore appeal to you to send a humanitarian team to see
for themselves what is really happening and what could be
achieved with help from Europe.

Next year marks the 50th anniversary of the ending of the
Second World War. Many Shans gave their lives fighting with
the British Army. Please help us in their memory.

Sincerely,

Khun Sa
President,
Shan State Restoration Council

APPENDIX E

A clear transcription of the The Panlong Agreement, 1947. Followed by a copy of the original document and signatories.

*NOTE: The Panlong Agreement forms the basis of the Shan's claim for the right to secede from the Union of Burma (Myanmar) and become an independent state. The Shan claim is reinforced by Chapter 10 in the Constitution of the Union of Burma, which deals with the Right of Secession. For example this extract is from Article 201 which states: —

Save as otherwise expressly provided in this Constitution or in any Act of Parliament made under section 109, every State shall have the right to secede from the Union in accordance with the conditions hereinafter prescribed.

THE PANGLONG AGREEMENT, 1947.

A Conference having been held at Panglong, attended by certain Members of the Executive Council of the Governor of Burma, all Saophas and representatives of the Shan States, the Kachin Hills and the Chin Hills :

The Members of the Conference, believing that freedom will be more speedily achieved by the Shans, the Kachins and the Chins by their immediate co-operation with the Interim Burmese Government :-

The Members of the Conference have accordingly, and without dissentients, agreed as follows :-

1. A Representative of the Hill Peoples, selected by the Governor on the recommendation of representatives of the Supreme Council of the United Hill Peoples (SCOUHP), shall be appointed a Counsellor to the Governor to deal with the Frontier Areas.

2. The said Counsellor shall also be appointed a Member of the Governor's Executive Council, without portfolio, and the subject of Frontier Areas brought within the purview of the Executive Council by Constitutional Convention as in the case of Defence and External Affairs. The Counsellor for Frontier Areas shall be given executive authority by similar means.

3. The said Counsellor shall be assisted by two Deputy Counsellors representing races of which he is not a member. While the two Deputy Counsellors should deal in the first instance with the affairs of their respective areas and the Counsellor with all the remaining parts of the Frontier Areas, they should by Constitutional Convention act on the principle of joint responsibility.

4. While the Counsellor, in his capacity of Member of the Executive Council, will be the only representative of the Frontier Areas on the Council, the Deputy Counsellors shall be entitled to attend meetings of the Council when subjects pertaining to the Frontier Areas are discussed.

5. Though the Governor's Executive Council will be augmented as agreed above, it will not operate in respect of the Frontier Areas in any manner which would deprive any portion of these Areas of the autonomy which it now enjoys in internal administration. Full autonomy in internal administration for the Frontier Areas is accepted in principle.

6. Though the question of demarcating and establishing a separate Kachin State within a Unified Burma is one which must be relegated for decision by the Constituent Assembly, it is agreed that such a State is desirable. As a first step towards this end, the Counsellor for Frontier Areas and the Deputy Counsellors shall be consulted in the administration of such areas in the Myitkyina and the Bhamo Districts as are Part II Scheduled Areas under the Government of Burma Act of 1935.

7. Citizens of the Frontier Areas shall enjoy rights and privileges which are regarded as fundamental in democratic countries.

8. The arrangements accepted in this Agreement are without prejudice to the financial autonomy now vested in the Federated Shan States.

9. The arrangements accepted in this Agreement are without prejudice to the financial assistance which the Kachin Hills and the Chin Hills are entitled to receive from the revenues of Burma, and the Executive Council will examine with the Frontier Areas Counsellor and Deputy Counsellors the feasibility of adopting for the Kachin Hills and the Chin Hills financial arrangements similar to those between Burma and the Federated Shan States.

Shan Committee.	Kachin Committee.	Burmese Government.
[signature] Saohpalong of Tawngpeng State.	*[signature]* (Sinwa Naw, Myitkyina)	*[signature]* 12/2/47
[signature] Saohpalong of Yawnghwe State.	*[signature]* (Zau Rip, Myitkyina)	
[signature] Saohpalong of North Hsenwi State.	*[signature]* (Dinra Tang, Myitkyina)	
[signature] Saohpalong of Laihka State.	*[signature]* (Zau La, Bhamo.)	
[signature] Saohpalong of Mong Pawn State.	*[signature]* (Zau Lawn, Bhamo)	
[signature] Saohpalong of Hsamonghkam State.	*[signature]* (Labang Grong, Bhamo)	
[signature] Representative of Kaahtung Saohpalong.	**Chin Committee.**	
[signature] (Hkun Pung)	*[signature]* (U Hlur Hmung, ATM, TDSM, B.S.M., Falam.)	
[signature] (U Tin E) *[signature]* (U Ntun Myint)	*[signature]* (U Thawng Za Khup, ATM, Tiddim.)	
[signature] (U Kya Bu) *[signature]* (Hkun Saw).		
[signature] (Sao Yape Hpa) *[signature]* (Hkun Htee)	*[signature]* (U Kio Mang, ATM, Haka)	

၂၆။ ပင်လုံစာချုပ်။

Panglong Agreement.

Dated Panlong the 12th February 1947

THE PANLONG AGREEMENT, 1947.

A conference having being held at Panlong, attended by certain Members of the Executive Council of the Government of Burma, Saophas and representatives of the Shan State, the Kachin Hills and the Chin Hills:

The Members of the Conference, believing that freedom will be more speedily achieved by the Shan, the Kachin and the Chins by their immediate co-operation with the Interim Burmese Government;

The Members of the Conference have accordingly, and without dissentients, agreed as follows:—

1   A Representative of the Hill Peoples, selected by the Governor on the recommendation of representatives of the Supreme Council of the United Hill Peoples (SCOUHP), shall be appointed a Counsellor to the Governor to deal with the Frontier Areas.

2   The said Counsellor shall also be appointed a Member of the Governor's Executive Council, without portfolio and the subject of the Frontier Areas brought within the purview of the Executive Council by Constitutional Convention as in the case of Defence and External Affairs. The Counsellor for Frontier Areas shall be given executive authority by similar means.

3   The said Counsellor shall be assisted by two Deputy Counsellors representing races of which he is not a member. While the two Deputy Counsellors shall deal in the first instance with the affairs of their respective areas and the Counsellor with all the remaining parts of the Frontier Areas. They should on Constitutional Convention act on the principle of joint responsibility.

4   While the Counsellor, in his capacity as Member of the Executive Council, will be the only representative of the frontier Areas on the Council, the Deputy Counsellor shall be entitled to attend meetings of the Council when subjects pertaining to the Frontier Areas are discussed.

5   Though the Governor's Executive Council will be augmented as agreed above, it will not cooperate in the Frontier Areas in any manner

which would deprive any portion of those Areas of the autonomy which it now enjoys in internal administration. Full autonomy in internal administration for the Frontier Areas is accepted in principle.

6   Though the question of demarcating and establishing a separate Kachin State within a United Burma is one which must be relegated for decision by the Constituent Assembly, it is agreed that such s State is desirable. As a first step towards this end, the Counsellor for Frontier Areas and the Deputy Counsellor shall be consulted in the administration of such areas in the Myitkyina and the Bhamo Districts as are Part II Scheduled Areas under the Government of Burma Act of 1935.

7   Citizens of the Frontier Areas shall enjoy rights and privileges which are regarded as fundamental in democratic countries.

8   The arrangements accepted in this Agreement are without prejudice to the financial autonomy now vested in the Federal Shan States.

9   The arrangements accepted in this Agreement are without prejudice to the financial assistance which the Kachin Hills and the Chin Hills are entitled to receive from the revenues of Burma, and the Executive Council will examine with the frontier Areas Counsellor and Deputy Counsellors the feasibility adopting for the Kachin Hills and the Chin Hills financial arrangements similar to those between Burma and the federal Shan States.

Signed by the Shan Committee, Kachin Committee and the Burmese Government.

APPENDIX F

A letter by Khun Sa to Lord Bottomley, who was the British Observer at the Conference in Panlong, in 1947. It's interesting to note that Khun Sa mentions his son in the text. The second letter is Lord Bottomley's reply to Patrick King's request for information.

```
11 November 1993

The Right Honorable Lord Arthur Bottomley
House of Lords
London SW1AO PW
UNITED KINGDOM
```

Dear Lord Bottomley,

It is with great pleasure that I write this letter,and I thank Mr Patrick King heartily for his offer to convey this letter to you.

As you undoubtedly know,things have not been well with the Shans as well as the neighboring Burmese since you had left us in 1948. Due the people's faith in myself,I have been since 1960 been in their service like my ancestord. (For your information,I still keep the Distinguished Service Gold Medal that my grandfather, the Myosa of Nawngleng,received from His Majesty's Government. My late uncle,Khun Ja,had also fought against the Japanese along-side the British during the War). I don't know how further it will take us to achieve at least the kind of peace and sense of well-being that we had enjoyed while you were here.

My son has also been to school in Britain. So,unlike his father, he thinks and acts like a Britisher except for the fact that he's not. With your permission,I would like him to visit you and pay respects on my behalf.

All the best for you.

Sincerely,

Khunsa

```
Contact Address
-------------------

Khernsai Jaiyen
P.O.Box 41
Maehongson 58000
THAILAND
```

LORD BOTTOMLEY O.B.E.
19 LICHFIELD RD
WOODFORD GREEN
ESSEX
IG8 9SU
TEL: 504 5782

29th January, 1994.

Dear Mr. King,

In reply to your letter dated 25th January, I was a member of the Cabinet sub-committee which met the Burmese delegation on the 26th September, 1946.

The talks in London occasionally ran into difficulties. In particular the Burmese were against a Committee of Enquiry to consider the association of the Frontier Area people with the rest of Burma. However, it was agreed that this subject was a proper matter for discussion. It was agreed that a special conference should be held in Panglong and I should be the British observer. The conference was held on 9th February, 1947, and I was accompanied by the Director if the Frontier Area Administration who was respected and trusted by the Frontier Area pdoples. He made sure that I met the leaders whenever they asked to see me. The leaders of the Frontier Areas people told me that they were in favour of a united Burma. I thought this was desirable, particularly in view of events in Europe to-day I have been proved right. The break up to Ygoslavia and other countries has had disastrous consequences.

Yours sincerely,

Patrick King, Esq.,
12, Woodstock Road,
LONDON,
NW11 8ER.

259

APPENDIX G

The original letter conferring a Shan Title of Distinction on Khun Yi Sai, Khun Sa's grandfather, signed in 1935 by the British Viceroy of India. The two medals awarded to Khun Ji, Khun Sa's uncle, in 1937 by the British to commemorate the Coronation of King George VI.

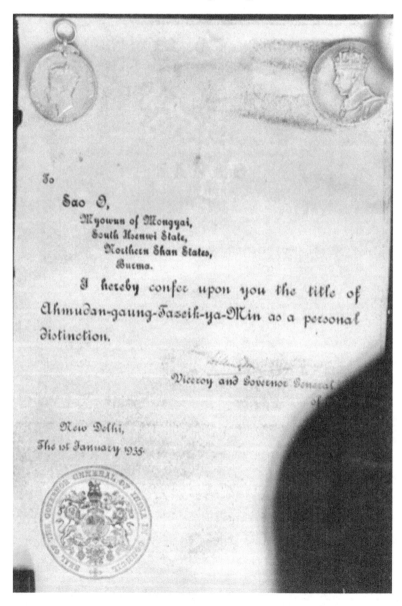

ACKNOWLEDGEMENTS

I owe a debt of gratitude to many people for their help with the writing of this book. In particular all the individuals in Southeast Asia, especially the Shans, whom I promised to keep their identities secret, in return for important information.

In America I would like to thank my good friend and book expert Jack McPherson. To Lieutenant Colonel Bo Gritz for giving me lots of fun and adventures, and also, if he can hear me, the late Jim Reser for his help, friendship and making me laugh so much.

In Italy I would like to thank television reporter Gabriella Simone and the executives at Fininvest, owners of Canale 5 television, for taking the chance and backing my first trip to the Golden Triangle when others wouldn't.

In England I remember my friend and mentor the late Tudor Gates who helped with important research. To Julie Bowden for proofreading. To Paul Fulcher for the maps. To Gabriel, Stefan, James, Joe and the team at Spiffingcovers for their advice and professional skill. To Ian Stuart Lynn, my friend and colleague on many films, for the video trailer. To broadcaster Roger Cook for giving me the break with Central Television with this story. To my old comrade-in-arms Tony Marriage for sharing adventures which finally led to this one! And of course to old friend Mike Borlace for accompanying me twice, covertly, into Burma.

Finally to my family and friends for their assistance and constant encouragement. And last but not least, to Isla St Clair for putting up with my moods and motivating me to get on with the job.

Printed in Great Britain
by Amazon

33865278R00145